T0094329

Getting Started with Advanced C#

Upgrade Your Programming Skills

Vaskaran Sarcar

Foreword by Deepak Seshadri

Apress®

Getting Started with Advanced C#: Upgrade Your Programming Skills

Vaskaran Sarcar
Kolkata, West Bengal, India

ISBN-13 (pbk): 978-1-4842-5933-7 ISBN-13 (electronic): 978-1-4842-5934-4
https://doi.org/10.1007/978-1-4842-5934-4

Managing Director, Apress Media LLC: Welmoed Spahr
Acquisitions Editor: Smriti Srivastava
Development Editor: Laura Berendson
Coordinating Editor: Shrikant Vishwakarma

Cover designed by eStudioCalamar

Cover image designed by Freepik (www.freepik.com)

Distributed to the book trade worldwide by Springer Science+Business Media New York, 233 Spring Street, 6th Floor, New York, NY 10013. Phone 1-800-SPRINGER, fax (201) 348-4505, e-mail orders-ny@springer-sbm.com, or visit www.springeronline.com. Apress Media, LLC is a California LLC and the sole member (owner) is Springer Science + Business Media Finance Inc (SSBM Finance Inc). SSBM Finance Inc is a **Delaware** corporation.

For information on translations, please e-mail rights@apress.com, or visit http://www.apress.com/rights-permissions.

Apress titles may be purchased in bulk for academic, corporate, or promotional use. eBook versions and licenses are also available for most titles. For more information, reference our Print and eBook Bulk Sales web page at http://www.apress.com/bulk-sales.

Any source code or other supplementary material referenced by the author in this book is available to readers on GitHub via the book's product page, located at www.apress.com/978-1-4842-5933-7. For more detailed information, please visit http://www.apress.com/source-code.

Printed on acid-free paper

*This book is dedicated to those people who can listen
to their inner voices and have the courage to follow their dreams
despite unfavorable circumstances.*

Table of Contents

About the Author

Vaskaran Sarcar obtained his master's degree in Software Engineering from Jadavpur University, Kolkata (India), and an MCA from Vidyasagar University, Midnapore (India). He was a National Gate Scholar (2007-2009) and has more than 12 years of experience in education and the IT industry. Vaskaran devoted his early career (2005-2007) to teaching at various engineering colleges. Later he joined HP India PPS R&D Hub Bangalore and worked there until August 2019. At the time of his retirement from the IT industry, he was a senior software engineer and team lead at HP. To follow his dream and passion, Vaskaran is now a full-time author. You can connect with him at vaskaran@rediffmail.com or find him on LinkedIn at `www.linkedin.com/in/vaskaransarcar`.

Other books by Vaskaran include

- *Design Patterns in C#, Second Edition (Apress, 2020 (Upcoming))*

- *Interactive Object-Oriented Programming in Java, Second Edition* (Apress, 2019)

- Java Design Patterns, Second Edition (Apress, 2019)

- *Design Patterns in C#* (Apress, 2018)

- *Interactive C#* (Apress, 2017)

- *Interactive Object-Oriented Programming in Java* (Apress, 2016)

- *Java Design Patterns* (Apress, 2016)

- *C# Basics: Test Your Skill* (CreateSpace, 2015)

- *Operating System: Computer Science Interview Series* (CreateSpace, 2014)

About the Technical Reviewer

 **Carsten Thomsen** is primarily a back-end developer but works with smaller front-end bits as well. He has authored and reviewed several books, and created numerous Microsoft Learning courses, all on software development. He works as a freelancer/contractor in various countries in Europe, working with tools such as Azure, Visual Studio, Azure DevOps, and GitHub. Being an exceptional troubleshooter who asks the right questions—including the less logical ones—in a most-logical-to-least-logical fashion, he also enjoys working with architecture, research, analysis, development, testing, and bug fixing. Carsten is a very good communicator with great skills in mentoring, team leadership, research, and presenting new material.

Acknowledgments

At first, I thank the Almighty. I sincerely believe that with His blessings only, could I complete this book. I extend my deepest gratitude and thanks to the following people.

Ratanlal Sarkar and Manikuntala Sarkar: my dear parents, with your blessings only, could I complete this work.

Indrani, my wife; Ambika, my daughter; and Aryaman, my son: sweethearts, once again, without your love, I could not proceed at all. I know that we need to limit many social gatherings and invitations to complete my books on time and each time. I promise you that I'll take a long break and spend more time with you.

Sambaran, my brother: Thank you for your constant encouragement towards me.

Carsten, my technical advisor: I know that whenever I was in need, your support was there. Thank you one more time.

Shekhar, my another technical advisor: I am always thankful for all your contributions in my previous books. I must acknowledge your support for the newly added chapter in this edition.

Deepak, my ex-colleague cum senior: A special thanks to you for investing your time in writing a foreword for my book. From the moment when experts like you agreed to write for me, I got additional motivation to enhance the quality of my work.

Celestin, Laura, Smriti, Shrikant: Thanks for giving me another opportunity to work with you and Apress.

Krishnan, Rajan, Ramraj, Selvakumar, Pushparaj: Thank you for your exceptional support to beautify my work. Your efforts are truly extraordinary.

Lastly, I extend my deepest gratitude to my publisher, the editorial board members, and everyone who directly or indirectly supported this book.

Foreword

"A tool is only as good as its user!"

Building on this truth, using a programming language is similar in that its effectiveness is only as good as the knowledge and skill of the person using it. This book is for people who have a basic understanding of how to write a C# program but want to leverage more advanced constructs for building optimized, scalable, long-lasting solutions.

C# has come a long way from being a Microsoft Windows tool a few years ago. Now it is also used in much larger ecosystems, such as Mac and Linux. This makes the code a lot more portable. Microsoft also integrated their recent acquisition of Mono into their portfolio, so that a coder can target the code to run on multiple platforms. As the popularity of the language increases, it is important that coders learn about its advanced features to make the best use of the framework.

I have spent a good part of my career programming and reviewing others' C# code. I realized that many developers do not use the language effectively because they are not aware of the more useful features that it has to offer. This book serves as a guide for exactly that—learning the more advanced concepts.

Today, it is more important than ever to not only consider how quickly a solution can be developed, but also about how the solution can be reused across multiple platforms and fine-tuned for each platform. Knowing advanced topics helps developers to easily fine-tune to the environment that their code runs on, so that they are optimized for that environment.

The book starts with concepts such as delegates and events. It then goes into finer detail, including programming with generics, multithreading, database connections, and more. In each chapter, Vaskaran explains the construct in a very simple way, with examples, and then proceeds to a Q and A session. It almost mimics a classroom session. This style engages the reader in learning the topic and answers questions. This is an excellent way to absorb the fundamental concepts and to ensure understanding them.

Vaskaran has worked with me for many years and has always been very passionate about C# and the nonfunctional aspects of programming, such as memory management, performance, and so forth. In this book, he has done a commendable job with putting together great examples that clearly explain the concepts. I am sure that this book will propel C# developers to the next level in a very short time.

Deepak Seshadri
Performance Architect
Printer Firmware, HP Inc.

Introduction

This book is an introductory guide to advanced programming in C#. The examples and code have been deliberately kept simple to allow you to concentrate on understanding important concepts in depth.

In 2015, I wrote *C# Basics: Test your Skill*, which covered fundamental concepts in C#. In 2018, the book was further enhanced and *Interactive C#* was published. Immediately after its release, it became the "#1 New Release" in the C# and object-oriented programming category on Amazon.com. The book was translated into Japanese in 2019. This kind of success motivated me to enhance the work further. I was involved in teaching since 2005, which was another motivation to introduce a book like this one. So, it is my privilege to present you with *Getting Started with Advanced C#: Upgrade Your Programming Skills*. Before I proceed further, I want to thank you for your support to motivate me to write a book like this.

If you ask me about the most fascinating characteristic of this book, I'd tell you that similar to *Interactive C#*, it is also interactive and simple, but this time, you start exploring advanced programming by using some important features in C#. In this book, my goal was not to demonstrate typical and tough programs using all the latest features of C#; instead, like my previous books, the goal is to fuel your creativity and encourage you to implement advanced concepts using core constructs in C#. I always believe that the word *core* is most important when you learn a programming language. Whatever is the latest feature today, will be outdated tomorrow but the core constructs are evergreen, and in most cases, they function behind the new features unnoticed. This is why although this book is for advanced programmers, in Part 1, I focus on the fundamental features of advanced C#. I show you how to incorporate them in different programming techniques in Part 2.

You'll probably agree that when you travel an unknown path to a destination, it helps to have a caring guide. Learning a new programming language through a book is a journey that was always on my mind. In this book, I not only explain topics in an informative way, I also made the book interactive by using Q&A sessions in each chapter. These sessions assist you in your learning process, and they act as "doubt-clearing sessions" that make you a feel that you are asking your guide questions (or expressing your doubts), and you are receiving answers from him in a simple one-to-one communication. In most cases, you'll get a full demonstration of programs along with the output, followed by important analysis to get maximum benefit. As a result, you can continue reading without interruption.

The aim of this book is to give you a classroom environment feeling, where you are *not* only a listener, you are also an active participant who can ask questions and get the answers to them. Before you jump into the topics, let me highlight few more points about the book, including the way the chapters are organized and who the intended readers are.

How the Book Is Organized

The book has two major parts.

- Part 1 consists of the first three chapters, in which you see the discussion and implementation of delegates, events, and lambda expressions. These are the building blocks for advanced programming in C#, and before you move to Part 2, you need to master them. If you have already gone through other C# books, you may be wondering why there are three separate chapters for delegates, events, and lambda expressions. In those books, you may see their presence in a single chapter with only some sample code. But as you go forward in this book, you'll clearly understand why a detailed discussion on these topics is vital to really mastering the advanced concepts and using built-in advanced features in C#.

- In Part 2, there are four chapters. You will experience advanced programming in detail by using the concepts/constructs that you learned in Part 1. You start with generic programming and then learn about thread programming and asynchronous programming to benefit from a multithreaded environment.

- In C#, database programming can be done in three different ways: using connected layers, using disconnected layers, or using Entity Framework (EF). This book is for the advanced C# beginners, and LINQ (which is the basis of EF) is *not* discussed. So, I excluded the discussion on EF. In the final chapter, you'll learn database programming using ADO.NET to connect to a MySQL database and how to exercise SQL statements and stored procedures through your C# applications. You will not find many materials that cover the use of C# with MySQL (instead, you may see other RDBMS; for example, Microsoft SQL Server), but I want to assure you that MySQL is a big name and considered a top player in RDBMS. Most importantly, its open source and widely used.

- I believe that the code in this book is compatible with all the latest and upcoming versions of C#. I have used Visual Studio, which is an integrated development environment (IDE) from Microsoft. Although you can run a C# application in many ways (for example, using Notepad and command prompts), I opted for Visual Studio because it's very common and widely used in C# applications.

- It's important to note that apart from a few special programs, I used .NET Core as my target framework, which simply uses C# 8.0. As per Microsoft, the latest C# compiler can determine the default language version based on the target framework(s). This is because the C# language may use features that are used in specific .NET implementation only. I recommend that you go to `https://docs.microsoft.com/en-us/dotnet/csharp/language-reference/configure-language-version` if you are interested in C# versioning.

- Please remember that as you learn about these concepts, try writing your own code; only then will you master an area.

- You can download all the source code in the book from Apress's website. I plan to maintain the errata, and I can also make any necessary updates/announcements there. I suggest that you visit the Errata pages to receive any corrections or updates.

Prerequisite Knowledge

The target readers for this book are those who are familiar with the basic language constructs in C# and know about object-oriented concepts like polymorphism, inheritance, abstraction, encapsulation, and most importantly, know how to compile or run a C# application in Visual Studio. This book does not invest time in topics that are easily available, such as how to install Visual Studio on your system, how to write a "Hello World" program in C#, or how to use an if-else statement or a while loop. Instead, the book starts with a discussion on delegates. As I said before, in this book, my focus is on the core constructs of advanced C#, and I explain how these concepts can be learned and used effectively. Finally, in Chapter 7, I have used some simple SQL queries. Though their usage are clearly described and shown, but a minimum knowledge of SQL can help you a lot.

Who This Book Is For

In short, you should read this book if the answer is "yes" to any of the following questions.

- Are you familiar with basic constructs in C# and familiar with basic object-oriented concepts like polymorphism, inheritance, abstraction, and encapsulation?

- Do you know how to set up your coding environment?

- Do you want to explore advanced programming in C# step by step?

- Do you want to explore the following advanced C# topics: generic programming, thread programming, asynchronous programming, and database programming (using ADO.NET and MySQL)?

- Are you want to know how the core constructs work behind the advanced features?

You probably shouldn't read this book if the answer is "yes" to any of the following questions.

- Are you totally new to C#?

- Do you want to learn advanced concepts in C# excluding the topics mentioned previously?

- Do you want to explore the latest features of C# only?

- Do you dislike a book that emphasizes Q&A sessions?

- "I do not like Windows, Visual Studio, and .NET Core. I want to learn and use C# without them." Is this statement true for you?

- "I prefer to use Entity Framework (EF) for my database programs, and I do not like MySQL." Is this statement true for you?

Guidelines for Using This Book

Here are some suggestions for you to use the book more effectively:

- The first six chapters of the book are linked. So, I suggest you go through the chapters sequentially. Also, it is possible that some fundamental questions are discussed in the "Q&A Session" of a previous chapter, and I have not repeated those in the later chapters.

- Most of these programs are tested with C# 8.0 and I have used Visual Studio (Community 2019, Version 16.3.9) IDE in a Windows 10 environment. When I started the book, I Started with the latest versions available at that time. But as expected, version updates are keep coming and I also kept updating. But all these versions details should not matter much to you because I have used the fundamental constructs of advanced C# only. So, I believe that these codes should execute smoothly in the upcoming versions of C#/Visual studio as well. There are only few exceptions, in which I used .NET Framework. For example, in chapter 6, when you learn Asynchronous programming, I have shown you implementations of `IAsyncResult` patterns and event based asynchronous patterns. These are not recommended (and supported) for upcoming development. If you execute these programs in .NET Core 3.0, you'll receive following exception saying `System.PlatformNotSupportedException: 'Operation is not supported on this platform.` So, for these examples, I used .NET Framework 4.7.2.

- I tested some of these codes in different systems and different environments (including online editors) and I always received the expected output. With these experiments, I believe that the results should not vary in other environments as well, but you know the nature of software—it is naughty. So, I recommend that if you want to see the exact same outputs, it will be better if you can mimic the same environment.

Conventions Used in This book

All the output and code in the book follow the same font and structure. To draw your attention, in some places, I have made the code bold. For example, consider the following output fragment and the lines in bold.

```
Assigning an instance method to a delegate object.
Calling CalculateSum(..) method of OutsideProgram class using a delegate.
Sum of 50 and 70 is: 120
delOb.Target=DelegateExample2.OutSideProgram
delOb.Target==null? False
delOb.Method=Int32 CalculateSum(Int32, Int32)
```

To print messages in a console, I used the traditional style, although you may prefer to use string interpolation (which basically replaced the need of String.Format(…) starting in C# 6.0). In most examples, I use the following format.

```
Console.WriteLine("-{0} from Method1() prints {1}", Thread.CurrentThread.Name, i);
```

But if you use string interpolation, you may write

```
Console.WriteLine($"{Thread.CurrentThread.Name} from MyMethod() prints {i}");
```

I agree that the second one is more readable but to support legacy code too, I opted for the traditional approach. Each of these approaches works fine and not a blocker for you to understand a C# code but the choice is up to you.

Final Words

I believe that the book is designed for you in such a way that upon its completion, you will have developed an adequate knowledge of the topics, you will have efficiently learned to use the advanced features of this powerful language, and most importantly, you'll know how to go further.

Lastly, I hope that this book can help you and you will value the effort.

PART I

Getting Familiar with Building Blocks

CHAPTER 1

Delegates

The concept of delegates is a very powerful feature in many programming languages, including C#. I believe that the discussion of advanced programming in C# cannot start without delegates. In this chapter, you learn about delegates and why they are essential.

Let's recall the fundamentals of class and object. To create an object—let's say, obA from a class A, you can write something like the following.

```
A obA=new A();
```

Here, the object reference obA points to an object of A. Similar to this, delegates are reference types, but the key difference is that they point to methods. Simply put, a delegate is an object that knows how to invoke a method. A delegate derives from System.Delegate class.

Let's look at it from another point of view. You know what a variable is and how it behaves. You have seen that you can put different boolean values (true/false), strings (or, words), numbers (integer, double, etc.) in respective types of variables. But when you use delegates, you can assign a method to a variable and pass it around.

In short, by using delegates, you can treat your methods like objects. So, you can store a delegate in a variable, pass it as method parameter, and return it from a method.

The use of delegates can help promote type-safety. (In a broad sense, the term *type-safety* simply tells you that you cannot assign one type to another type if they are not compatible. The check for type-safety may appear both at compile time and runtime). This is why delegates are often referred to as *type-safe function pointers*.

In demonstration 1, a method called Sum takes two integer (int) parameters and returns an integer, like the following.

```
public static int Sum(int a, int b)
{
    return a + b;
}
```

© Vaskaran Sarcar 2020
V. Sarcar, *Getting Started with Advanced C#*, https://doi.org/10.1007/978-1-4842-5934-4_1

In this case, you can declare a delegate to point to the Sum method, as follows.

```
DelegateWithTwoIntParameterReturnInt delOb = new
DelegateWithTwoIntParameterReturnInt (Sum);
```

But before that, you need to define the `DelegateWithTwoIntParameterReturnInt` delegate, which must have the same signature, as follows.

```
delegate int DelegateWithTwoIntParameterReturnInt(int x, int y);
```

The return type, the parameters, and their corresponding order are the same for both the Sum method and the `DelegateWithTwoIntParameterReturnInt` delegate. I chose a long name for my delegate for better readability. You can always choose your own delegate name.

The first important point to understand is that once you have `DelegateWithTwoIntParameterReturnInt`, you can use it to keep track of any method that takes two integers as input parameters and returns an integer; for example, to calculate the sum of two ints, the difference of two ints, the multiplication of two ints, the division of two ints, and so forth.

POINTS TO REMEMBER

- A delegate instance contains details of a method rather than data.

- You can use delegates for methods that match the delegate's signature. For example, as the name suggests, `DelegateWithTwoIntParameterReturnInt` is compatible with any method that accepts two **int** parameters and returns an **int.**

- When you use a delegate to invoke a method, at a high level, the overall process can be divided into two parts. In the first part, you (the caller) invoke the delegate, and in the second part, the delegate calls your target method. This mechanism decouples a caller from a target method.

Definition

A delegate is a reference type derived from System.Delegate, and its instances are used to call methods with matching signatures and return types. Later in this chapter, you'll learn about variances, and you'll discover that the word *compatible* is more suitable than the word *matching* in this context. I'm trying to make things as simple as possible.

The dictionary meaning of the word *delegate* is "a representative or an agent." The delegates in C# programming represent methods with matching signatures. This is the general form of a delegate declaration.

‹modifier› delegate ‹return type› (parameter list);

The following are examples of delegate declarations.

```
delegate void DelegateWithNoParameter();
public delegate int MyDelegateWithOneIntParameter(int i);
public delegate double MakeTotal(double firstNo, double secondNo);
delegate int DelegateWithTwoIntParameterReturnInt(int x, int y);
```

You may notice that these are similar to methods without a body. But, when the compiler sees the keyword *delegate*, it understands that you are using the type that derives from System.Delegate.

To begin with delegates, in the following example, I show you two cases. The first case will look familiar to you. You simply invoke a method without using a delegate. In the second case, you use a delegate to invoke a method.

Demonstration 1

In this demonstration, note the following segment of code.

```
// Creating a delegate instance
// DelegateWithTwoIntParameterReturnInt delOb = new DelegateWithTwoInt
   ParameterReturnInt(Sum);
// Or, simply write as follows:
DelegateWithTwoIntParameterReturnInt delOb = Sum;
```

I kept the comments that say that I'm using the short form when I create the delegate instance. You can use any of them.

You can also make the code size shorter when you use delOb(25,75) instead of delOb.Invoke(25,75). This is why I also kept the following comments.

```
// delOb(25,75) is shorthand for delOb.Invoke(25,75)
```

When you use the short form (i.e., you assign the method name to the delegate instance without using a new operator or explicitly invoking the delegate's constructor), you are using a feature known as method group conversion. This form has been allowed since C# version 2.0.

Now let's go through the complete example and the corresponding output and analysis.

```csharp
using System;

namespace DelegateExample1
{
    delegate int DelegateWithTwoIntParameterReturnInt(int x, int y);

    class Program
    {
        public static int Sum(int a, int b)
        {
            return a + b;
        }

        static void Main(string[] args)
        {
            Console.WriteLine("***A simple delegate demo.***");
            Console.WriteLine("\n Calling Sum(..) method without using a
            delegate:");
            Console.WriteLine("Sum of 10 and 20 is : {0}", Sum(10, 20));

            //Creating a delegate instance
            //DelegateWithTwoIntParameterReturnInt delOb = new DelegateWith
            //  TwoIntParameterReturnInt(Sum);
            //Or,simply write as follows:
            DelegateWithTwoIntParameterReturnInt delOb = Sum;
            Console.WriteLine("\nCalling Sum(..) method using a delegate.");
            int total = delOb(10, 20);
```

```
Console.WriteLine("Sum of 10 and 20 is: {0}", total);

/* Alternative way to calculate the aggregate of the numbers.*/
//delOb(25,75) is shorthand for delOb.Invoke(25,75)
Console.WriteLine("\nUsing Invoke() method on delegate instance,
calculating sum of 25 and 75.");
total = delOb.Invoke(25,75);
Console.WriteLine("Sum of 25 and 75 is: {0}", total);
Console.ReadKey();
        }
    }
}
```

Output

The following is the output from running this program.

```
***A simple delegate demo.***

Calling Sum(..) method without using a delegate:
Sum of 10 and 20 is : 30

Calling Sum(..) method using a delegate.
Sum of 10 and 20 is: 30

Using Invoke() method on delegate instance, calculating sum of 25 and 75.
Sum of 25 and 75 is: 100
```

Analysis

Let's take a closer look at the code. To make it easier to understand, Figure 1-1 presents a partial screenshot of the IL code.[1]

---

[1]You know that when we compile our .net program using any .Net obedient language like C#, initially our source code will be converted into an intermediate code, which is known as MSIL (Microsoft Intermediate Language). This IL code is interpreted by CLR (Common Language Runtime). Upon program execution, this IL code will be converted into the binary executable binary code or native code.

And CLR is a framework layer that exists above OS and handles all the execution of the .net applications. The programs must go through the CLR so that there will be no direct communication with the OS.

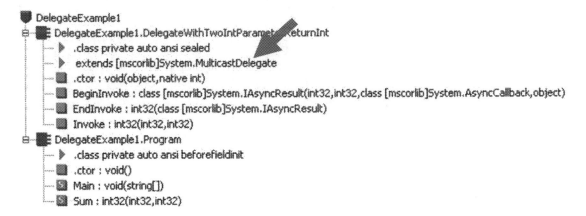

Figure 1-1. Partial screenshot of IL code for DelegateExample1

Notice that when you create a delegate, the C# compiler turns it into a class that extends from `MulticastDelegate`. Let's go one level deeper. If you see the implementation of `MulticastDelegate`, you see that it derives from the `System.Delegate` class. For your reference, **Figure 1-2** presents a partial screenshot from Visual Studio 2019.

```
namespace System
{
    //
    // Summary:
    //     Represents a multicast delegate; that is, a delegate that can have more than
    //     one element in its invocation list.
    [ComVisible(true)]
    public abstract class MulticastDelegate : Delegate
    {
        ...protected MulticastDelegate(object target, string method);
        ...protected MulticastDelegate(Type target, string method);
```

Figure 1-2. Partial screenshot of MulticastDelegate class from Visual Studio IDE 2019

Figure 1-3 shows the IL code for the `Main` method in demonstration 1.

```
IL_003c:   stloc.0
IL_003d:   ldstr       "\nCalling Sum(..) method using a delegate."
IL_0042:   call        void [mscorlib]System.Console::WriteLine(string)
IL_0047:   nop
IL_0048:   ldloc.0
IL_0049:   ldc.i4.s    10
IL_004b:   ldc.i4.s    20
IL_004d:   callvirt    instance int32 DelegateExample1.DelegateWithTwoIntParameterReturnInt::Invoke(int32,
                                                                                                      int32)
IL_0052:   stloc.1
IL_0053:   ldstr       "Sum of 10 and 20 is: {0}"
IL_0058:   ldloc.1
IL_0059:   box         [mscorlib]System.Int32
IL_005e:   call        void [mscorlib]System.Console::WriteLine(string,
                                                                object)
IL_0063:   nop
IL_0064:   ldstr       "\nUsing Invoke() method on delegate instance, calcu"
+ "lating sum of 25 and 75."
IL_0069:   call        void [mscorlib]System.Console::WriteLine(string)
IL_006e:   nop
IL_006f:   ldloc.0
IL_0070:   ldc.i4.s    25
IL_0072:   ldc.i4.s    75
IL_0074:   callvirt    instance int32 DelegateExample1.DelegateWithTwoIntParameterReturnInt::Invoke(int32,
                                                                                                      int32)
```

Figure 1-3. *Partial screenshot of IL code for the* `Main` *method in prior demonstration*

In Figure 1-3, the line that the arrow points to shows that `delOb(10,20)` is the syntactic shortcut for `delOb.Invoke(10,20)`.

POINTS TO REMEMBER

- The .NET Framework defines the **delegate** and the **MulticastDelegate** class. When you create a delegate, the C# compiler makes a class that derives from **MulticastDelegate**, which derives from the **Delegate** class.

- Only the C# compiler can create a class that derives from the Delegate class or the `MulticastDelegate` class, but you cannot do the same. In other words, these delegate types are implicitly sealed. You will get a compile-time error if you write something like the following.

  ```
  class MyClass : Delegate { }
  ```

  or,

  ```
  class MyClass : MulticastDelegate { }
  ```

- In the demonstration, you saw that delOb(10,20) is a syntactic shortcut for delOb.Invoke(10,20). So, in real-world programming, it's always better to do a null check prior to invoke the operation.

- Delegate methods are also referred to as *callable entities*.

Q&A Session

1.1 In demonstration 1, you define the delegate outside of the Program class. Is this mandatory?

No. Since it's a class type, you can define it inside of a class, outside of a class, or at the beginning of the namespace.

1.2 You said that only the C# compiler can create a class that derives from the Delegate class or the MulticastDelegate class, but you cannot do the same. Do you mean that these delegate types are implicitly sealed?

Yes.

1.3 Is the use of delegates limited to static methods?

You can refer both static and non-static methods using delegates. Delegates do not care about the object type that is invoking the method. So, this delegate

```
delegate int MyDelegate(int aNumber);
```

it can refer the instance method.

```
public int Factorial(int i)
{
    // method body
}
```

can also refer the following static method.

```
public static int MyStaticMethod(int a)
{
    // method body
}
```

But there are some important differences when you use a static method or a non-static method in the context of a delegate. You'll see a case study on this shortly.

Comparing a Static Method with an Instance Method

I already said that you can assign both the static methods and the instance methods to a delegate object. To demonstrate this, I modified demonstration 1. I added a new class, OutsideProgram, and placed one instance method, called CalculateSum, in it. I've assigned both the static method, Sum, and instance method, CalculateSum, to the delegate instance, delOb, and analyzed each case.

In each case, you see the following lines of code.

```
Console.WriteLine("delOb.Target={0}", delOb.Target);
Console.WriteLine("delOb.Target==null? {0}", delOb.Target == null);
Console.WriteLine("delOb.Method={0}",delOb.Method);
```

The output for these lines of code show you that when you assign a non-static method to a delegate object, the object maintains a reference not only to the method, but also to the instance to which this method belongs.

The Target property in the Delegate class can be used to verify this. This is why you may notice different output for the first two lines when you compare a static method and an instance method in this context. For your reference, I'm showing you the description of the Target property from Visual Studio, which is as follows.

```
// Summary:
// Gets the class instance on which the current delegate invokes
//the instance method.
//
// Returns:
//The object on which the current delegate invokes the instance
//method, if the delegate represents an instance method; null
//if the delegate represents a static method.
[NullableAttribute(2)]
public object? Target { get; }
```

This description from Visual Studio also says that if you assign a static method to the delegate object delOb, then delOb.Target will contain null.

Demonstration 2

```
using System;

namespace DelegateExample2
{
    delegate int DelegateWithTwoIntParameterReturnInt(int x, int y);

    class Program
    {
        public static int Sum(int a, int b)
        {
            return a + b;
        }

        static void Main(string[] args)
        {
            Console.WriteLine("***Comparing the behavior of a static
            method and  instance method when assign them to a delegate
            instance.***");
            Console.WriteLine("Assigning a static method to a delegate
            object.");
            //Assigning a static method to a delegate object.
            DelegateWithTwoIntParameterReturnInt delOb = Sum;
            Console.WriteLine("Calling Sum(..) method of Program Class
            using a delegate.");
            int total = delOb(10, 20);
            Console.WriteLine("Sum of 10 and 20 is: {0}", total);
            Console.WriteLine("delOb.Target={0}", delOb.Target);
            Console.WriteLine("delOb.Target==null? {0}", delOb.Target ==
            null);//True
            Console.WriteLine("delOb.Method={0}", delOb.Method);
            OutSideProgram outsideOb = new OutSideProgram();
            Console.WriteLine("\nAssigning an instance method to a delegate
            object.");
```

```
            //Assigning an instance method to a delegate object.
            delOb = outsideOb.CalculateSum;
            Console.WriteLine("Calling CalculateSum(..) method of
            OutsideProgram class using a delegate.");
            total = delOb(50, 70);
            Console.WriteLine("Sum of 50 and 70 is: {0}", total);
            Console.WriteLine("delOb.Target={0}", delOb.Target);
            //delOb.Target=DelegateEx1.OutSideProgramClass
            Console.WriteLine("delOb.Target==null? {0}", delOb.Target ==
            null);//False
            Console.WriteLine("delOb.Method={0}", delOb.Method);
            Console.ReadKey();
        }
    }
    class OutSideProgram
    {
        public int CalculateSum(int x, int y)
        {
            return x + y;
        }

    }
}
```

Output

This is the output. I made a few lines bold to draw your attention.

```
***Comparing the behavior of a static method and  instance method when
assign them to a delegate instance.***
Assigning a static method to a delegate object.
Calling Sum(..) method of Program Class using a delegate.
Sum of 10 and 20 is: 30
```
delOb.Target=
delOb.Target==null? True
```
delOb.Method=Int32 Sum(Int32, Int32)
```

Assigning an instance method to a delegate object.
Calling CalculateSum(..) method of OutsideProgram class using a delegate.
Sum of 50 and 70 is: 120
delOb.Target=DelegateExample2.OutSideProgram
delOb.Target==null? False
delOb.Method=Int32 CalculateSum(Int32, Int32)

Using Multicast Delegates

By using a delegate instance, you can refer to multiple target methods. You can do this by using the += operator. When a delegate is used to encapsulate more than one method of a matching signature, it is a *multicast delegate*. These delegates are subtypes of System. MulticastDelegate, which is a subclass of System.Delegate.

In the following example, you target three methods. To demonstrate a general case, I combined both static and instance methods to the delegate object. The following code segment with supportive comments were used.

```
// Target a static method
MultiDelegate multiDel = MethodOne;
// Target another static method
multiDel += MethodTwo;
// Target an instance method
multiDel += new OutsideProgram().MethodThree;
```

In a case like this, the delegates are invoked in the order that you added them in your calling chain. When you invoke multiDel(), all three methods are invoked.

POINTS TO REMEMBER

- The following two lines of code are functionally equivalent.

  ```
  multiDel += MethodTwo;
  //Same as the following line
  multiDel = multiDel+MethodTwo;
  ```

- When you use a multicast delegate, the delegates are invoked in the order that you added them in your calling chain.

You can increase the chain of methods by using the += operator. Similarly, you can reduce the chain by using the -= operator. To demonstrate this, before I invoke multiDel() for the second time in the following example, I removed MethodTwo from the chain using the following line of code.

```
multiDel -= MethodTwo;
```

Now go through the following example, which shows a complete demonstration of using a multicast delegate.

Demonstration 3

```
using System;

namespace MulticastDelegateExample1
{
    delegate void MultiDelegate();
    class Program
    {
        public static void MethodOne()
        {
            Console.WriteLine("A static method of Program class-
            MethodOne() executed.");
        }
        public static void MethodTwo()
        {
            Console.WriteLine("A static method of Program class-
            MethodTwo() executed.");
        }
        static void Main(string[] args)
        {
            Console.WriteLine("***Example of a Multicast Delegate.***");
            // Target a static method
            MultiDelegate multiDel = MethodOne;
            // Target another static method
            multiDel += MethodTwo;
```

```
            //Target an instance method
            multiDel += new OutsideProgram().MethodThree;
            multiDel();
            //Reducing the delegate chain
            Console.WriteLine("\nReducing the length of delegate chain by
            discarding MethodTwo now.");
            multiDel -= MethodTwo;
            //The following invocation will call MethodOne and MethodThree now.
            multiDel();
            Console.ReadKey();
        }
    }
    class OutsideProgram
    {
        public void MethodThree()
        {
            Console.WriteLine("An instance method of OutsideProgram class
            is executed.");
        }
    }
}
```

Output

The following is the output from running this program.

```
***Example of a Multicast Delegate.***
A static method of Program class- MethodOne() executed.
A static method of Program class- MethodTwo() executed.
An instance method of OutsideProgram class is executed.
```

   Reducing the length of delegate chain by discarding MethodTwo now.

```
A static method of Program class- MethodOne() executed.
An instance method of OutsideProgram class is executed.
```

Analysis

In demonstration 3, you saw that the target methods have a void return type. This is because multicast delegates are often used for methods with void return types.

Q&A Session

1.4 You said that multicast delegates are often used for methods with void return types. What is the reason for this?

A multicast delegate targets multiple methods from an invocation list. However, a single method or delegate invocation can return only a single value. If you use multiple methods with non-void return types in your multicast delegate invocation, you will get the return value from the last method in the invocation list. Although other methods are also called, those values are discarded. The following example gives you a clearer picture of this.

Demonstration 4

```
using System;

namespace MulticastDelegateExample2
{
    delegate int MultiDelegate();
    class Program
    {
        public static int MethodOne()
        {
            Console.WriteLine("A static method of Program class-
            MethodOne() executed.");
            return 1;
        }
        public static int MethodTwo()
        {
            Console.WriteLine("A static method of Program class-
            MethodTwo() executed.");
            return 2;
        }
```

```
        public static int MethodThree()
        {
            Console.WriteLine("A static method of Program class-
            MethodThree() executed.");
            return 3;
        }
        static void Main(string[] args)
        {
            Console.WriteLine("***A case study with a multicast delegate
            when we target non-void methods.***");
            // Target MethodOne
            MultiDelegate multiDel = MethodOne;
            // Target MethodTwo
            multiDel += MethodTwo;
            // Target MethodThree
            multiDel += MethodThree;
            int finalValue=multiDel();
            Console.WriteLine("The final value is {0}", finalValue);
            Console.ReadKey();
        }
    }
}
```

Output

The following is the output from running this program.

```
***A case study with a multicast delegate when we target non-void
methods.***
A static method of Program class- MethodOne() executed.
A static method of Program class- MethodTwo() executed.
A static method of Program class- MethodThree() executed.
The final value is 3
```

Analysis

The three methods from the invocation list (MethodOne(), MethodTwo(), and MethodThree()) were called, but the final returned value was 3, which comes from MethodThree.

Q&A Session

1.5 I understand that multicast delegates are not useful for methods with a non-void return type because the intermediate return values are discarded. But I believe that nothing is preventing me from storing those values and using them in different ways. Is this correct?

Absolutely. You can always gather those values and use them as you wish; but it is rarely done. Also, at the time of writing, there was no syntactical shortcut for this in C# language specification. So, if you use multicast delegates for methods with a non-void return type, the intermediate return values will be lost, which is often considered a functionality loss.

In addition, you need to pay special attention to exception handling. If a method in your invocation list throws an exception, other methods will not get a chance to handle it.

1.6 Can you provide an example that demonstrates why exception handling is a concern when I use multicast delegates?

Let's modify MethodOne() in demonstration 3 as follows.

```
public static void MethodOne()
{
    Console.WriteLine("A static method of Program class- MethodOne()
    executed.");
    // For Q&A 1.6
    // Let's say, some code causes an exception
    // like the following
    int a = 10, b = 0,c;
    c = a / b;
    Console.WriteLine("c={0}",c);
}
```

Now execute the program again. This time, you'll get the following exception, and as a result, the next method in the invocation list will not execute. This is why MethodTwo()

will not run; it does not have a chance to handle the exception. Figure 1-4 is a runtime screenshot from Visual Studio.

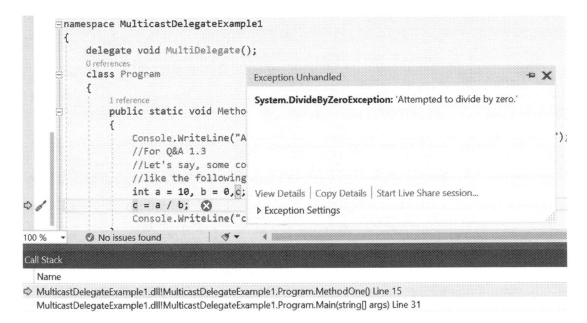

Figure 1-4. *A runtime error screenshot from Visual Studio IDE*

1.7 In demonstration 1, you used the following line:

```
DelegateWithTwoIntParameterReturnInt delOb = Sum;
```

Now I'm worried. What will happen if I overload Sum methods?

It does not matter. Delegates act like type-safe function pointers because they can track full method signatures (for example, the number of parameters, the type of parameters, the return type of methods) accurately.

When you use delegates and have overloaded methods, the compiler can bind the correct method for you. To investigate this, consider the following example, where the Sum method is overloaded (I used static methods, but you can use instance methods too). There are two overloaded versions of the Sum method. In one case, the Sum method accepts two int parameters, and in the other case, it accepts three int parameters; but DelegateWithTwoIntParameterReturnInt can bind the intended method properly.

Demonstration 5

```
using System;

namespace CaseStudyWithOverloadedMethods
{
    delegate int DelegateWithTwoIntParameterReturnInt(int x, int y);
    class Program
    {
        public static int Sum(int a, int b)
        {
            return a + b;
        }
        public static int Sum(int a, int b, int c)
        {
            return a + b + c;
        }
        static void Main(string[] args)
        {
            Console.WriteLine("***A case study with overloaded
            methods.***");
            DelegateWithTwoIntParameterReturnInt delOb = Sum;
            Console.WriteLine("\nCalling Sum(..) method using a delegate.");
            int total = delOb(10, 20);
            Console.WriteLine("Sum of 10 and 20 is: {0}", total);
            Console.ReadKey();
        }
    }
}
```

Output

You get the following output when you run this program.

```
***A case study with overloaded methods.***

Calling Sum(..) method using a delegate.
Sum of 10 and 20 is: 30
```

Analysis

It is important to note that if you do not have the correct overloaded version, you'll get a compile-time error. For example, if you comment out the intended method as follows,

```
//public static int Sum(int a, int b)
//{
//    return a + b;
//}
```

you'll get the following compilation error:

```
No Overload for 'Sum' matches delegate
'DelegateWithTwoIntParameterReturnInt'
```

Figure 1-5 is a partial screenshot from Visual Studio IDE.

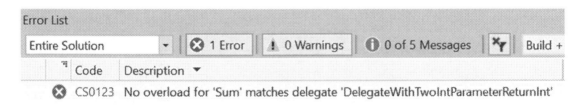

Figure 1-5. *A compile-time error screenshot from Visual Studio IDE*

Q&A Session

1.8 How are delegates commonly used?

You see the use of delegates in event handling and callback methods (particularly in asynchronous programming). I'll discuss this in later chapters of the book.

1.9 Can I use delegates to point to constructors?

No. But programmatically, you can achieve a similar effect. For example, consider demonstration 2. Let's provide a public constructor to the OutsideProgram class. After this modification, it looks like the following.

```
class OutSideProgram
    {
        //For Q&A 1.9
        public OutSideProgram()
```

```
    {
        Console.WriteLine("\nOutSideProgram constructor is called.");
    }
    public int CalculateSum(int x, int y)
    {
        return x + y;
    }

}
```

Let's define a delegate, as follows.

```
delegate OutSideProgram ConsGenerator();
```

Now, inside Main, you can write the following lines (I used a lambda expression here. You'll learn about lambda expressions in Chapter 3).

```
// For Q&A 1.9
ConsGenerator consGenerator =() =>
{
    return new OutSideProgram();
};
consGenerator();
```

If you execute the program now, you'll see the message "OutSideProgram constructor is called" in your output. In short, you can use a method that can mimic the behavior of a constructor. I used the lambda expression there because I haven't introduced any new method that can do the same.

1.10 I learned that in method overloading, the method's return type doesn't matter, but in the context of delegates, it looks as if it matters. Is this correct?

Yes. It's an important point to remember.

Variance in Delegates

When you instantiate a delegate, you can assign it a method that has a "more derived" return type than the originally specified return type. This support is available in C# version 2.0 and onward. On the other hand, contravariance allows a method with parameter types that are less derived than in the delegate type. Collectively, covariance and contravariance are known as method group variance.

To get a better understanding, let's begin with mathematics and explore the important terms from a mathematical point of view. Let's suppose that you have a domain of integers.

For case 1, assume that you have a function, $f(x) = x + 2$ (for all, x belongs to the integer). If $x \leq y$, then you can also say that $f(x) \leq f(y)$ for all x. The projection (function f) is preserving the direction of size (I mean, before you use the function, if the part on the left hand side is smaller (or, bigger) than the part of right hand side, after applying the function, same will preserve).

For case 2, let's consider another function: $f(x) = -x$ (for all, x belongs to the integer). In this case, you can see $10 \leq 20$ but $f(10) \geq f(20)$ (since $f(10) = -10$, $f(20) = -20$ and $-10 > -20$). So, the projection is reversing the direction of size.

For case 3, let's consider the following function, $f(x) = x*x$ (for all, x belongs to the integer). In this case, you can see $-1 \leq 0$ and $f(-1) > f(0)$. On the other hand, $1 < 2$ and $f(1) < f(2)$. The projection (function f) neither preserves the direction of size nor reverses the direction of size.

In case 1, function f is covariant; in case 2, function f is contravariant; and in case 3, function f is invariant.

In C# programming, you can assign a method to a delegate with a matching signature. But there may be a case, when the return type of your method doesn't match exactly with the delegate's return type, but you identify that this method's return type is a derived type of the delegate's return type. In this case, covariance allows you to match the method with the delegate. So, in simple words, *covariance allows you to match the method which has a "more derived" return type than the "original return type" that defined in the delegate.*

Contravariance deals with parameters. It allows a method to have a parameter type that is less derived than those in the delegate type.

POINTS TO REMEMBER

Let's remember the following points.

- **Covariance** allows you to pass a derived type where a parent type was expected; and with delegates, you apply the concept to the return types.

- **Contravariance** allows you to use a more generic (less derived) type than originally specified. Using delegates, you can assign a method with base class parameters to a delegate that expects to get the derived class parameters.

- **Invariance** allows you to use only the type originally specified. It's neither covariant nor contravariant.

Covariance and contravariance are collectively known as *variance*.

The concept of covariance has supported arrays since C#1.0. You can write this:

```
Console.WriteLine("***Covariance in arrays(C#1.0 onwards)***");
// It is not type safe
object[] myObjArray = new string[5];
// Following line will cause run-time error
myObjArray[0] = 10;
```

But this segment of code will cause a runtime error that outputs the following.

```
System.ArrayTypeMismatchException: 'Attempted to access an element as a
type incompatible with the array.'
```

Covariance in Delegates

Covariance and contravariance has been supported by delegates since C# version 2.0. Support for generic type parameters, generic interfaces, and generic delegates began with C# 4.0. I have not yet discussed generic types. This section deals with non-generic delegates and starts with covariance. In the upcoming examples, Bus class derives from Vehicle class. So, you can easily understand that I use Vehicle as the base type and Bus as the derived type.

Demonstration 6

```csharp
using System;

namespace CovarianceWithNonGenericDelegate
{
    class Vehicle
    {
        public Vehicle CreateVehicle()
        {
            Vehicle myVehicle = new Vehicle();
            Console.WriteLine(" Inside Vehicle.CreateVehicle, a vehicle
            object is created.");
            return myVehicle;
        }
    }
    class Bus : Vehicle
    {
        public Bus CreateBus()
        {
            Bus myBus = new Bus();
            Console.WriteLine(" Inside Bus.CreateBus, a bus object is
            created.");
            return myBus;
        }
    }

    class Program
    {
        public delegate Vehicle VehicleDelegate();
        static void Main(string[] args)
        {
            Vehicle vehicleOb = new Vehicle();
            Bus busOb = new Bus();
            Console.WriteLine("***Testing covariance with delegates.
            It is allowed C# 2.0 onwards.***\n");
            // Normal case:
```

```
          /* VehicleDelegate is expecting a method with return type
          Vehicle.*/
          VehicleDelegate vehicleDelegate1 = vehicleOb.CreateVehicle;
          vehicleDelegate1();
          /* VehicleDelegate is expecting a method with return type
          Vehicle(i.e. a basetype) but you're assigning a method with
          return type Bus( a derived type) Covariance allows this kind of
          assignment.*/
          VehicleDelegate vehicleDelegate2 = busOb.CreateBus;
          vehicleDelegate2();
          Console.ReadKey();
        }
    }
}
```

Output

The following is the output from running this program.

```
***Testing covariance with delegates. It is allowed C# 2.0 onwards.***

 Inside Vehicle.CreateVehicle, a vehicle object is created.
 Inside Bus.CreateBus, a bus object is created.
```

Analysis

Note this line of code with supporting comments from the preceding program.

```
/* VehicleDelegate is expecting a method with return type
Vehicle(i.e. a basetype)but you're assigning a method with
return type Bus( a derived type)
Covariance allows this kind of assignment.*/
VehicleDelegate vehicleDelegate2 = busOb.CreateBus;
```

The compiler did not complain about this line because covariance offers this kind of flexibility.

Contravariance in Delegates

Contravariance is related to parameters. Suppose that a delegate can point to a method that accepts a derived type parameter. Using contravariance, you can use the same delegate to point to a method that accepts a base type parameter.

Demonstration 7

```
using System;

namespace ContravarianceWithNonGenegicDelegate
{
    class Vehicle
    {
        public void ShowVehicle(Vehicle myVehicle)
        {
            Console.WriteLine("Vehicle.ShowVehicle is called.");
                Console.WriteLine("myVehicle.GetHashCode() is: {0}",
                myVehicle.GetHashCode());
        }
    }
    class Bus : Vehicle
    {
        public void ShowBus(Bus myBus)
        {
            Console.WriteLine("Bus.ShowBus is called.");
            Console.WriteLine("myBus.GetHashCode() is: {0}", myBus.
            GetHashCode());
        }
    }

    class Program
    {
        public delegate void BusDelegate(Bus bus);
        static void Main(string[] args)
        {
```

```
Console.WriteLine("***Demonstration-7.Exploring Contravariance
with non-generic delegates***");
Vehicle myVehicle = new Vehicle();
Bus myBus = new Bus();
//Normal case
BusDelegate busDelegate = myBus.ShowBus;
busDelegate(myBus);

// Special case
// Contravariance:
/*
 * Note that the following delegate expected a method that
   accepts a Bus(derived) object parameter but still it can point
   to the method that accepts Vehicle(base) object parameter
 */
BusDelegate anotherBusDelegate = myVehicle.ShowVehicle;
anotherBusDelegate(myBus);
// Additional note:you cannot pass vehicle object here
// anotherBusDelegate(myVehicle);//error
Console.ReadKey();
        }
    }
}
```

Output

The following is the output from running this program.

```
***Demonstration-7.Exploring Contravariance with non-generic delegates***
Bus.ShowBus is called.
myBus.GetHashCode() is: 58225482
Vehicle.ShowVehicle is called.
myVehicle.GetHashCode() is: 58225482
```

Analysis

You can see that in the previous example, `BusDelegate` accepts one `Bus` type parameter. Still using contravariance, when you instantiate a `BusDelegate` object, you can point to a method that accepts a `Vehicle` type parameter. So, contravariance allows the following type of assignment.

```
BusDelegate anotherBusDelegate = myVehicle.ShowVehicle;
```

In both cases, I passed the same object to both delegate objects. As a result, you see the same hash code in the output. The supporting comments were kept in this example to help your understanding.

Q&A Session

1.11 You used the term *method group variance*. Why is it called a method group? MSDN highlights the following points.

- A method group, which is a set of overloaded methods resulting from a member lookup.

- A method group is permitted in an invocation_expression (*i*nvocation expressions), a delegate_creation_expression (*d*elegate creation expressions) and as the left-hand side of an is operator, and can be implicitly converted to a compatible delegate type (*m*ethod group conversions). In any other context, an expression classified as a method group causes compile-time error.

The demonstration 5 case study with overloaded methods included the following line.

```
DelegateWithTwoIntParameterReturnInt delOb = Sum;
```

Here, `Sum` refers to a method group. When you use this kind of statement (i.e., no parentheses with method arguments), all methods in the group are available in the same context but the method group conversion can create the delegate that calls the intended method. But in cases where you include parentheses with arguments, the method call can be identified easily and unambiguously.

Final Words

You can always create and use your own delegate, but in real-world programming, it may help to use ready-made constructs to save time and effort. In this context, the `Func`, `Action`, and `Predicate` delegates are very useful. But you can use them effectively when you learn advanced topics later in the book; for example, lambda expressions and generic programming. Let's skip this for now and jump to the next topic: events.

Summary

This chapter covered the following key questions.

- What is a delegate?

- What is a multicast delegate?

- When should you use a multicast delegate?

- How do you differentiate a static method from an instance method when you target these methods with delegates?

- How do you implement covariance and contravariance using delegates?

- How are delegates commonly used?

CHAPTER 2

Events

The support for events is considered one of the most exciting features in C#.

The following are some fundamental characteristics of events. I suggest that you go through these points multiple times before you code with events.

- The backbone of events are delegates, so it's essential to learn delegates before you use events.

- When using events, one segment of code can send a notification to another segment of code.

- Events are commonly used in GUI applications. For example, when you click a button or select a radio button, you may notice some interesting changes in the UI layout.

- In a publisher-subscriber model, one object raises a notification (event) and one or multiple objects listen to those events. The object that raises the event is called a *sender* (or publisher or broadcaster), and the object that receives the event is called a *receiver* (or subscriber). The sender does not care how the receiver interprets the events. It may not care who is registering to receive or unregistering to stop receiving the events or notifications. You can relate this to Facebook or Twitter. If you follow someone, you can get notifications when that person updates his profile. If you do not want to get notifications, you can always unsubscribe. In short, a subscriber can decide when to start listening to events or when to stop listening to events. (In programming terms, when to register for events and when to unregister the events).

- In .NET, events are implemented as multicast delegates.

© Vaskaran Sarcar 2020
V. Sarcar, *Getting Started with Advanced C#*, https://doi.org/10.1007/978-1-4842-5934-4_2

- Publishers contain the delegate. Subscribers register by using += on the publisher's delegate and unregister by using -= on that delegate. So, when we apply += or -= to an event, there is a special meaning (in other words, they are not shortcuts for assignments).

- Subscribers do not communicate with each other. As a result, you can make a loosely coupled system. This is often the key goal in an event-driven architecture.

- In GUI applications, the Visual Studio IDE can make your life easier when you deal with events. (I believe that since these concepts are the core of C#, it's better to learn from the basics.)

- The .NET framework provides a generic delegate that supports standard event design patterns, as follows:

```
public delegate void EventHandler<TEventArgs>(object
sendersource, TEventArgs e), where TEventArgs :
EventArgs;.
```

  I haven't discussed generics yet, so you can skip this point for now. But it's interesting to know that to support backward compatibility, many events in the .NET framework follow a non-generic custom delegate pattern.

- Here is an example of an event declaration:

```
public event EventHandler MyIntChanged;
```

  This simply indicates that MyIntChanged is the name of the event and EventHandler is the corresponding delegate.

  The modifier does not need not to be public. You may choose non-public modifiers, like private, protected, internal, and so forth, for your event. You can also use keywords like static, virtual, override, abstract, sealed, and new in this context.

Demonstration 1

Now you are ready to code. Before you declare an event, you need a delegate. In the example, you see the following line of code.

```
public event EventHandler MyIntChanged;
```

But you do not see the delegate declaration because I'm using a predefined EventHandler delegate.

Now let's focus on our implementation. There are two classes: Sender and Receiver. Sender plays the role of the broadcaster; it raises the MyIntChanged event when you change the myInt instance value. The Receiver class plays the role of the consumer. It has a method called GetNotificationFromSender. To get notifications from the sender, note the following line of code.

```
// Receiver is registering for a notification from sender
sender.MyIntChanged += receiver.GetNotificationFromSender;
```

Here the sender is a Sender class object, and the receiver is a Receiver class object. Eventually, the receiver is no longer interested in getting further notifications from the sender and unsubscribes from the event by using following code.

```
// Unregistering now
sender.MyIntChanged -= receiver.GetNotificationFromSender;
```

It's worth noting that the sender can send notifications to itself. To demonstrate this, inside the final lines of Main, you see the following code.

```
// Sender will receive its own notification now onwards
sender.MyIntChanged += sender.GetNotificationItself;
using System;

namespace EventEx1
{
    class Sender
    {
        private int myInt;
        public int MyInt
```

```csharp
        {
            get
            {
                return myInt;
            }
            set
            {
                myInt = value;
             //Whenever we set a new value, the event will fire.
                OnMyIntChanged();
            }
        }
        //EventHandler is a predefined delegate which is used to
        //handle simple events.
        //It has the following signature:
        //delegate void System.EventHandler(object sender,System.EventArgs e)
        //where the sender tells who is sending the event and
        //EventArgs is used to store information about the event.
        public event EventHandler MyIntChanged;
        public void OnMyIntChanged()
        {
            if(MyIntChanged!=null )
            {
                MyIntChanged(this, EventArgs.Empty);
            }
        }

        public void GetNotificationItself(Object sender, System.EventArgs e)
        {
            Console.WriteLine("Sender himself send a notification: I have
            changed myInt value  to {0} ", myInt);
        }
    }
    class Receiver
    {
```

```
    public void GetNotificationFromSender(Object sender, System.
    EventArgs e)
    {
     Console.WriteLine("Receiver receives a notification: Sender
     recently has changed the myInt value . ");
    }
}
class Program
{
    static void Main(string[] args)
    {
        Console.WriteLine("***Exploring events.***");
        Sender sender = new Sender();
        Receiver receiver = new Receiver();
        //Receiver is registering for a notification from sender
        sender.MyIntChanged += receiver.GetNotificationFromSender;

        sender.MyInt = 1;
        sender.MyInt = 2;
        //Unregistering now
        sender.MyIntChanged -= receiver.GetNotificationFromSender;
        //No notification sent for the receiver now.
        sender.MyInt = 3;
        //Sender will receive its own notification now onwards.
        sender.MyIntChanged += sender.GetNotificationItself;
        sender.MyInt = 4;

        Console.ReadKey();

    }
  }
}
```

Output

The following is the output from running this program.

```
***Exploring events.***
Receiver receives a notification: Sender recently has changed the myInt value.
Receiver receives a notification: Sender recently has changed the myInt value.
Sender himself send a notification: I have changed myInt value  to 4
```

Analysis

Initially, I changed the sender's myInt value using the MyInt property. When I changed the value to 1 or 2, the Receiver object (receiver) received notifications because it subscribed to the event. Then the receiver unsubscribed. So, when I changed the value to 3, there was no notification for the receiver. Then sender subscribed to the event notification. As a result, when I changed the value to 4, the sender received a notification.

Note   In a real-world application, once you subscribe to an event, you should also unsubscribe from the event before you leave; otherwise, you may see the impact of memory leak.

Q&A Session

2.1 Can I use any method on a specific event?

No. It should match the delegate signature. For example, let's assume that the Receiver class has another method called UnRelatedMethod, as follows.

```
public void UnRelatedMethod()
{
    Console.WriteLine(" An unrelated method. ");
}
```

In demonstration 1, if you attached this method with MyIntChanged by using the statement

```
sender.MyIntChanged += receiver.UnRelatedMethod;//Error
```

you would get the following compile-time error:

```
CS0123    No overload for 'UnRelatedMethod' matches delegate 'EventHandler'
```

Creating Custom Events

In demonstration 1, you saw a built-in delegate, but in many cases, you may need your own event to handle specific scenarios. Let's exercise a program on a custom event. To make the example sort and simple, let's assume that the sender does not need to send any notification to itself. So, there is no method like GetNotificationItself in the Sender class now.

To make the changes align with the prior example, let's follow these steps.

1. Create a delegate. By convention, choose the delegate name with the EventHandler suffix; something like the following:

    ```
    delegate void MyIntChangedEventHandler(Object sender,
    EventArgs eventArgs);
    ```

2. Define your event. As a convention, you can drop the EventHandler suffix from the delegate name and set your event name.

    ```
    public event MyIntChangedEventHandler MyIntChanged;
    ```

3. Raise the event. Let's use the following method in the Sender class. In general, instead of making the method public, it is suggested that you make the method protected virtual.

    ```
    protected virtual void OnMyIntChanged()
    {
        if (MyIntChanged != null)
        {
            MyIntChanged(this, EventArgs.Empty);
        }
    }
    ```

4. Handle the event. Let's use a Receiver class, which has the
    following method to handle the event when it is raised. Let's keep
    it the same as in demonstration 1.

```
class Receiver
{
    public void GetNotificationFromSender(Object sender,
    System.EventArgs e)
    {
        Console.WriteLine("Receiver receives a notification:
        Sender recently has changed the myInt value . ");
    }
}
```

Demonstration 2

Now go through the complete demonstration.

```
using System;

namespace EventsEx2
{
    //Step 1-Create a delegate.
    //You can pick an name (this name will be your event name)
    //which has the suffix EventHandler.For example, in the following case
    //'MyIntChanged' is the event name which has the suffix 'EventHandler'

    delegate void MyIntChangedEventHandler(Object sender, EventArgs eventArgs);

    //Create a Sender or Publisher for the event.
    class Sender
    {
        //Step-2: Create the event based on your delegate.
        public event MyIntChangedEventHandler MyIntChanged;

        private int myInt;
        public int MyInt
        {
            get
```

```csharp
        {
            return myInt;
        }
        set
        {
            myInt = value;
         //Raise the event.
         //Whenever we set a new value, the event will fire.
            OnMyIntChanged();
        }
    }

    /*
    Step-3.
    In the standard practise, the method name is the event name with a prefix
    'On'.For example, MyIntChanged(event name) is prefixed with 'On' here.
    Also, in normal practises, instead of making the method 'public',
    you make the method 'protected virtual'.
    */
    protected virtual void OnMyIntChanged()
    {
        if (MyIntChanged != null)
        {
            MyIntChanged(this, EventArgs.Empty);
        }
    }
}
//Step-4: Create a Receiver or Subscriber for the event.
class Receiver
{
    public void GetNotificationFromSender(Object sender, System.
    EventArgs e)
    {
        Console.WriteLine("Receiver receives a notification: Sender
        recently has changed the myInt value . ");
    }
```

```
    }
    class Program
    {
        static void Main(string[] args)
        {
            Console.WriteLine("***Exploring a custom event.***");
            Sender sender = new Sender();
            Receiver receiver = new Receiver();
            //Receiver is registering for a notification from sender
            sender.MyIntChanged += receiver.GetNotificationFromSender;

            sender.MyInt = 1;
            sender.MyInt = 2;
            //Unregistering now
            sender.MyIntChanged -= receiver.GetNotificationFromSender;
            //No notification sent for the receiver now.
            sender.MyInt = 3;
            Console.ReadKey();
        }
    }
}
```

Output

The following is the output from running this program.

```
***Exploring a custom event.***
Receiver receives a notification: Sender recently has changed the myInt value .
Receiver receives a notification: Sender recently has changed the myInt value .
```

Analysis

You can see that by using the MyInt property, I'm changing the myInt value. When the value was set to 1 or 2, there was a notification for the receiver, but when myInt value was changed to 3, the receiver didn't get a notification because the event notification was unsubscribed.

Passing Data to an Event Argument

Let's take another look at the OnMyIntChanged method. In the previous two demonstrations, I used the following line of code in the method.

```
MyIntChanged(this, EventArgs.Empty);
```

I didn't pass anything in the event argument. But in real-world programming, you may need to pass something meaningful. Let's analyze such a case in demonstration 3.

Demonstration 3

In this demonstration, I followed these steps.

1. Create a subclass of EventArgs. This class has a JobNo property to set the value of the jobNo instance variable.

2. Modify the OnMyIntChanged method to encapsulate the intended data (which is the job number in this case) with the event. Now the method looks like the following:

```
protected virtual void OnMyIntChanged()
{
    if (MyIntChanged != null)
    {
      // Combine your data with the event argument
      JobNoEventArgs jobNoEventArgs = new JobNoEventArgs();
      jobNoEventArgs.JobNo = myInt;
      MyIntChanged(this, jobNoEventArgs);
    }}
```

3. I kept the steps same in this demonstration.

Here is the full demonstration.

```
using System;

namespace EventsEx3
{
    // Create a subclass of System.EventArgs
```

```csharp
class JobNoEventArgs : EventArgs
{
    int jobNo = 0;
    public int JobNo
    {
        get { return jobNo; }
        set { jobNo = value; }
    }
}

// Create a delegate.
delegate void MyIntChangedEventHandler(Object sender, JobNoEventArgs
eventArgs);
// Create a Sender or Publisher for the event.
class Sender
{
    // Create the event based on your delegate.
    public event MyIntChangedEventHandler MyIntChanged;

    private int myInt;
    public int MyInt
    {
        get
        {
            return myInt;
        }
        set
        {
            myInt = value;
            // Raise the event.
            // Whenever you set a new value, the event will fire.
            OnMyIntChanged();
        }
    }
}
```

```
        /*
In the standard practise, the method name is the event name with a prefix
'On'.For example, MyIntChanged(event name) is prefixed with 'On' here.Also,
in normal practises, instead of making the method 'public',you make the
method 'protected virtual'.
        */
        protected virtual void OnMyIntChanged()
        {
            if (MyIntChanged != null)
            {   // Combine your data with the event argument
                JobNoEventArgs jobNoEventArgs = new JobNoEventArgs();
                jobNoEventArgs.JobNo = myInt;
                MyIntChanged(this, jobNoEventArgs);
            }
        }
    }
    // Create a Receiver or Subscriber for the event.
    class Receiver
    {
        public void GetNotificationFromSender(Object sender, JobNoEventArgs e)
        {
            Console.WriteLine("Receiver receives a notification: Sender
            recently has changed the myInt value to {0}.",e.JobNo);
        }
    }
    class Program
    {
        static void Main(string[] args)
        {
            Console.WriteLine("***Passing data in the event argument.***");
            Sender sender = new Sender();
            Receiver receiver = new Receiver();
            // Receiver is registering for a notification from sender
            sender.MyIntChanged += receiver.GetNotificationFromSender;

            sender.MyInt = 1;
```

```
                sender.MyInt = 2;
                // Unregistering now
                sender.MyIntChanged -= receiver.GetNotificationFromSender;
                // No notification sent for the receiver now.
                sender.MyInt = 3;
                Console.ReadKey();
            }
        }
}
```

Output

The following is the output from running this program.

```
***Passing data in the event argument.***
Receiver receives a notification: Sender recently has changed the myInt
value to 1.
Receiver receives a notification: Sender recently has changed the myInt
value to 2.
```

Using Event Accessors

Let's make some interesting changes to demonstration 3. Instead of using

```
public event MyIntChangedEventHandler MyIntChanged;
```

use the following segment of code.

```
private MyIntChangedEventHandler myIntChanged;
public event MyIntChangedEventHandler MyIntChanged
{
    add
    {
        myIntChanged += value;
```

```
    }
    remove
    {
    myIntChanged -= value;
    }
}
```

To accommodate this change, let's update the OnMyIntChanged method as follows.

```
protected virtual void OnMyIntChanged()
{
    if (myIntChanged != null)
    {
        // Combine your data with the event argument
        JobNoEventArgs jobNoEventArgs = new JobNoEventArgs();
        jobNoEventArgs.JobNo = myInt;
        myIntChanged(this, jobNoEventArgs);
    }
}
```

Now if you execute the program, you receive the same output. How is this possible? The compiler works in a way that is similar to when you declared the event. Let's go back to the fundamentals of events.

An event is a special kind of multicast delegate, and you can invoke it only from the class that contains the event. A receiver can subscribe to the event, and it handles the event with a method in it. So, the receiver passes the method reference when subscribing to the event. As a result, this method is added to the delegate's subscription list through event accessors. These event accessors are similar to property accessors except they are named add and remove.

Normally, you do not need to supply custom event accessors. But when you define them, you are instructing the C# compiler to not generate the default field and accessors for you.

At the time of writing, applications based on the .NET Framework target C# 7.3; whereas .NET Core applications target C# 8.0. If you execute the same program in the .NET Framework (let's rename it EventEx3DotNetFramework) and investigate the IL code, you will notice the presence of add_<EventName> and remove_<EventName> in the IL code. Figure 2-1 is a partial screenshot of the IL code.

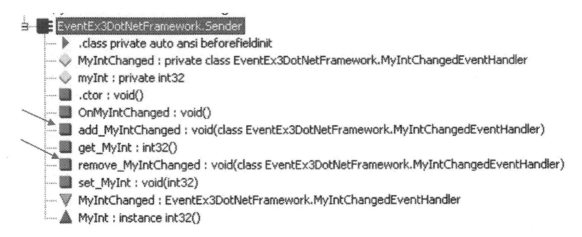

Figure 2-1. *Partial screenshot of IL code*

Demonstration 4

Let's go through a complete demonstration, which is as follows.

```
using System;

namespace EventsEx4
{
    //Create a subclass of System.EventArgs
    class JobNoEventArgs : EventArgs
    {
        int jobNo = 0;
        public int JobNo
        {
            get { return jobNo; }
            set { jobNo = value; }
        }
    }

    // Create a delegate.
    delegate void MyIntChangedEventHandler(Object sender, JobNoEventArgs
    eventArgs);

    // Create a Sender or Publisher for the event.
    class Sender
```

```csharp
{
    // Create the event based on your delegate.
    #region equivalent code
    // public event MyIntChangedEventHandler MyIntChanged;
    private MyIntChangedEventHandler myIntChanged;
    public event MyIntChangedEventHandler MyIntChanged
    {
        add
        {
            Console.WriteLine("***Inside add accessor.Entry
            point.***");
            myIntChanged += value;
        }
        remove
        {
            myIntChanged -= value;
            Console.WriteLine("***Inside remove accessor.Exit point.***");
        }
    }
    #endregion

    private int myInt;
    public int MyInt
    {
        get
        {
            return myInt;
        }
        set
        {
            myInt = value;
            // Raise the event.
            // Whenever we set a new value, the event will fire.
            OnMyIntChanged();
        }
    }
}
```

```csharp
    protected virtual void OnMyIntChanged()
    {
        // if (MyIntChanged != null)
        if (myIntChanged != null)
        {
            // Combine your data with the event argument
            JobNoEventArgs jobNoEventArgs = new JobNoEventArgs();
            jobNoEventArgs.JobNo = myInt;
            // MyIntChanged(this, jobNoEventArgs);
            myIntChanged(this, jobNoEventArgs);
        }
    }
}
// Create a Receiver or Subscriber for the event.
class Receiver
{
    public void GetNotificationFromSender(Object sender, JobNoEventArgs e)
    {
        Console.WriteLine("Receiver receives a notification: Sender
        recently has changed the myInt value to {0}.", e.JobNo);
    }
}
class Program
{
    static void Main(string[] args)
    {
        Console.WriteLine("***Using event accessors.***");
        Sender sender = new Sender();
        Receiver receiver = new Receiver();
        // Receiver is registering for a notification from sender
        sender.MyIntChanged += receiver.GetNotificationFromSender;

        sender.MyInt = 1;
        sender.MyInt = 2;
        // Unregistering now
        sender.MyIntChanged -= receiver.GetNotificationFromSender;
```

```
            // No notification sent for the receiver now.
            sender.MyInt = 3;
            Console.ReadKey();
        }
    }
}
```

Output

The following is the output from running this program.

```
***Using event accessors.***
***Inside add accessor.Entry point.***
Receiver receives a notification: Sender recently has changed the myInt
value to 1.
Receiver receives a notification: Sender recently has changed the myInt
value to 2.
***Inside remove accessor.Exit point.***
```

Analysis

When you use event accessors, keep in mind one important suggestion: implement the locking mechanism. For example, demonstration 4 can be improved when you write the following segment of code.

```
public object lockObject = new object();
private MyIntChangedEventHandler myIntChanged;
public event MyIntChangedEventHandler MyIntChanged
{
    add
    {
        lock (lockObject)
        {
            Console.WriteLine("***Inside add accessor.Entry point.***");
            myIntChanged += value;
        }
    }
```

```
    remove
    {
        lock (lockObject)
        {
            myIntChanged -= value;
            Console.WriteLine("***Inside remove accessor.Exit point.***");
        }
    }
}
```

Q&A Session

2.2 What are the key benefits of using user-defined event accessors?

Let's take a closer look at the following segment of code.

```
private  MyIntChangedEventHandler myIntChanged;
public event MyIntChangedEventHandler MyIntChanged
{
    add
    {
        myIntChanged += value;
    }
    remove
    {
        myIntChanged -= value;
    }
}
```

Note that these event accessors are similar to property accessors, except they are named add and remove. Here you use a property-like wrapper around your delegate. As a result, only the containing class can invoke the delegate directly; outsiders cannot do this. This promotes better security and control over your code.

Handling Interface Events

An interface can contain events. You need to follow the same rule when you implement an interface method or a property. The following example shows such an implementation.

Demonstration 5

In this example, IMyInterface has a MyIntChanged event. I used Sender and Receiver, which are identical to prior examples. The only difference is that this time, the Sender class is implementing the IMyInterface interface.

```
using System;

namespace EventEx5
{
    interface IMyInterface
    {
        // An interface event
        event EventHandler MyIntChanged;
    }
    class Sender : IMyInterface
    {
        // Declare the event here and raise from your intended location
        public event EventHandler MyIntChanged;
        private int myInt;
        public int MyInt
        {
            get
            {
                return myInt;
            }
            set
            {
                // Setting a new value prior to raise the event.
                myInt = value;
```

```
                OnMyIntChanged();
            }
        }

        protected virtual void OnMyIntChanged()
        {
            if (MyIntChanged != null)
            {
                MyIntChanged(this, EventArgs.Empty);
            }
        }
    }
    class Receiver
    {
        public void GetNotificationFromSender(Object sender, System.
        EventArgs e)
        {
            Console.WriteLine("Receiver receives a notification: Sender
            recently has changed the myInt value . ");
        }
    }
    class Program
    {
        static void Main(string[] args)
        {
            Console.WriteLine("***Exploring an event with an
            interface.***");
            Sender sender = new Sender();
            Receiver receiver = new Receiver();
            // Receiver is registering for a notification from sender
            sender.MyIntChanged += receiver.GetNotificationFromSender;

            sender.MyInt = 1;
            sender.MyInt = 2;
            // Unregistering now
            sender.MyIntChanged -= receiver.GetNotificationFromSender;
```

```
            // No notification sent for the receiver now.
            sender.MyInt = 3;

            Console.ReadKey();
        }
    }
}
```

Output

The following is the output from running this program.

```
***Exploring an event with an interface.***
Receiver receives a notification: Sender recently has changed the myInt value .
Receiver receives a notification: Sender recently has changed the myInt value .
```

Q&A Session

2.3 How can my class implement multiple interfaces when the interface events have the same name?

Yes, this situation is interesting. When your class implements multiple interfaces that have events with a common name, you need to follow explicit interface implementation techniques. But there is one important restriction that says that in a case like this, you need to supply add and remove event accessors. Normally, the compiler can supply these accessors, but in this case, it cannot. The following section provides a complete demonstration.

Handling Explicit Interface Events

To keep things simple, this example aligns with previous examples. Let's assume that now you have two interfaces: IBeforeInterface and IAfterInterface. Further assume that each contains an event called MyIntChanged.

The Sender class implements these interfaces. Now you have two receivers: ReceiverBefore and ReceiverAfter. These Receiver classes want to get notifications when myInt is changed. In this example, a ReceiverBefore object gets notification prior to a myInt change, and a ReceiverAfter object gets the notification after a myInt change.

You saw how to implement event accessors in demonstration 4. The same mechanism is followed here. This time, I followed Microsoft's recommendation, so you see the use of locks inside event accessors.

Demonstration 6

Go through the following complete demonstration.

```
using System;

namespace EventEx6
{
    interface IBeforeInterface
    {
        public event EventHandler MyIntChanged;
    }
    interface IAfterInterface
    {
        public event EventHandler MyIntChanged;
    }
    class Sender : IBeforeInterface, IAfterInterface
    {
        // Creating two separate events for two interface events
        public event EventHandler BeforeMyIntChanged;
        public event EventHandler AfterMyIntChanged;
        // Microsoft recommends this, i.e. to use a lock inside accessors
        object objectLock = new Object();

        private int myInt;
        public int MyInt
        {
            get
            {
                return myInt;
            }
```

```csharp
    set
    {
        // Fire an event before we make a change to myInt.
        OnMyIntChangedBefore();
        Console.WriteLine("Making a change to myInt from {0} to
        {1}.",myInt,value);
        myInt = value;
        // Fire an event after we make a change to myInt.
        OnMyIntChangedAfter();
    }
}
// Explicit interface implementation required.
// Associate IBeforeInterface's event with
// BeforeMyIntChanged
event EventHandler IBeforeInterface.MyIntChanged
{
    add
    {
        lock (objectLock)
        {
            BeforeMyIntChanged += value;
        }
    }

    remove
    {
        lock (objectLock)
        {
            BeforeMyIntChanged -= value;
        }
    }
}
// Explicit interface implementation required.
// Associate IAfterInterface's event with
// AfterMyIntChanged
```

```csharp
event EventHandler IAfterInterface.MyIntChanged
{
    add
    {
        lock (objectLock)
        {
            AfterMyIntChanged += value;
        }
    }

    remove
    {
        lock (objectLock)
        {
            AfterMyIntChanged -= value;
        }
    }
}
// This method uses BeforeMyIntChanged event
protected virtual void OnMyIntChangedBefore()
{
    if (BeforeMyIntChanged != null)
    {
        BeforeMyIntChanged(this, EventArgs.Empty);
    }
}
// This method uses AfterMyIntChanged event
protected virtual void OnMyIntChangedAfter()
{
    if (AfterMyIntChanged != null)
    {
        AfterMyIntChanged(this, EventArgs.Empty);
    }
}
}
```

```
// First receiver: ReceiverBefore class
class ReceiverBefore
{
    public void GetNotificationFromSender(Object sender, System.
    EventArgs e)
    {
        Console.WriteLine("ReceiverBefore receives : Sender is about to
        change the myInt value . ");
    }
}
// Second receiver: ReceiverAfter class
class ReceiverAfter
{
    public void GetNotificationFromSender(Object sender, System.
    EventArgs e)
    {
        Console.WriteLine("ReceiverAfter receives : Sender recently has
        changed the myInt value . ");
    }
}
class Program
{
    static void Main(string[] args)
    {
        Console.WriteLine("***Handling explicit interface events.***");
        Sender sender = new Sender();
        ReceiverBefore receiverBefore = new ReceiverBefore();
        ReceiverAfter receiverAfter = new ReceiverAfter();
        // Receiver's are registering for getting
        //notifications from Sender
        sender.BeforeMyIntChanged += receiverBefore.
        GetNotificationFromSender;
        sender.AfterMyIntChanged += receiverAfter.
        GetNotificationFromSender;
```

```
        sender.MyInt = 1;
        Console.WriteLine("");
        sender.MyInt = 2;
        // Unregistering now
        sender.BeforeMyIntChanged -= receiverBefore.
        GetNotificationFromSender;
        sender.AfterMyIntChanged -= receiverAfter.
        GetNotificationFromSender;
        Console.WriteLine("");
        // No notification sent for the receivers now.
        sender.MyInt = 3;

        Console.ReadKey();
    }
  }
}
```

Output

The following is the output from running this program.

```
***Handling explicit interface events.***
ReceiverBefore receives : Sender is about to change the myInt value .
Making a change to myInt from 0 to 1.
ReceiverAfter receives : Sender recently has changed the myInt value .

ReceiverBefore receives : Sender is about to change the myInt value .
Making a change to myInt from 1 to 2.
ReceiverAfter receives : Sender recently has changed the myInt value .

Making a change to myInt from 2 to 3.
```

Q&A Session

2.4 Delegates are the backbone for events, and in general, we follow an observer design pattern when we write code for events and register and unregister those events. Is this correct?

Yes.

2.5 In the beginning of the chapter, you said I can also use the "new" keyword when I write a program on an event. Can you give an example?

I basically used the short form. For example, in demonstration 1, you saw the following line of code when I registered the event.

```
sender.MyIntChanged += receiver.GetNotificationFromSender;
```

Now if you recall the short form used in the context of delegates from Chapter 1, you can write equivalent code, as follows.

```
sender.MyIntChanged += new EventHandler(receiver.
GetNotificationFromSender);
```

Apart from this, consider another case in which your Sender class contains a sealed event. If you have a derived class of Sender, it cannot use the event. Instead, the derived class can use the "new" keyword to indicate that it is not overriding the base class event.

2.6 Can you give an example of an abstract event?

See demonstration 7.

Demonstration 7

Microsoft says that for an abstract event, you do not get compiler-generated add and remove event accessor blocks. So, your derived class needs to provide its own implementation. Let's make it simple and modify demonstration 1 slightly. Like demonstration 2, let's assume that in this example, the sender does not need to send notifications to itself. The GetNotificationItself method is absent inside the Sender class in this demonstration.

Now let's focus on the key part. The Sender class contains an abstract event, which is as follows.

```
public abstract event EventHandler MyIntChanged;
```

Since the class contains an abstract event, the class itself becomes abstract.

I'll now introduce another class, called ConcreteSender, which derives from Sender. It overrides the event and completes the event invocation process.

Here is the implementation of ConcreteSender.

```
class ConcreteSender : Sender
{
    public override event EventHandler MyIntChanged;
    protected override void OnMyIntChanged()
    {
        if (MyIntChanged != null)
        {
            MyIntChanged(this, EventArgs.Empty);
        }
    }
}
```

Now let's go through the complete program and output.

```
using System;

namespace EventsEx7
{
    abstract class Sender
    {
        private int myInt;
        public int MyInt
        {
            get
            {
                return myInt;
            }
            set
            {
                myInt = value;
                // Whenever we set a new value, the event will fire.
                OnMyIntChanged();
            }
        }
```

```csharp
        // Abstract event.The containing class becomes abstract for this.
        public abstract event EventHandler MyIntChanged;
        protected virtual void OnMyIntChanged()
        {
            Console.WriteLine("Sender.OnMyIntChanged");
        }
    }
    class ConcreteSender : Sender
    {
        public override event EventHandler MyIntChanged;
        protected override void OnMyIntChanged()
        {
            if (MyIntChanged != null)
            {
                MyIntChanged(this, EventArgs.Empty);
            }
        }
    }

class Receiver
{
    public void GetNotificationFromSender(Object sender, System.EventArgs e)
    {
        Console.WriteLine("Receiver receives a notification: Sender
        recently has changed the myInt value . ");
    }

}
class Program
{
    static void Main(string[] args)
    {
        Console.WriteLine("***Exploring an abstract event.***");
        Sender sender = new ConcreteSender();
        Receiver receiver = new Receiver();
        // Receiver is registering for a notification from sender
```

```
        sender.MyIntChanged += receiver.GetNotificationFromSender;
        sender.MyInt = 1;
        sender.MyInt = 2;
        // Unregistering now
        sender.MyIntChanged -= receiver.GetNotificationFromSender;
        // No notification sent for the receiver now.
        sender.MyInt = 3;

        Console.ReadKey();
    }
}}
```

Output

The following is the output from running this program.

```
***Exploring an abstract event.***
Receiver receives a notification: Sender recently has changed the myInt
value .
Receiver receives a notification: Sender recently has changed the myInt
value .
```

Q&A Session

2.7 I understand that EventHandler **is a predefined delegate. But in many places, I've seen people using the term** *event handler* **in a broad sense. Is there any special meaning associated with it?**

Simply put, an event handler is a procedure, and you decide what to do when a specific event is raised. For example, when a user clicks a button in a GUI application. It is important to note that your event can have multiple handlers, and at the same time, the method that handles the event can also change dynamically. In this chapter, you saw how events work, and particularly, how a Receiver class handles events. But if you use a ready-made construct like Windows Form Designer in Visual Studio, you can code events very easily.

2.8 It would be helpful to have an example of how to add an event handler in a GUI application.

Let's look at demonstration 8.

Demonstration 8

In this demonstration, I create a simple UI application to demonstrate a simple event handling mechanism. The steps to do it are as follows.

1. Create a Windows Form app.

2. From the Toolbox, drag a button onto the form. Let's name it **Test**. Figure 2-2 shows what it may look like.

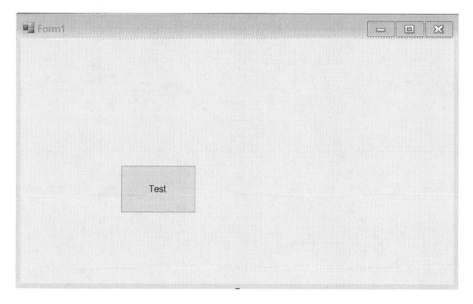

Figure 2-2. *Test button placed on Form1*

3. Select the button. Open the Properties window and click the **Events** button. Name the Click event TestBtnClickHandler (see Figure 2-3).

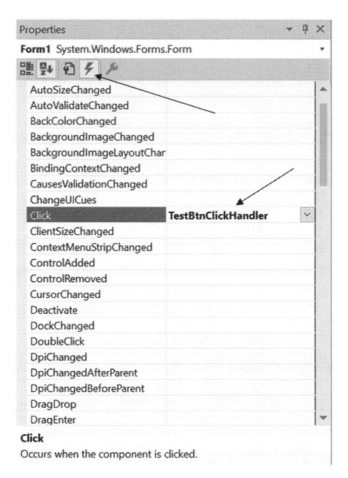

Figure 2-3. *Setting the Click event name as* `TestBtnClickHandler`

4. Double-click the Test button. This opens the Form1.cs file, in which you can write the following code for your event handler.

```
private void TestBtnClickHandler(object sender, EventArgs e)
{
 MessageBox.Show("Hello Reader.");
}
```

Output

Run your application and click the Test button. You see the output shown in Figure 2-4. (To take a better screenshot, I dragged the message box window on Form1.)

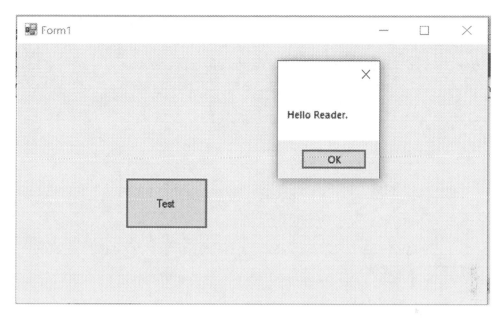

Figure 2-4. *Output screenshot from Visual Studio when you click the Test button*

Note   Demonstration 8 was executed in .NET Framework but not in .NET Core. At the time of writing, Visual Designer was labeled as a "preview feature" for .NET Core applications, and it was suffering from a lot of issues (For more information, go to `https://github.com/dotnet/winforms/blob/master/Documentation/designer-releases/0.1/knownissues.md`). When you click the Form1.cs file in Solution Explorer, you cannot see Form1.cs[Design] in a .NET Core application.

Final Words

In demonstration 2, you saw the following code segment.

```
if (MyIntChanged != null)
{
    MyIntChanged(this, EventArgs.Empty);
}
```

Actually, you see this kind of null check before raising your event in all examples. This is important, because if there is no listener (or receiver) for the event, you may encounter with an exception called `NullReferenceException`. In such cases, Visual Studio shows you the screen shown in Figure 2-5.

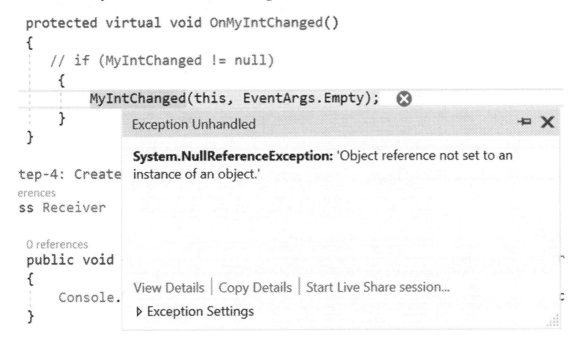

Figure 2-5. *A NullReferenceException occurred due to the absence of event listeners and the proper null check*

A null check is important prior to raising an event. But you can assume that in a real-world application, if you need to do several null checks, it'll make your code clumsy. In that case, you can use a feature available since C# 6.0. You can use the null conditional operator to avoid sudden surprises.

I provide an alternate code segment using this operator. (I kept the dead code with comments so that you can compare both code segments at the same time).

```
//if (MyIntChanged != null)
//{
//    MyIntChanged(this, EventArgs.Empty);
//}
//Alternate code
MyIntChanged?.Invoke(this, EventArgs.Empty);
```

This is all about events. Now lets move on to Chapter 3, where you learn to use another powerful feature in C#: lambda expressions.

Summary

This chapter addressed the following key questions.

- What is an event? How do you use the built-in support for events?

- How do you write a custom event?

- How do you pass data to your event argument?

- How do you use event accessors? Why are they useful?

- How do you use different interface events?

- How do you apply different modifiers and keywords to an event?

- How can you implement an event handling mechanism in a simple UI application?

CHAPTER 3

Lambda Expressions

Lambda expressions and anonymous methods are two important concepts in advanced programming. Collectively, they are often referred to as anonymous functions. The concept of anonymous methods came in C# 2.0, and lambda expressions were introduced in C# 3.0. Over time, lambda expressions became more popular than anonymous methods. If you target .NET Framework 3.5 or later, it is recommended that you use lambda expressions. This chapter shows you different ways to use lambda expressions and how they are used effectively in advanced programming.

The Usefulness of Lambda Expressions

A lambda expression is an anonymous method written in a form that is easily readable. What is an anonymous method and why is it useful? As the name suggests, an anonymous method is a method that does not have a name. In certain situations, they are very helpful. For example, when you point a method using a delegate but the method is present in a different location in the source file (or, in an extreme case, it is in a different source file). This segregated code is difficult to understand, debug, and maintain. In such situations, anonymous methods are helpful because you can define an "in-line" method without a name to serve your purpose.

The word *lambda* comes from lambda calculus, which simulates a Turing machine. It is spelled with the Greek letter lambda (λ), which your keyboard does not have. To denote a lambda operator, you use the => symbols. The left side of the operator specifies the input parameters (if any) and the right side of the operator specifies either an expression or a statement block. The => is right associative, and its precedence is the same as =. When reading code that contains a lambda operator, you replace the lambda operator with *goes to*, *go to*, *arrow*, or *become(s)*. For example, you read x=> x+5; as x goes to x+5. Similarly, you read (x,y)=>x+y; as x and y go to x+y.

© Vaskaran Sarcar 2020
V. Sarcar, *Getting Started with Advanced C#*, https://doi.org/10.1007/978-1-4842-5934-4_3

The C# compiler can convert a lambda expression to either a delegate instance or an expression tree (it is often used in LINQ). This book does not discuss LINQ in detail, but you have learned about delegates and saw several examples on them in Chapter 1. Let's focus on delegate instances here.

Note   When a lambda expression is converted to a delegate type, the result depends on the input parameters and return type. If a lambda expression doesn't have a return type, it can be converted to one of the Action delegates types; if it has a return type, it can be converted to one of the Func delegate types. Func and Action are generic delegates, which you learn about in Chapter 4.

Demonstration 1

I start with a simple program that calculates the sum of two integers (21 and 79) by using various approaches. The first approach uses a normal method (which you are familiar with). You can use this method to calculate the sum of the ints. Next, I show you how to use a delegate instance to do the same. The last two segments of code show you the use of an anonymous method and a lambda expression, respectively. Each program segment generates the same output. The program lets you choose the approach. For readability, go through the supportive comments.

```csharp
using System;

namespace LambdaExpressionEx1
{
    public delegate int Mydel(int x, int y);

    class Program
    {
        public static int Sum(int a, int b) { return a + b; }

        static void Main(string[] args)
        {
            Console.WriteLine("***Exploring the use of a lambda expression
            and comparing it with other techniques. ***");
```

```
// Without using delgates or lambda expression
Console.WriteLine(" Using a normal method.");
int a = 21, b = 79;
Console.WriteLine(" Invoking the Sum() method in a common way
without using a delegate.");
Console.WriteLine("Sum of {0} and {1} is : {2}", a,b, Sum(a, b));

/* Using Delegate(Initialization with a named method)*/
Mydel del1 = new Mydel(Sum);
Console.WriteLine("\n Using delegate now.");
Console.WriteLine("Invoking the Sum() method with the use of a
delegate.");
Console.WriteLine("Sum of {0} and {1} is : {2}", a, b, del1(a, b));

// Using Anonymous method (C# 2.0 onwards)
Mydel del2 = delegate (int x, int y) { return x + y; };
Console.WriteLine("\n Using anonymous method now.");
Console.WriteLine("Invoking the Sum() method using an anonymous
method.");
Console.WriteLine("Sum of {0} and {1} is : {2}", a, b, del2(a, b));

// Using Lambda expression(C# 3.0 onwards)
Console.WriteLine("\n Using lambda expression now.");
Mydel sumOfTwoIntegers = (x, y) => x + y;
Console.WriteLine("Sum of {0} and {1} is : {2}", a, b,
sumOfTwoIntegers(a, b));
Console.ReadKey();
        }
    }
}
```

Output

The following is the output from running this program.

```
***Exploring the use of a lambda expression and comparing it with other
techniques.***
Using a normal method.
```

Invoking the Sum() method in a common way without using a delegate.
Sum of 21 and 79 is : 100

 Using delegate now.
Invoking the Sum() method with the use of a delegate.
Sum of 21 and 79 is : 100

 Using anonymous method now.
Invoking the Sum() method using an anonymous method.
Sum of 21 and 79 is : 100

 Using lambda expression now.
Sum of 21 and 79 is : 100

Analysis

Let's review the statements used for the anonymous method and the lambda expression. For the anonymous method, I used

```
delegate (int x, int y) { return x + y; };
```

For the lambda expression, I used

```
(x, y) => x + y;
```

If you are familiar with anonymous methods but not lambda expressions, you can use the following steps to get a lambda expression from an anonymous method.

For step 1, remove the delegate keyword from the anonymous method expression, which results in what's shown in Figure 3-1.

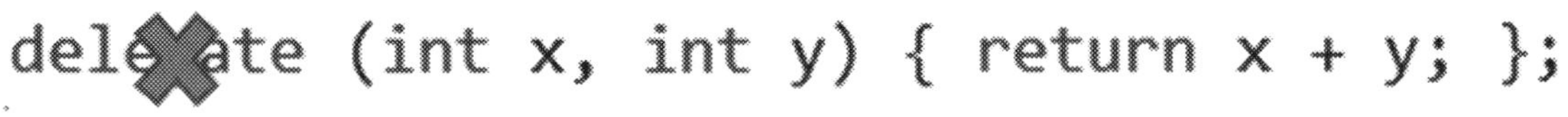

Figure 3-1. *Removing the delegate keyword from the anonymous method expression*

That is, you get (int x, int y) {return x + y; };.

In step 2, add a lambda operator, which results in what's shown in Figure 3-2. (It also results in a valid lambda expression.)

```
(int x, int y)  => { return x + y; };
```

Figure 3-2. *Adding the lambda operator in step1 expression*

Notice that in this case, I am dealing with a single return statement. In a case like this, as step 3, you can remove curly braces, semicolons, and the return, which results in what's shown in Figure 3-3 (it is a valid lambda statement).

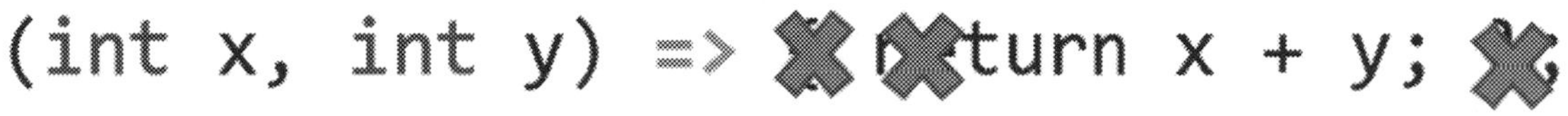

```
(int x, int y) => 🟥 🟥turn x + y; 🟥
```

Figure 3-3. *Removing curly braces, semicolons, and "return" from the expression in step 2*

That is, you get: `(int x, int y) => x + y;`

In most cases, compilers can identify the input parameters and return type when it deals with a lambda expression. In programming terms, this is called *type inference*. Still, in some special cases, you may need to keep this type information to let the compiler evaluate the expression properly. But this is a very simple case, and the compiler can understand it properly (in this context, note the delegate declaration), even if you do not mention the type of the input parameters. As a result, for step 4, you can remove that type information from input parameters and make the expression shorter, as shown in Figure 3-4.

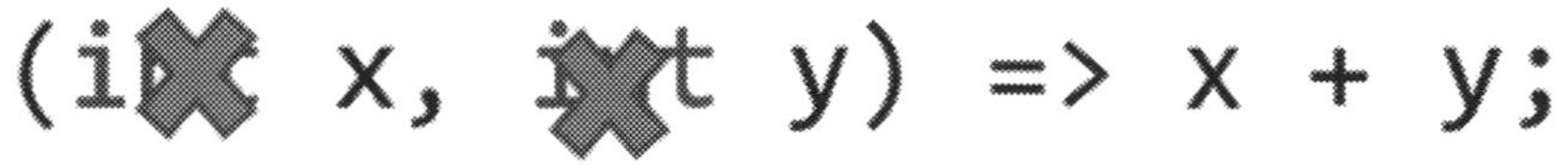

```
(i🟥 x, 🟥t y) => x + y;
```

Figure 3-4. *Removing type info from the expression in step 3 to get the shortest expression*

That is, you get `(x, y) => x + y;`.

Lambda Expression with (and Without) Parameters

A lambda expression can accept one or multiple parameters. You can also use a lambda expression that does not accept any parameters.

In demonstration 1, you saw that when a lambda expression uses multiple parameters, you list them in parentheses separated by commas, like `(x, y)=> x+y;`.

If a lambda expression accepts only one parameter, you can omit the parentheses. For example, you can use either `(x)=> x*x;` or `x=>x*x;`. Both serve the same purpose.

Finally, `() => Console.WriteLine("No parameter.");` is an example of a lambda expression that does not have any parameters. Demonstration 2 features all the cases.

Demonstration 2

This demonstration covers the usage of lambda expressions with different parameters.

```
using System;

namespace LambdaExpTest2
{
    class Program
    {
        public delegate void DelegateWithNoParameter();
        public delegate int DelegateWithOneIntParameter(int x);
        public delegate void DelegateWithTwoIntParameters(int x, int y);
        static void Main(string[] args)
        {
            Console.WriteLine("***Experimenting lambda expressions with
            different parameters.***\n");
            // Without lambda exp.
            Method1(5, 10);

            // Using Lambda expression

            DelegateWithNoParameter delWithNoParam = () => Console.
            WriteLine("Using lambda expression with no parameter, printing
            Hello");
            delWithNoParam();
```

```
            DelegateWithOneIntParameter delWithOneIntParam = (x) => x * x;
            Console.WriteLine("\nUsing a lambda expression with one
            parameter, square of 5 is {0}", delWithOneIntParam(5));

            DelegateWithTwoIntParameters delWithTwoIntParam = (int x, int y) =>
              {
                  Console.WriteLine("\nUsing lambda expression with two
                  parameters.");
                  Console.WriteLine("It is called a statement lambda
                  because it has a block of statements in it's body.");
                  Console.WriteLine("This lambda accepts two parameters.");
                  int sum = x + y;
                  Console.WriteLine("Sum of {0} and {1} is {2}", x, y, sum);
              };

            delWithTwoIntParam(10,20);

            Console.ReadKey();
        }

        private static void Method1(int a, int b)
        {
           Console.WriteLine("\nThis is Method1() without lambda expression.");
            int sum = a + b;
            Console.WriteLine("Sum of {0} and {1} is {2}", a, b, sum);
        }
    }
}
```

Output

The following is the output from running this program.

```
***Experimenting lambda expressions with different parameters.***
This is Method1() without lambda expression.
Sum of 5 and 10 is 15

Using lambda expression with no parameter, printing Hello
```

Using a lambda expression with one parameter, square of 5 is 25

Using lambda expression with two parameters.
It is called a statement lambda because it has a block of statements in
it's body.
This lambda accepts two parameters.
Sum of 10 and 20 is 30

Types of Lambda Expressions

Ideally, lambda expressions are used for the single-line methods. But in demonstration 2, you saw that a lambda expression can be more than one line.

In programming terms, you categorize lambda expressions as expression lambdas and statement lambdas. An expression lambda has a single expression, whereas a statement lambda contains a block of statements. Statement lambdas may use curly braces, semicolons, and return statements. A statement lambda can contain any number of statements, but in general, they contain two or three statements. If you use more than three lines in a lambda expression, it may complicate its understanding; in those cases, you may prefer a normal method over a lambda expression.

Expression-Bodied Members

Lambda expressions first appeared in C# 3.0, but starting in C# 6.0, they offered additional flexibility: if you have a non-lambda method inside a class, you can use the same expression syntax to define the same method. For example, in the following demonstration, there is a class called Test.

```
class Test
{
    public int CalculateSum1(int a, int b)
    {
        int sum = a + b;
        return sum;
    }
}
```

```
        // Expression-bodied method is not available in C#5
        public int CalculateSum2(int a, int b) => a + b; // ok
    }
```

Note the non-lambda method CalculateSum1. It is a simple method that accepts two ints, calculates their sum, and returns the result (which is also an int).

Since C# 6.0 onward, you can write a lambda expression to define an equivalent version of CalculateSum1. The following is such an expression.

public int CalculateSum2(int a, int b) => a + b;

If you use this in a C# version prior to C# 6.0 (say, in C# 5.0), you get the following compile-time error.

```
CS8026: Feature 'expression-bodied method' is not available in C# 5. Please
use language version 6 or greater.
```

Figure 3-5 is a Visual Studio IDE screenshot for your reference.

CS8026   Feature 'expression-bodied method' is not available in C# 5. Please use language version 6 or greater

Figure 3-5. *Feature 'expression-bodied method' is not available in C# 5*

I kept the comments to help you understand. But it is important to note that you can use this concept when your method can be expressed with a single expression (i.e., there is only one line of code in the method implementation). In other words, it is applicable to *expression lambda* syntax, but you cannot use it for *statement lambda* syntax. In demonstration 3, if you uncomment the following code segment, you get a compile-time error.

```
//int CalculateSum3(int a, int b) =>{
//    int sum = a + b;
//    return sum;
//}
```

Demonstration 3

This complete demonstration shows the use of an expression-bodied method.

```
using System;

namespace ExpressionBodiedMethodDemo
{
    class Test
    {
        public int CalculateSum1(int a, int b)
        {
            int sum = a + b;
            return sum;
        }
        /*
        Expression-bodied method is not available in C#5.
        C#6.0 onwards,you can use same expression syntax to define a
        non-lambda method within a class
        It is ok for single expression, i.e. for
        expression lambda syntax,but not for statement lambda.
        */

        public int CalculateSum2(int a, int b) => a + b;//ok

        // Following causes compile-time error
        // For expression-bodied methods, you cannot use
        // statement lambda
        //int CalculateSum3(int a, int b) =>{
        //    int sum = a + b;
        //    return sum;
        //}
    }
```

```
class Program
{
    static void Main(string[] args)
    {
        Console.WriteLine("***Experimenting lambda expression with
        expression-bodied method.***\n");
        // Using Normal method
        Test test = new Test();
        int result1 = test.CalculateSum1(5, 7);
        Console.WriteLine("\nUsing a normal method, CalculateSum1(5, 7)
        results: {0}", result1);
        // Using expression syntax

        int result2 = test.CalculateSum2(5, 7);
        Console.WriteLine("\nUsing expression syntax for
        CalculateSum2(5,7),result is: {0}", result2);
        Console.ReadKey();
    }
}
}
```

Output

The following is the output from running this program.

```
***Experimenting lambda expression with expression-bodied method.***

Using a normal method, CalculateSum1(5, 7) results: 12

Using expression syntax for CalculateSum2(5,7),result is: 12
```

POINTS TO REMEMBER

Expression syntax to define non-lambda methods are not applicable for *statement lambdas*. You can use it only for *expression lambdas*.

Demonstration 4

Demonstration 3 showed you the use of an expression-bodied method, but it is also applicable to properties, constructors, and finalizers. In demonstration 4, you see how it is used with a constructor, a read-only property, and a read-write property. So, let's focus on the important segments of code and compare them with the usual implementations.

Suppose that you have an `Employee` class in which there is employee ID, company name, and employee name. In the code, I represented them as `empId`, `company`, and `name`, respectively. You supply the `empId` when you initialize an `Employee` object. `Company` is a read-only property and `Name` is a read-write property.

The following is the usual implementation of the public constructor, which takes only one argument.

```
public Employee(int id)
{
 empId = id;
}
```

The following shows the expression-bodied constructor.

```
public Employee(int id) => empId = id;
```

Here is the usual implementation of the read-only `Company` property.

```
public string Company
{
  get
  {
    return company;
  }
}
```

The following shows the expression-body definition of the read-only property.

```
public string Company => company;
```

Here is the usual implementation of the read-write Name property.

```
public string Name
{
  get
  {
    return name;
  }
  set
  {
    name = value;
  }
}
```

The following shows the expression-body definition of the read-write property.

```
public string Name
 {
    get => name;
    set => name = value;
 }
```

Let's go through the complete demonstration and output, which are as follows.

```
using System;

namespace Expression_BodiedPropertiesDemo
{
    class Employee
    {
        private int empId;
        private string company = "XYZ Ltd.";
        private string name = String.Empty;

        //Usual implementation of a constructor.
        //public Employee(int id)
        //{
        //    empId = id;
        //}
```

```csharp
//Following shows an expression-bodied constructor
public Employee(int id) => empId = id;//ok

//Usual implementation of a read-only property
//public string Company
//{
//    get
//    {
//        return company;
//    }
//}
//Read-only property.C#6.0 onwards.
public string Company => company;

//Usual implementation
//public string Name
//{
//    get
//    {
//        return name;
//    }
//    set
//    {
//        name = value;
//    }
//}

//C#7.0 onwards , we can use expression-body definition for the get
//and set accessors.
public string Name
{
    get => name;
    set => name = value;
}
}
```

```
class Program
{
    static void Main(string[] args)
    {
        Console.WriteLine("***Experimenting lambda expressions with
        expression-bodied properties.***");
        Employee empOb = new Employee(1);
        //Error.Company is read-only
        //empOb.Company = "ABC Co.";
        empOb.Name = "Rohan Roy ";//ok
        Console.WriteLine("{0} works in {1} as an employee.",
        empOb.Name,empOb.Company);
        Console.ReadKey();
    }
}
}
```

Output

The following is the output from running this program.

```
***Experimenting lambda expressions with expression-bodied properties.***
Rohan Roy  works in XYZ Ltd. as an employee.
```

POINTS TO REMEMBER

In C# 6.0, we got support for expression-bodied methods and read-only properties. In C# 7.0, the support was extended to properties, indexers, constructors, and finalizers.

Local Variables in a Lambda Expression

You may have noticed the use of local variables in a lambda expression. In this case, the variable must be in scope. Demonstration 5 shows a simple use of a local variable inside a lambda expression.

Demonstration 5

This demonstration draws your attention to the following points.

- You can use either query syntax or method call syntax in your program. I've shown the usage of both. (If you are familiar with LINQ programming, you know about query syntax; otherwise, you can skip that segment of code until you learn about it.) Consider the following code, particularly the bold portions:

  ```
  IEnumerable<int> numbersAboveMidPoint = intList.Where(x =>
  x > midPoint);
  ```

- midPoint is a local variable. A lambda expression can access this variable because it is in scope at this location.

- List<int> and IEnumerable<int> are used in this example. They are the simplest constructs in generic programming. If you are new to generics, you can skip this example for now and come back after covering generic programming in Chapter 4.

Let's go through the demonstration.

```
using System;
using System.Collections.Generic;
using System.Linq;

namespace TestingLocalVariableScopeUsingLambdaExpression
{
    class Program
    {
        static void Main(string[] args)
        {
            Console.WriteLine("***Testing local variable scope with a
            lambda expression.***\n");
            #region Using query syntax
            /* Inside lambda Expression,you can access the variable that
            are in scope (at that location).*/
            int midPoint = 5;
```

```
List<int> intList = new List<int> { 1, 2, 3, 4, 5, 6, 7, 8, 9, 10 };
var myQueryAboveMidPoint = from i in intList
                           where i > midPoint
                           select i;
Console.WriteLine("Numbers above mid point(5) in intList are as
follows:");
foreach (int number in myQueryAboveMidPoint)
{
    Console.WriteLine(number);
}
#endregion
#region Using method call syntax
// Alternative way( using method call syntax)
Console.WriteLine("Using a lambda expression, numbers above mid
point(5) in intList are as follows:");
IEnumerable<int> numbersAboveMidPoint = intList.Where(x => x >
midPoint);
foreach (int number in numbersAboveMidPoint)
{
    Console.WriteLine(number);
}
#endregion
Console.ReadKey();
        }
    }
}
```

Output

The following is the output from running this program.

```
***Testing local variable scope with a lambda expression.***
Numbers above mid point(5) in intList are as follows:
6
7
8
```

```
9
10
Using a lambda expression, numbers above mid point(5) in intList are as
follows:
6
7
8
9
10
```

Using Tuples in a Lambda Expression

Since C# 7.0, there has been built-in support for tuples. In many applications, tuples have built-in delegates (for example, Func, Action, etc.) and lambda expressions. You learn about built-in delegates in Chapter 4. For now, let's use tuples in the context of user-defined delegates.

In the following example, I'm passing a tuple to a method. For simplicity, let's assume that the tuple has only two components. You want to pass this tuple to a method argument, and in turn, you want a tuple in which you get the doubles of each component. The following method represents such a sample.

```
static Tuple<int, double> MakeDoubleMethod(Tuple<int, double> input)
{
    return Tuple.Create(input.Item1 * 2, input.Item2 * 2);
}
```

You can see that inside the tuple, the first component is an int, and the second one is a double. I'm just multiplying the input arguments by two to get the double of each component and returning the result with another tuple.

Inside Main method, I called this method as follows.

```
var resultantTuple = MakeDoubleMethod(inputTuple);
```

Since I'm invoking the method from a static context, I made MakeDoubleMethod static.

Now you know how to use tuples with a method. Let's implement the concept using a lambda expression.

First, declare a delegate, as follows.

```
delegate Tuple<int, double> MakeDoubleDelegate(Tuple<int, double> input);
```

Now you have the delegate, so you can use a lambda expression, like the following.

```
MakeDoubleDelegate delegateObject =
                (Tuple<int, double> input) => Tuple.Create(input.Item1 * 2,
                input.Item2 * 2);
```

If you do not use a named component, by default, the fields of the tuple are named Item1, Item2, Item3, and so forth. To get the intended result, you can use the following lines of code.

```
var resultantTupleUsingLambda= delegateObject(inputTuple);
Console.WriteLine("Using lambda expression, the content of resultant tuple
is as follows:");
Console.WriteLine("First Element: " + resultantTupleUsingLambda.Item1);
Console.WriteLine("Second Element: " + resultantTupleUsingLambda.Item2);
```

Like many other examples in this book, I kept both ways to get the intended result. It can help to compare the use of a lambda expression with a normal method in a similar context. Next is a complete demonstration.

Demonstration 6

```
using System;

namespace UsingTuplesInLambdaExp
{
    delegate Tuple<int, double> MakeDoubleDelegate(Tuple<int, double> input);
    class Program
    {
        static void Main(string[] args)
        {
            Console.WriteLine("***Using Tuples in Lambda Expression.***");
            var inputTuple = Tuple.Create(1, 2.3);
```

```
            Console.WriteLine("Content of input tuple is as follows:");
            Console.WriteLine("First Element: " + inputTuple.Item1);
            Console.WriteLine("Second Element: " + inputTuple.Item2);
            var resultantTuple = MakeDoubleMethod(inputTuple);

            Console.WriteLine("\nPassing tuple as an input argument in a
            normal method which again returns a tuple.");
            Console.WriteLine("Content of resultant tuple is as follows:");
            Console.WriteLine("First Element: " + resultantTuple.Item1);
            Console.WriteLine("Second Element: " + resultantTuple.Item2);

            Console.WriteLine("\nUsing delegate and lambda expression with
            tuple now.");
            MakeDoubleDelegate delegateObject =
                (Tuple<int, double> input) => Tuple.Create(input.Item1 * 2,
                input.Item2 * 2);
            var resultantTupleUsingLambda= delegateObject(inputTuple);
            Console.WriteLine("Using lambda expression, the content of
            resultant tuple is as follows:");
            Console.WriteLine("First Element: " +
            resultantTupleUsingLambda.Item1);
            Console.WriteLine("Second Element: " +
            resultantTupleUsingLambda.Item2);
            Console.ReadKey();
        }
        static Tuple<int, double> MakeDoubleMethod(Tuple<int, double> input)
        {
            return Tuple.Create(input.Item1 * 2, input.Item2 * 2);
        }
    }
}
```

Output

The following is the output from running this program.

```
***Using Tuples in Lambda Expression.***
Content of input tuple is as follows:
```

```
First Element: 1
Second Element: 2.3
```

Passing tuple as an input argument in a normal method which again returns a tuple.

```
Content of resultant tuple is as follows:
First Element: 2
Second Element: 4.6
```

Using delegate and lambda expression with tuple now.

```
Using lambda expression, the content of resultant tuple is as follows:
First Element: 2
Second Element: 4.6
```

Event Subscription with Lambda Expressions

You can use lambda expressions with events.

Demonstration 7

To demonstrate a case, let's look at the first program in Chapter 2 and modify it. Since we're focusing on lambda expressions, this time, you do not need to make a Receiver class, which had a method called GetNotificationFromSender, to handle the event notification when myInt is changing inside a Sender class object. In that example, the Sender class also had a GetNotificationItself method to handle its own event. It was presented to demonstrate you that a Sender class can also handle its own event.

This is the complete demonstration.

```
using System;

namespace UsingEventsAndLambdaExp
{
    class Sender
    {
        private int myInt;
        public int MyInt
```

```
        {
            get
            {
                return myInt;
            }
            set
            {
                myInt = value;
                //Whenever we set a new value, the event will fire.
                OnMyIntChanged();
            }
        }
        // EventHandler is a predefined delegate which is used to handle
        //simple events.
        // It has the following signature:
        //delegate void System.EventHandler(object sender,System.EventArgs e)
        //where the sender tells who is sending the event and
        //EventArgs is used to store information about the event.
        public event EventHandler MyIntChanged;
        public void OnMyIntChanged()
        {
            if (MyIntChanged != null)
            {
                MyIntChanged(this, EventArgs.Empty);
            }
        }
    }

    class Program
    {
        static void Main(string[] args)
        {
            Console.WriteLine("***Demonstration-.Exploring events with
            lambda expression.***");
            Sender sender = new Sender();
```

```
//Using lambda expression as an event handler
//Bad practise
//sender.MyIntChanged += (Object sender, System.EventArgs e) =>
// Console.WriteLine("Using lambda expression, inside Main
method, received a notification: Sender recently has changed
the myInt value . ");
//Better practise
EventHandler myEvent =
   (object sender, EventArgs e) =>
   Console.WriteLine("Using lambda expression, inside Main
   method, received a notification: Sender recently has changed
   the myInt value . ");
sender.MyIntChanged += myEvent;

sender.MyInt = 1;
sender.MyInt = 2;
//Unregistering now
//sender.MyIntChanged -= receiver.GetNotificationFromSender;
//No notification sent for the receiver now.
//but there is no guarantee if you follow the bad practise
//sender.MyIntChanged -= (Object sender, System.EventArgs e) =>
// Console.WriteLine("Unregistered event notification.");

//But now it can remove the event properly.
sender.MyIntChanged -= myEvent;
sender.MyInt = 3;

Console.ReadKey();

      }
    }
}
```

Output

The following is the output from running this program.

```
***Demonstration-.Exploring events with lambda expression.***
Using lambda expression, inside Main method, received a notification:
Sender recently has changed the myInt value .
Using lambda expression, inside Main method, received a notification:
Sender recently has changed the myInt value .
```

Q&A Session

3.1 Why are you writing additional code? I'm seeing that you could simply write the following to subscribe to the event.

```
sender.MyIntChanged += (Object sender, System.EventArgs e) =>
  Console.WriteLine("Using lambda expression, inside Main method, received
  a notification: Sender recently has changed the myInt value . ");
```

And you could use it to replace the following lines.

```
EventHandler myEvent = (object sender, EventArgs e) =>
Console.WriteLine("Using lambda expression, inside Main method, received a
notification: Sender recently has changed the myInt value . ");
sender.MyIntChanged += myEvent;
```

Is this correct?

Nice catch, but it was necessary. Let's say that you use the following lines to subscribe the event.

```
sender.MyIntChanged += (Object sender, System.EventArgs e) =>
Console.WriteLine("Using lambda expression, inside Main method, received a
notification: Sender recently has changed the myInt value . ");
```

And, then later unsubscribe from it with the following line.

```
sender.MyIntChanged -= (Object sender, System.EventArgs e) =>
  Console.WriteLine("Unregistered event notification.");
```

There is no guarantee that the compiler will unsubscribe from the correct event. For example, in this case, when I execute the program, I notice a third case in the output that is unwanted (because before I set myInt's value to 3, I wanted to unsubscribe from the event notification). The following is the output.

```
***Demonstration-.Exploring events with lambda expression.***
Using lambda expression, inside Main method, received a notification:
Sender recently has changed the myInt value .
Using lambda expression, inside Main method, received a notification:
Sender recently has changed the myInt value .
Using lambda expression, inside Main method, received a notification:
Sender recently has changed the myInt value .
```

So, experts recommend that in such a case, you should store the anonymous method /lambda expression in a delegate variable, and then add this delegate to the event. As a result, you can keep track of it, and if you want, you can unsubscribe from it properly. It is generally recommended to not use anonymous functions to subscribe to an event when you want to unsubscribe from the event later. It is because, to avoid memory leaks in real-world applications, once you subscribe to an event, you should unsubscribe from it once the intended job is done.

3.2 What is an expression?

According to Microsoft, an expression can be a combination of operators and operands. It can be evaluated to a single value, method, object, or namespace. An expression can include a method call, an operator with the operands, a literal value (a literal is a constant value that does not have a name), or simply the name of a variable, type member, method parameter, namespace, or type.

The following is a simple example of an expression statement.

```
int i=1;
```

Here, i is a simple name, and 1 is the literal value. Literals and simple names are two of the simplest types of expression.

3.3 What is a Turing machine?

A Turing machine is an abstract machine that can manipulate symbols of a tape by following rules. It is the mathematical basis of many programming languages.

3.4 What is the difference between a statement lambda and an expression lambda?

An expression lambda has only one expression, but a statement lambda has a statement block on the right side of the lambda operator. With a statement lambda, you can have any number of statements within curly braces. At the time of writing, you cannot use a statement lambda for expression-bodied methods, but you can use an expression lambda in those contexts.

In expression trees, only expression lambdas can be used; but you cannot use statement lambda's in those contexts. I excluded the discussion of expression trees because it is a LINQ-related feature, which is beyond the scope of this book.

3.5 If you do not supply parameters, the compiler can still can determine the types. But when you supply them, they must match the delegate type. Is this correct?

Yes. But sometimes the compiler can't infer it. In that case, you need to supply the parameters. In this context, you need to remember that input parameters must be implicit or explicit.

3.6 You said that input parameters must be implicit or explicit. What does that mean?

Let's suppose that you have the following delegate.

```
delegate string MyDelegate(int a, int b);
```

If you write the following segment of code, you get a compile-time error, as shown in Figure 3-6.

```
MyDelegate resultOfLambdaExp =(int x,  y)=> (x > y) ? "Yes." : "No.";
```

❌ CS0748 Inconsistent lambda parameter usage; parameter types must be all explicit or all implicit

Figure 3-6. *Compile-time error due to inconsistent lambda parameter usage*

The remedy is as follows.

```
MyDelegate resultOfLambdaExp =(int x, int y)=> (x > y) ? "Yes." : "No.";
```

Or, you can remove both ints, as follows.

```
MyDelegate resultOfLambdaExp =( x, y)=> (x > y) ? "Yes." : "No.";
```

3.7 What are the restrictions associated with lambda expressions?

Lambda expressions are supersets of anonymous methods. All restrictions that are applicable to anonymous methods are also applicable to lambda expressions (for example, in the context of an anonymous method, you cannot use ref or out parameters of the defining method). For reference, remember the following points.

- Lambdas are not allowed on the left side of an "is" or "as" operator. In this context, you may remember the statement from C# 6.0 specification, which says, "An anonymous function doesn't have a value or type in and of itself but in convertible to a compatible delegate or expression tree type."

- You cannot use break, goto, or continue to jump out from the lambda expression scope.

- You cannot exercise unsafe codes inside a lambda expression. For example, let's suppose that you have the following delegate:

```
delegate void DelegateWithNoParameter();
```

If you write the following segment of code, you get a compile-time error in all the places (which I marked with comments) where you manipulated the pointers.

```
DelegateWithNoParameter delOb = () =>
    {
        int a = 10;
        //CS 0214:Pointers and fixed sized buffers may
        //only be used only in an unsafe context
        int* p = &a;//Error
        //Console.WriteLine("a={0}", a);
        //Printing using string interpolation
        Console.WriteLine($"a={a}");
        Console.WriteLine($"*p={*p}");//Error CS0214
    };
```

3.8 You said that in the context of an anonymous method, you cannot use the ref or out parameters of the defining method. Can you please elaborate?

Let's consider our Sum method in demonstration1 and modify it as follows.

```
public static int Sum(ref int a, ref int b)
        {
            //return a + b;
            //Using Anonymous method(C# 2.0 onwards)
            Mydel del2 = delegate (int x, int y)
            {
                //Following segment will NOT work
                x = a;//CS1628
                y = b;//CS1628
                return x + y;

                //Following segment will work
                //return x + y;
            };
            return del2(a, b);
        }
Where the Mydel delegate is unchanged and as follows:
public delegate int Mydel(int x, int y);
```

You will get a compile-time error (marked with CS1628) for this code segment. CS1628 says that you cannot use the *ref, out,* or *in* parameters inside an anonymous method or a lambda expression. Figure 3-7 is a Visual Studio 2019 error screenshot for your reference.

❌ CS1628 Cannot use ref, out, or in parameter 'b' inside an anonymous method, lambda expression, query expression, or local function

❌ CS1628 Cannot use ref, out, or in parameter 'a' inside an anonymous method, lambda expression, query expression, or local function

Figure 3-7. *Compile-time error. You cannot use ref, out, or in parameter inside an anonymous method or lambda expression*

You can refer to a potential solution that is shown using a commented line in the prior code segment.

Final Words

That's all about lambdas for now. Before you leave this chapter, I want to remind you that although cool features are very tempting to use, readability and understandability of the code should be your topmost priority.

Next, we move to Part 2 (which starts with Chapter 4) of the book, where you see usage of the concepts that you've learned so far. Although Part 2 is heart of this book, the contents of Part 1 (Chapters 1, 2, and 3) are the building blocks for them.

Summary

This chapter addressed the following key questions.

- Why are anonymous methods and lambda expressions useful?

- How can you convert an anonymous method to a lambda expression?

- How can you use lambda expressions that accept a different number of parameters?

- How can you use a local variable with a lambda expression?

- What is an expression lambda?

- What is a statement lambda?

- How can you use expression syntax to define non-lambda methods? And what are its usage limitations?

- What are the key restrictions applicable to lambda expressions?

PART II

Exploring Advanced Programming

- Chapter 4: Generic Programming
- Chapter 5: Thread Programming
- Chapter 6: Asynchronous Programming
- Chapter 7: Database Programming

CHAPTER 4

Generic Programming

In this chapter, you learn about generic programming and you are introduced to *generics*, one of the coolest features of C#. It is an integral part of advanced programming. Generic programming simply means the efficient use of generics. It first appeared in C# 2.0. Over time, additional flexibilities were added to this powerful feature, and nowadays, you find rare real-life applications that do not use generics at their core.

The Motivation Behind Generics

When you use a generic type in your application, you do not commit to a specific type for your instances. For example, when you instantiate a generic class, you can say that you want your object to deal with int types, but at another time you can say that you want your object to deal with double types, string types, object types, or so forth. In short, this kind of programming allows you to make a type-safe class without having to commit to any particular type.

This is not a new concept, and it is definitely not limited to C#. You see similar kinds of programming in other languages as well, for example, Java and C++ (using templates). The following are some of the advantages of using a generic application.

- Your program is reusable.

- Your program is enriched with better type-safety.

- Your program can avoid typical runtime errors that may arise due to improper casting.

To address these points, I'll start with a simple nongeneric program and analyze the potential drawbacks. After that, I'll show you a corresponding a generic program and give a comparative analysis to discover the advantages of generic programming. Let's start.

© Vaskaran Sarcar 2020

V. Sarcar, *Getting Started with Advanced C#*, https://doi.org/10.1007/978-1-4842-5934-4_4

Demonstration 1

Demonstration 1 has a class called NonGenericEx. This class has two instance methods: DisplayMyInteger and DisplayMyString.

```
public int DisplayMyInteger(int myInt)
{
 return myInt;
}
public string DisplayMyString(string myStr)
{
 return myStr;
}
```

Did you notice that both methods are basically doing the same operation, but one method is dealing with an int and the other is dealing with a string? Not only is this approach ugly, it also suffers from another potential drawback, which you'll see in the analysis section. But before we analyze it, let's execute the program.

```
using System;

namespace NonGenericProgramDemo1
{
    class NonGenericEx
    {
        public int DisplayMyInteger(int myInt)
        {
            return myInt;
        }
        public string DisplayMyString(string myStr)
        {
            return myStr;
        }
    }
    class Program
    {
        static void Main(string[] args)
```

```
        {
            Console.WriteLine("***A non-generic program demonstration.***");
            NonGenericEx nonGenericOb = new NonGenericEx();
            Console.WriteLine("DisplayMyInteger returns :{0}",
            nonGenericOb.DisplayMyInteger(123));
            Console.WriteLine("DisplayMyString returns :{0}", nonGenericOb.
            DisplayMyString("DisplayMyString method inside NonGenericEx is
            called."));
            Console.ReadKey();
        }
    }
}
```

Output

This is the output.

```
***A non-generic program demonstration.***
DisplayMyInteger returns :123
DisplayMyString returns :DisplayMyString method inside NonGenericEx is
called.
```

Analysis

Let's suppose that now you need to deal with another datatype—a double. Using the current code, add the following line inside Main.

```
Console.WriteLine("ShowDouble returns :{0}", nonGenericOb.
DisplayMyDouble(25.5));//error
```

You get the following compile-time error.

```
Error CS1061  'NonGenericEx' does not contain a definition for
'DisplayMyDouble' and no accessible extension method 'DisplayMyDouble'
accepting a first argument of type 'NonGenericEx' could be found (are you
missing a using directive or an assembly reference?)
```

This is because you do not have a `DisplayMyDouble` method yet. At the same time, you cannot use any existing methods to deal with a `double` datatype. An obvious approach is to introduce a method that looks like the following.

```
public double DisplayMyDouble(double myDouble)
{
 return myDouble;
}
```

But how long can you tolerate this? If your code size kept growing in the same manner for all the other datatypes, your code would not be reusable for different datatypes. And at the same time, as the code grew, it would look ugly and the overall maintenance would become hectic. Fortunately, you have a simple solution when you prefer generic programming over its counterpart nongeneric programming.

First, the following are the key points that you should remember.

- Generic classes and methods promote reusability, type-safety, and efficiency. Their nongeneric counterparts don't have these qualities. You often see the use of generics with collections and the methods that work on them.

- The .NET Framework class library includes a `System.Collections.Generic` namespace that has several generic-based collection classes. This namespace was added in version 2.0. This is why Microsoft recommends that any application that targets .NET Framework 2.0 (or later) should use generic collection classes instead of their nongeneric counterparts, such as `ArrayList`.

- Angle brackets <> are used in generic programs. A generic type is placed in angle brackets; for example, <T> in your class definition. T is the most common single letter to indicate a generic type when you deal with a single generic type only.

- You can define a class with placeholders for the type of its methods, fields, parameters, and so forth, in a generic program; later, these placeholders are replaced with the particular type that you want to use.

- Here is the simple generic class used in demonstration 2:

```
class GenericClassDemo<T>
{
    public T Display(T value)
    {
        return value;
    }
}
```

- T is called a generic type parameter.

- The following is an example of instantiation from a generic class:

```
GenericClassDemo<int> myGenericClassIntOb = new
GenericClassDemo<int>();
```

  Note that the type parameter is replaced with int in this case.

- You may notice multiple generic type parameters in a particular declaration. For example, the following class has multiple generic types:

```
public class MyDictionary<K,V>{//Some code}
```

- A generic method might use its type parameter as its return type. It can also use the type parameter as a type of a formal parameter. Inside GenericClassDemo<T> class, the Display method uses T as a return type. This method also uses T as the type of its formal parameter.

- You can place constraints on a generic type. This is explored later in this chapter.

Now go through demonstration 2.

Demonstration 2

Demonstration 2 is a simple generic program. Before you instantiate a generic class, you need to specify the actual types to substitute with the type parameters. In this demonstration, the following lines of code are inside Main.

```
GenericClassDemo<int> myGenericClassIntOb = new GenericClassDemo<int>();
GenericClassDemo<string> myGenericClassStringOb = new
GenericClassDemo<string>();
GenericClassDemo<double> myGenericClassDoubleOb = new
GenericClassDemo<double>();
```

These three lines of code tell you that the first line substitutes the type parameter with an int; the second line substitutes the type parameter with a string; and the third line substitutes the type parameter with a double.

When you do this kind of coding, the type substitutes the type parameter everywhere it appears. As a result, you get a type-safe class that is constructed based on your chosen type. When you choose an int type and use the following line of code,

```
GenericClassDemo<int> myGenericClassIntOb = new GenericClassDemo<int>();
```

you can use the following line to get an int from the Display method.

```
Console.WriteLine("Display method returns :{0}", myGenericClassIntOb.
Display(1));
```

This is the complete demonstration.

```
using System;

namespace GenericProgramDemo1
{
    class GenericClassDemo<T>
    {
        public T Display(T value)
        {
            return value;
        }
    }
    class Program
    {
        static void Main(string[] args)
        {
            Console.WriteLine("***Introduction to Generic
            Programming.***");
            GenericClassDemo<int> myGenericClassIntOb = new
            GenericClassDemo<int>();
            Console.WriteLine("Display method returns :{0}",
            myGenericClassIntOb.Display(1));
            GenericClassDemo<string> myGenericClassStringOb = new
            GenericClassDemo<string>();
```

```
        Console.WriteLine("Display method returns :{0}",
        myGenericClassStringOb.Display("A generic method is called."));
        GenericClassDemo<double> myGenericClassDoubleOb = new
        GenericClassDemo<double>();
        Console.WriteLine("Display method returns :{0}",
        myGenericClassDoubleOb.Display(12.345));
        Console.ReadKey();
    }
  }
}
```

Output

This is the output.

```
***Introduction to Generic Programming.***
Display method returns :1
Display method returns :A generic method is called.
Display method returns :12.345
```

Analysis

Let's do a comparative analysis of demonstration 1 (a nongeneric program) and demonstration 2 (a generic program). Both programs are doing the same operations but there are some key distinctions between them, as follows.

- In demonstration 1, you need to specify methods like DisplayInteger, DisplayString, DisplayDouble, and so forth to handle the datatypes. But in demonstration 2, only one generic Display method is sufficient enough to handle the different datatypes, and you can accomplish this task with fewer lines of code.

- When the DisplayDouble method was absent inside Main in demonstration 1, we encountered a compile-time error when we wanted to deal with the double datatype. But in demonstration 2, there was no need to define any additional methods to handle a double datatype (or any other datatype). So, you can see that this generic version is much more flexible than the nongeneric version.

Now consider demonstration 3.

Demonstration 3

This demonstration shows a nongeneric program that uses the ArrayList class. The size of an ArrayList can grow dynamically. It has a method called Add, which can help you to add an object to at the end of the ArrayList. In the upcoming demonstration, I used the following lines.

```
myList.Add(1);
myList.Add(2);
// No compile time error
myList.Add("InvalidElement");
```

Since the method expects objects as arguments, these lines are compiled successfully. But you'll face the problem if you fetch the data using the following code segment.

```
foreach (int myInt in myList)
{
 Console.WriteLine((int)myInt); //downcasting
}
```

The third element is not an int (it is a string), and as a result, you encounter a runtime error. A runtime error is worse than a compile-time error, because at this stage, you can hardly do anything fruitful.

This is the complete demonstration.

```
using System;
using System.Collections;

namespace NonGenericProgramDemo2
{
    class Program
    {
        static void Main(string[] args)
        {
            Console.WriteLine("***Use Generics to avoid runtime error***");
            ArrayList myList = new ArrayList();
            myList.Add(1);
            myList.Add(2);
            //No compile time error
```

```
        myList.Add("InvalidElement");
        foreach (int myInt in myList)
        {
        /*Will encounter run-time exception for the final
        element  which is not an int */
            Console.WriteLine((int)myInt); //downcasting
        }
        Console.ReadKey();
        }
    }
}
```

Output

The program does not raise any compile-time errors, but at runtime, you see the exception shown in Figure 4-1.

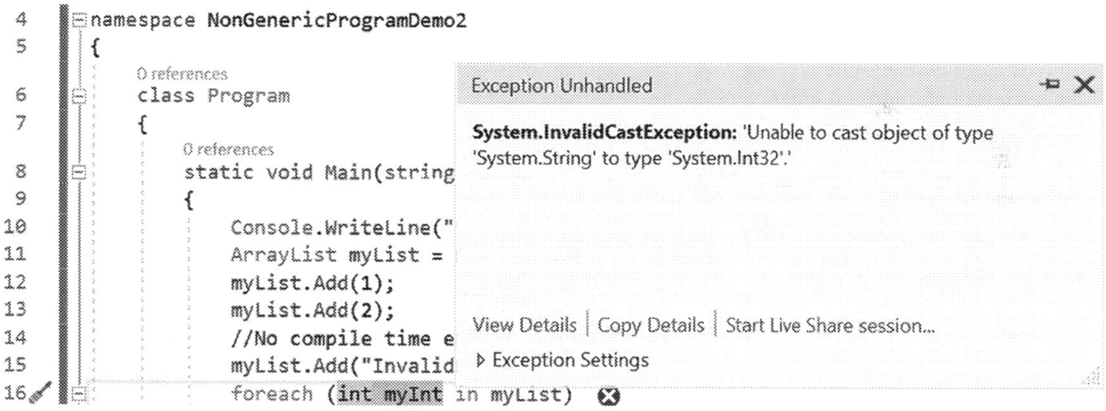

Figure 4-1. *Runtime error InvalidCastException occurred*

Now you understand that you encounter this runtime error because the third element (i.e., myList [2] in the ArrayList) was supposed to be an int, but I stored a string. At compile time, I did not encounter any issues because it was stored as an object.

Analysis

The prior demonstration also suffers from performance overhead due to boxing and downcasting.

111

A Quick Look into the List Class

Before you go further, let's have a quick look at the built-in List class. This class is very common and widely used. It is made for generics, so when you instantiate a List class, you can mention the type that you want to put in your list. For example, in the following

```
List<int> myList = new List<int>(); contains a list of ints.
List<double> myList = new List<double>(); contains a list of doubles.
List<string> myList = new List<string>(); contains a list of strings
```

The List class has many built-in methods. I recommend that you go through them. These ready-made constructs make your programming life easier. For now, let's use the Add method. Using this method, you can add items to the end of your list.

This is the method description from Visual IDE.

```
//
// Summary:
//    Adds an object to the end of the System.Collections.Generic.List`1.
//
// Parameters:
//    item:
//       The object to be added to the end of the
//       System.Collections.Generic.List`1. The value can be null
//       for reference types.
public void Add(T item);
```

The following segment of code creates a list of ints and then adds two items to it.

```
List<int> myList = new List<int>();
myList.Add(10);
myList.Add(20);
```

Now come to the important part. If you add a string to this list by mistake, you get a compile-time error.

This is the erroneous code segment.

```
//Compile time error: Cannot convert from 'string' to 'int'
//myList.Add("InvalidElement");//error
```

Demonstration 4

To compare with demonstration 3, in the following example, let's use List<int> instead of ArrayList and then review the concepts that we've discussed so far.

This is the complete program.

```
using System;
using System.Collections.Generic;

namespace GenericProgramDemo2
{
    class Program
    {
        static void Main(string[] args)
        {
            Console.WriteLine("***Using Generics to avoid run-time error.***");
            List<int> myList = new List<int>();
            myList.Add(10);
            myList.Add(20);
            //Cannot convert from 'string' to 'int'
            myList.Add("InvalidElement");//Compile-time error
            foreach (int myInt in myList)
            {
                Console.WriteLine((int)myInt);//downcasting
            }
            Console.ReadKey();
        }
    }
}
```

Output

In this program, you get the following compile-time error

```
CS1503    Argument 1: cannot convert from 'string' to 'int'
```

for the following line of code.

```
myList.Add("InvalidElement");
```

113

You cannot add a `string` in `myList` because it was intended to hold integers only (note that I'm using `List<int>`). Since the error is caught at compile time, you do not need to wait until runtime to catch this defect.

Once you comment out the erroneous line, you can compile this program and generate the following output.

```
***Using Generics to avoid run-time error.***
1
2
```

Analysis

When you compare demonstration 3 with demonstration 4, you see that

- To avoid runtime errors, you should prefer the generic version over its counterpart—the nongeneric version.

- Generic programming helps you avoid penalties caused by boxing/unboxing.

- To store strings, you can use something like `List<string> myList2 = new List<string>();` to create a list that holds only the string types. Similarly, List<T> can be used for other datatypes. This shows that the `List<T>` version is more flexible and usable than the nongeneric version `ArrayList`.

Generic Delegates

In Chapter 1, you learned about user-defined delegates and their importance. Now, let's discuss generic delegates. In this section, I cover three important built-in generic delegates—called `Func`, `Action`, and `Predicate`, which are very common in generic programming. Let's start.

Func Delegate

There are 17 overloaded versions of the `Func` delegate. They can take 0 to 16 input parameters but always have one return type. For example,

```
Func<out TResult>
Func<in T, out TResult>
Func<in T1, in T2,out TResult>
Func<in T1, in T2, in T3, out TResult>
```

● ● ● ● ● ●

```
Func<in T1, in T2, in T3,in T4, in T5, in T6,in T7,in T8,in T9,in T10,in
T11,in T12,in T13,in T14,in T15,in T16, out TResult>
```

To understand the usage, let's consider the following method.

```
private static string DisplayEmployeeDetails(string name, int empId, double
salary)
{
    return string.Format("Employee Name:{0},id:{1}, salary:{2}$", name,
    empId,salary);
}
```

To invoke this method using a custom delegate, you can follow these steps.

1. Define a delegate (say, Mydel); something like this:

    ```
    public delegate string Mydel(string n, int r, double d);
    ```

2. Create a delegate object and point the method using a code;
    something like the following:

    ```
    Mydel myDelOb = new Mydel(DisplayEmployeeDetails);
    Or in short,
    Mydel myDelOb = DisplayEmployeeDetails;
    ```

3. Invoke the method like this:

    ```
    myDelOb.Invoke("Amit", 1, 1025.75);
    ```

    Or, simply with this:

    ```
    myDelOb("Amit", 1, 1025.75);
    ```

If you use the built-in Func delegate, you can make your code simpler and shorter. In this case, you can use it as follows.

```
Func<string, int, double, string> empOb = new Func<string, int, double,string>
(DisplayEmployeeDetails);
Console.WriteLine(empOb("Amit", 1,1025.75));
```

The Func delegate is perfectly considering all three input arguments (a string, an int, and a double, respectively) and returning a string. You may be confused and want to know which parameter denotes the return type. If you move your cursor on it in Visual Studio, you can see that the last parameter (TResult) is considered the return type of the function, and the others are considered input types (see Figure 4-2).

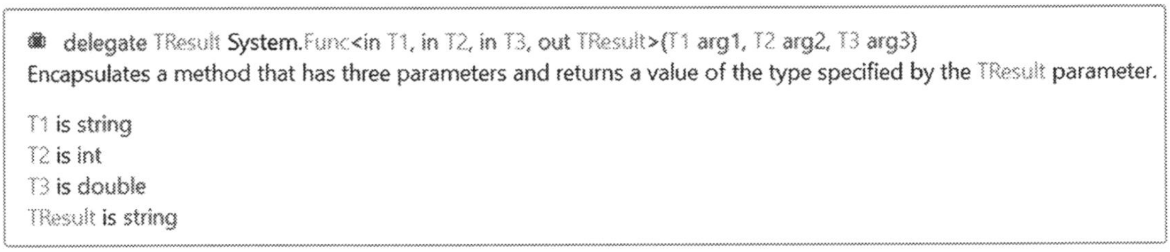

Figure 4-2. *Details of Func<in T1, in T2, in T3, outTResult> delegate*

Note   The magic of in and out parameters will be revealed to you shortly.

Q&A Session

4.1 In the previous code segment, DisplayEmployeeDetails has three parameters, and its return type was string. Usually, I have different methods that can take a different number of input parameters. How can I use Func in those contexts?

Func delegates can consider 0 to 16 input parameters. You can use the overloaded version that suits your needs. For example, if you have a method that takes one string, and one int as input parameters, and whose return type is a string, and the method is something like the following.

```
private static string DisplayEmployeeDetailsShortForm(string name, int empId)
{
    return string.Format("Employee Name:{0},id:{1}", name, empId);
}
```

You can use following overloaded version of Func.

```
Func<string, int, string> empOb2 = new Func<string, int, string>
(DisplayEmployeeDetailsShortForm);
Console.WriteLine(empOb2("Amit", 1));
```

Action Delegate

Visual studio describes the following about an Action delegate:

> Encapsulates a method that has no parameters and does not return a value.

```
public delegate void Action();
```

But normally you'll notice the generic version of this delegate which can take 1 to 16 input parameters but do not have a return type. The overloaded versions are as follows.

```
Action<in T>
Action<in T1,in T2>
Action<in T1,in T2, in T3>
....
Action<in T1, in T2, in T3,in T4, in T5, in T6,in T7,in T8,in T9,in T10,in
T11,in T12,in T13,in T14,in T15,in T16>
```

Let's suppose that you have a method called CalculateSumOfThreeInts that takes three ints as input parameters and whose return type is void, as follows.

```
private static void CalculateSumOfThreeInts(int i1, int i2, int i3)
{
    int sum = i1 + i2 + i3;
    Console.WriteLine("Sum of {0},{1} and {2} is: {3}", i1, i2, i3, sum);
}
```

You can use an Action delegate to get the sum of three integers, as follows.

```
Action<int, int, int> sum = new Action<int, int, int>(CalculateSumOfThreeInts);
sum(10,3,7);
```

Predicate Delegate

A Predicate delegate evaluates something. For example, let's assume that you have a method that defines some criteria, and you need to check whether an object can meet the criteria or not. Let's consider the following method.

```
private static bool GreaterThan100(int myInt)
{
    return myInt > 100 ? true : false;
}
```

You can see that this method evaluates whether an int is greater than 100 or not. So, you can use a Predicate delegate to perform the same test, as follows.

```
Predicate<int> isGreater = new Predicate<int>(IsGreaterThan100);
Console.WriteLine("101 is greater than 100? {0}", isGreater(101));
Console.WriteLine("99 is greater than 100? {0}", isGreater(99));
```

Demonstration 5

This is the complete program that demonstrates all the concepts discussed so far.

```
using System;

namespace GenericDelegatesDemo
{
    class Program
    {
        static void Main(string[] args)
        {
            Console.WriteLine("***Using Generic Delegates.***");
            // Func
            Console.WriteLine("Using Func delegate now.");
            Func<string, int, double,string> empOb = new Func<string, int,
            double,string>(DisplayEmployeeDetails);
            Console.WriteLine(empOb("Amit", 1,1025.75));
            Console.WriteLine(empOb("Sumit", 2,3024.55));
```

```csharp
    // Action
    Console.WriteLine("Using Action delegate now.");
    Action<int, int, int> sum = new Action<int, int,
    int>(CalculateSumOfThreeInts);
    sum(10, 3, 7);
    sum(5, 10, 15);
    /*
    Error:Keyword 'void' cannot be used in this context
    //Func<int, int, int, void> sum2 = new Func<int, int, int, void>
    (CalculateSumOfThreeInts);
    */

    // Predicate
    Console.WriteLine("Using Predicate delegate now.");
    Predicate<int> isGreater = new Predicate<int>(IsGreater
    Than100);
    Console.WriteLine("101 is greater than 100? {0}",
    isGreater(101));
    Console.WriteLine("99 is greater than 100? {0}",
    isGreater(99));

    Console.ReadKey();
}
private static string DisplayEmployeeDetails(string name,
int empId, double salary)
{
    return string.Format("Employee Name:{0},id:{1}, salary:{2}$",
    name, empId,salary);
}
private static void CalculateSumOfThreeInts(int i1, int i2, int i3)
{
    int sum = i1 + i2 + i3;
    Console.WriteLine("Sum of {0},{1} and {2} is: {3}", i1, i2, i3, sum);
}
private static bool IsGreaterThan100(int input)
```

```
        {
            return input > 100 ? true : false;
        }
    }
}
```

Output

```
***Using Generic Delegates.***
Using Func delegate now.
Employee Name:Amit,id:1, salary:1025.75$
Employee Name:Sumit,id:2, salary:3024.55$
Using Action delegate now.
Sum of 10,3 and 7 is: 20
Sum of 5,10 and 15 is: 30
 Using Predicate delegate now.
101 is greater than 100? True
99 is greater than 100? False
```

Q&A Session

4.2 I've seen the use of built-in generic delegates. How can I use my own generic delegates?

I used the built-in generic delegates because they make your life easier. No one is restricting you from using your own generic delegate. I suggest you follow the construct of these generic delegates before you use your own, however. For example, in the previous demonstration, I used the Action delegate as follows.

```
Action<int, int, int> sum = new Action<int, int,
int>(CalculateSumOfThreeInts);
sum(10, 3, 7);
```

Now, instead of using the built-in delegate, you can define your own generic delegate (say, CustomAction) as follows.

```
// Custom delegate
public delegate void CustomAction<in T1, in T2, in T3>(T1 arg1, T2 arg2, T3 arg3);
```

And then you could use it as follows.

```
CustomAction<int, int, int> sum2 = new CustomAction<int, int,
int>(CalculateSumOfThreeInts);
sum2(10, 3, 7);
```

4.3 I'm seeing that when you created delegate instances, you didn't use the short form. Is there any reason for that?

Good find. You can always use the short form. For example, instead of using

```
Action<int, int, int> sum = new Action<int, int,
int>(CalculateSumOfThreeInts);
```

I could simply use

```
Action<int, int, int> sum = CalculateSumOfThreeInts;
```

But since you have only started to learn about delegates, these long forms can often help you to understand the code better.

4.4 Can I use Func delegate to point to a method that returns void?

When you have a method with a void return type, it is recommended that you use the Action delegate. If you use the following line of code in prior demonstration by mistake, you get a compile-time error because the target method return type is void.

```
//Error:Keyword 'void' cannot be used in this context
Func<int, int, int, void> sum2 = new Func<int, int, int, void>(CalculateSum
OfThreeInts);//error
```

4.5 Can I have generic methods?

In demonstration 2, you saw a generic method, as follows.

```
public T Display(T value)
{
    return value;
}
```

It shows that you can opt for a generic method when you have a set of methods that are identical except for the types, it works on.

For example, in Demonstration2, you have seen that I used the same named method when I invoked: Display(1), Display("A generic method is called.") and Display(12.345).

The Default Keyword in Generics

It shows that you have seen the use of *default* keyword in `switch` statements, where *default* refers to a default case. In generic programming, it has a special meaning. You can use `default` to initialize generic types with the default values. In this context, you may note the following points.

- The default value for a reference type is `null`.

- The default value of a value type (other than struct and bool type) is 0.

- For a bool type, the default value is `false`.

- For a struct (which is a value type) type, the default value is an object of that struct with all fields set with their default values (i.e., the default value of a struct is value produced by setting all value types fields to their default values and all reference type fields to null.)

Demonstration 6

Consider the following example with the output.

```
using System;

namespace UsingdefaultKeywordinGenerics
{
    class MyClass
    {
        // Some other stuff as per need
    }
    struct MyStruct
    {
        // Some other stuff as per need
    }
    class Program
    {
        static void PrintDefault<T>()
        {
            T defaultValue = default(T);
```

```
            string printMe = String.Empty;
            printMe = (defaultValue == null) ? "null" : defaultValue.
            ToString();
            Console.WriteLine("Default value of {0} is {1}", typeof(T), printMe);
            // C# 6.0 onwards,you can use interpolated string
            //Console.WriteLine($"Default value of {typeof(T)} is
            {printMe}.");
        }
        static void Main(string[] args)
        {
            Console.WriteLine("***Using default keyword in Generic
            Programming.***");
            PrintDefault<int>();//0
            PrintDefault<double>();//0
            PrintDefault<bool>();//False
            PrintDefault<string>();//null
            PrintDefault<int?>();//null
            PrintDefault<System.Numerics.Complex>(); //(0,0)
            PrintDefault<System.Collections.Generic.List<int>>(); // null
            PrintDefault<System.Collections.Generic.List<string>>(); // null
            PrintDefault<MyClass>(); //null
            PrintDefault<MyStruct>();
            Console.ReadKey();
        }
    }
}
```

Output

This is the output.

```
***Using default keyword in Generic Programming.***
Default value of System.Int32 is 0
Default value of System.Double is 0
Default value of System.Boolean is False
Default value of System.String is null
Default value of System.Nullable`1[System.Int32] is null
```

```
Default value of System.Numerics.Complex is (0, 0)
Default value of System.Collections.Generic.List`1[System.Int32] is null
Default value of System.Collections.Generic.List`1[System.String] is null
Default value of UsingdefaultKeywordinGenerics.MyClass is null
Default value of UsingdefaultKeywordinGenerics.MyStruct is
UsingdefaultKeywordinGenerics.MyStruct
```

Note   The last line of the output is printing the `<namespace>.<Name of the structure>`; basically you can't set a default value for a structure. More specifically, the default value of a struct is the value returned by the default constructor of the struct. As said before, the default value of a struct is value produced by setting all value types fields to their default values and all reference type fields to null. The implicit parameterless constructor in each struct sets these default values. You cannot define an explicit parameterless constructor for your own use. It is also useful to know that the simple types in C# such as int, double, bool etc. are often called as struct types.

Q&A Session

4.6 How is the default keyword used in generic programming?

You have seen that the default keyword helps you find the default value of a type. In generic programming, sometimes you may want to provide a default value for a generic type. In the previous example, you saw that a default value differs according to a value type or a reference type. In that example, note the `PrintDefault<T>()` method carefully.

Instead of using the following line of code

```
T defaultValue = default(T);
```

if you use something like

```
T defaultValue = null;//will not work for value types
```

you get a compile-time error that says,

```
Error  CS0403  Cannot convert null to type parameter 'T' because it could
be a non-nullable value type. Consider using 'default(T)' instead.
```

Or, if you use the following line of code

```
T defaultValue = 0;//will not work for reference types
```

you get compile-time error that says,

```
Error  CS0029  Cannot implicitly convert type 'int' to 'T'
```

Implementing Generic Interface

Just like generic classes, you can have generic interfaces. A generic interface can contain both generic and nongeneric methods. If you want to implement a generic interface method, you can follow the same approach that you use when you normally implement a nongeneric interface method. The following program demonstrates how to implement methods of a generic interface.

Demonstration 7

To cover both scenarios, in this example, the generic interface GenericInterface<T> has a generic method called GenericMethod(T param) and a nongeneric method called NonGenericMethod(). The first method has a generic return type, T, and the second one has a void return type.

The remaining parts are easy to understand, and I kept the comments for your reference.

```
using System;

namespace ImplementingGenericInterface
{
    interface GenericInterface<T>
    {
        //A generic method
        T GenericMethod(T param);
        //A non-generic method
        public void NonGenericMethod();

    }
```

```
//Implementing the interface
class ConcreteClass<T>:GenericInterface<T>
{
    //Implementing interface method
    public T GenericMethod(T param)
    {
        return param;
    }

    public void NonGenericMethod()
    {
        Console.WriteLine("Implementing NonGenericMethod of
        GenericInterface<T>");
    }
}
class Program
{
    static void Main(string[] args)
    {
        Console.WriteLine("***Implementing generic interfaces.***\n");
        //Using 'int' type
        GenericInterface<int> concreteInt = new ConcreteClass<int>();
        int myInt = concreteInt.GenericMethod(5);
        Console.WriteLine($"The value stored in myInt is : {myInt}");
        concreteInt.NonGenericMethod();

        //Using 'string' type now
        GenericInterface<string> concreteString = new
        ConcreteClass<string>();
        string myStr = concreteString.GenericMethod("Hello Reader");
        Console.WriteLine($"The value stored in myStr is : {myInt}");
        concreteString.NonGenericMethod();

        Console.ReadKey();
    }
}
}
```

Output

This is the output.

```
***Implementing generic interfaces.***
```

```
The value stored in myInt is : 5
Implementing NonGenericMethod of GenericInterface<T>
The value stored in myStr is : 5
Implementing NonGenericMethod of GenericInterface<T>
```

Analysis

There are some interesting points to note in the previous example. Let's check them.

- If you have another concrete class that wants to implement
  GenericInterface<T>, and you write following code block, you get
  compile-time errors.

```
class ConcreteClass2 : GenericInterface<T>//Error
{
    public T GenericMethod(T param)
    {
        throw new NotImplementedException();
    }

    public void NonGenericMethod()
    {
        throw new NotImplementedException();
    }
}
```

  This is because I did not pass type argument T to ConcreteClass2.
  You have three compile-time errors with the same "Error CS0246
  The type or namespace name 'T' could not be found (are you
  missing a using directive or an assembly reference?)." *message.*

- You get the same errors if you write the following segment of code:

```
class ConcreteClass2<U> : GenericInterface<T>//Error
```

The reason is obvious: T is not found.

When you implement the generic interface, the implementing class needs to work on the same T type parameter. This is why the following segment of code is valid.

```
class ConcreteClass<T> : GenericInterface<T>
{//remaining code}
```

Q&A Session

4.7 In the previous example, can my implementing class work on multiple type parameters?

Yes. Both of the following code segments are also valid.

```
class ConcreteClass2<U,T> : GenericInterface<T>//valid
{//remaining code}
```

```
class ConcreteClass2<T, U> : GenericInterface<T>//also valid
{remaining code}
```

The key thing to remember is that your implementing class needs to supply the argument(s) required by the interface (for example, in this case, an implementor class must include the T parameter, which is present in the GenericInterface<T> interface.

4.8 Suppose you've got the following two interfaces.

```
interface IFirstInterface1<T> { }
interface ISecondInterface2<T, U> { }
```

Can you predict whether the following segments of code will compile or not?

Segment 1:
```
class MyClass1<T> : IFirstInterface<T> { }
```
Segment 2:
```
class MyClass2<T> : ISecondInterface<T, U> { }
```
Segment 3:
```
class MyClass3<T> : ISecondInterface<T, string> { }
```
Segment 4:
```
class MyClass4<T> : ISecondInterface<string, U> { }
```
Segment 5:

```
class MyClass5<T> : ISecondInterface<string, int> { }
```
Segment 6:
```
class MyClass6 : ISecondInterface<string, int> { }
```

Only segment 2 and segment 4 will not compile. In segment 2, MyClass2 doesn't include the U parameter. In segment 4, MyClass4 doesn't include the T parameter.

In segment 1 and segment 3, MyClass1 and MyClass3 have the required parameter(s), respectively.

Segments 5 and 6 had no issues at all, because in these cases, the respective classes worked on interfaces whose constructions are closed.

Generic Constraints

You can place restrictions on generic type parameters. For example, you may opt that your generic type must be a reference type or a value type, or it should derive from any other base type and so forth. But why should you allow constraints in your code? The simple answer is that by using constraints, you can have lots of control on your code, and you allow a C# compiler to know in advance about the type you are going to use. As a result, a C# compiler can help you detect bugs during compile time.

To specify a constraint, you use the where keyword and a colon (:) operator, such as in the following.

```
class EmployeeStoreHouse<T> where T : IEmployee
```

or,

```
class EmployeeStoreHouse<T> where T : IEmployee,new()
```

IEmployee is an interface.

In general, the following constraints are used.

- where T: struct means that type T must be a value type. (Remember that a struct is a value type.)

- where T: class means that type T must be a reference type. (Remember that a class is a reference type.)

- where T: IMyInter means that type T must implement the IMyInter interface.

- `where T: new()` means that type T must have a default (parameterless) constructor. (If you use it with other constraints, place it in the last position.)

- `where T: S` means that type T must be derived from another generic type S. It is sometimes referred to as a *naked type constraint*.

Now let's go through a demonstration.

Demonstration 8

In demonstration 8, the `IEmployee` interface contains an abstract `Position` method. I use this method to set the designation of an employee before I store the details of the employee in an employee store (think of it as a simple database of employees). The `Employee` class inherits from `IEmployee`, so it needs to implement this interface method. The `Employee` class has a public constructor that can take two arguments: the first one sets the employee name, and the second one indicates the years of experience. I'm setting a designation based on employee experience. (Yes, for simplicity, I'm considering only the years of experience to set a position.)

In this demonstration, you see the following line.

```
class EmployeeStoreHouse<T> where T : IEmployee
```

It is the constraint for your generic parameter that simply tells you that the generic type T must implement the `IEmployee` interface.

Lastly, I used range-based switch statements, which are supported in C# 7.0 onward. If you're using a legacy version, you can replace the code segment with traditional switch statements.

This is the complete demonstration.

```
using System;
using System.Collections.Generic;

namespace UsingConstratintsinGenerics
{
    interface IEmployee
    {
        string Position();
    }
```

```csharp
class Employee : IEmployee
{
    public string Name;
    public int YearOfExp;
    //public Employee() { }
    public Employee(string name, int yearOfExp)
    {
        this.Name = name;
        this.YearOfExp = yearOfExp;
    }
    public string Position()
    {
        string designation;
//C#7.0 onwards range based switch statements are allowed.
        switch (YearOfExp)
        {
            case int n when (n <= 1):
                designation = "Fresher";
                break;

            case int n when (n >= 2 && n <= 5):
                designation = "Intermediate";
                break;
            default:
                designation = "Expert";
                break;
        }
        return designation;
    }
}
class EmployeeStoreHouse<T> where T : IEmployee
{
    private List<Employee> EmpStore = new List<Employee>();
    public void AddToStore(Employee element)
    {
```

```
            EmpStore.Add(element);
        }
        public void DisplayStore()
        {
            Console.WriteLine("The store contains:");
            foreach (Employee e in EmpStore)
            {
                Console.WriteLine(e.Position());
            }
        }
    }

    class Program
    {
        static void Main(string[] args)
        {
            Console.WriteLine("***Using constraints in generic
            programming.***\n");
            //Employees
            Employee e1 = new Employee("Suresh", 1);
            Employee e2 = new Employee("Jack", 5);
            Employee e3 = new Employee("Jon", 7);
            Employee e4 = new Employee("Michael", 2);
            Employee e5 = new Employee("Amit", 3);

            //Employee StoreHouse
            EmployeeStoreHouse<Employee> myEmployeeStore = new EmployeeStore
            House<Employee>();
            myEmployeeStore.AddToStore(e1);
            myEmployeeStore.AddToStore(e2);
            myEmployeeStore.AddToStore(e3);
            myEmployeeStore.AddToStore(e4);
            myEmployeeStore.AddToStore(e5);

            //Display the Employee Positions in Store
            myEmployeeStore.DisplayStore();
```

```
        Console.ReadKey();
      }
    }
}
```

Output

This is the output.

```
***Using constraints in generic programming.***

The store contains:
Fresher
Intermediate
Expert
Intermediate
Intermediate
```

Q&A Session

4.9 Why am I getting multiple compile-time errors in the following line?

```
class EmployeeStoreHouse<T> where T : new(),IEmployee
```

There are currently two issues. First, you haven't placed the new() constraint as the last constraint. Second, the Employee class does not have a public parameterless constructor. Visual Studio gives you a clue about both errors; an error screenshot is shown in Figure 4-3.

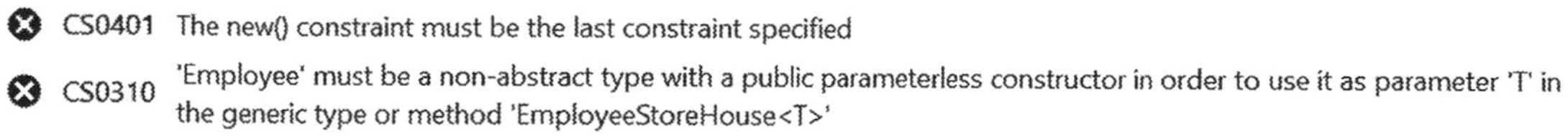

❌ CS0401   The new() constraint must be the last constraint specified

❌ CS0310   'Employee' must be a non-abstract type with a public parameterless constructor in order to use it as parameter 'T' in the generic type or method 'EmployeeStoreHouse<T>'

Figure 4-3. *Compile-time error due to improper usage of new() constraint*

The simple remedy is

- Place a new() constraint in the last position

- Define a public parameterless constructor in the Employee class, such as

```
public Employee() { }
```

4.10 Can I apply constraints on constructors?

When you use a new() constraint for your generic type, you actually place the constraints on the constructor. For example, in the following code, the type must have a parameterless constructor.

```
public class MyClass<T> where T:new()
```

In this context, it is important to note that you cannot use a "parameterful" constructor constraint. For example, if you use something like new(int), in the following code, you get several compile-time errors.

```
class EmployeeStoreHouse<T> where T : IEmployee,new(int) //Error
```

One error says,

```
Error CS0701 'int' is not a valid constraint. A type used as a constraint
must be an interface, a nonsealed class or a type parameter.
```

4.11 Can I apply multiple interfaces as constraints on a single type?

Yes. For example, if you use the ready-made List class, you see the following.

```
public class List<[NullableAttribute(2)]T>
    : ICollection<T>, IEnumerable<T>, IEnumerable, IList<T>,
      IReadOnlyCollection<T>, IReadOnlyList<T>, ICollection, IList
  {//some other stuff}
```

You can see that ICollection<T>, IEnumerable<T>, and IList<T> are applied on List<T>.

Using Covariance and Contravariance

In the discussion on delegates in Chapter 1, you learned that covariance and contravariance support delegates first appeared in C# 2.0. Since C# 4.0, these concepts can be applied to generic type parameters, generic interfaces, and generic delegates. Chapter 1 also explored these concepts with nongeneric delegates. In this chapter, we continue to explore these concepts with additional cases.

Before going forward, recall the following points.

- Covariance and contravariance deal with type conversion with arguments and return types.

- In .NET 4 onward, you can use these concepts in generic delegates and generic interfaces. (In earlier versions, you got compile-time errors.)

- Contravariance is generally defined as an adjustment or modification. When you try to implement these concepts in the coding world, you understand the following truths (or similar truths).

  - All soccer players are athletes, but the reverse is not true (because there are many athletes who play golf, basketball, hockey, etc.) Similarly, you can say that all buses or trains are vehicles, but the reverse is not necessarily true.

  - In programming terminology, all derived classes are of type-based classes, but the reverse is not true. For example, suppose that you have a class called Rectangle that is derived from a class called Shape. Then you can say that all Rectangles are Shapes, but the reverse is not true.

  - According to MSDN, covariance and contravariance deal with implicit reference conversion for arrays, delegates, and generic types. Covariance preserves assignment compatibility, and contravariance reverses it.

Starting with the .NET Framework 4, in C#, there are keywords to mark the generic type parameters of interfaces and delegates as covariant or contravariant. For covariant interfaces and delegates, you see the use of the out keyword (to indicate that values are coming out). Contravariant interfaces and delegates are associated with the in keyword (to indicate that values are going in).

Consider a built-in C# construct. Let's check the definition of IEnumerable<T> in Visual Studio, as shown in Figure 4-4.

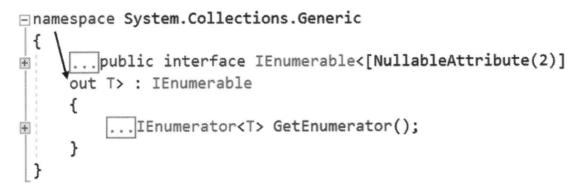

```
namespace System.Collections.Generic
{
    ...public interface IEnumerable<[NullableAttribute(2)]
    out T> : IEnumerable
    {
        ...IEnumerator<T> GetEnumerator();
    }
}
```

Figure 4-4. *Partial screenshot of IEnumerable<T> interface from Visual Studio 2019*

You can see that out is associated with IEnumerable. It simply means that you can assign IEnumerable<DerivedType> to IEnumerable<BaseType>. This is why you can assign IEnumerable<string> to IEnumerable<object>. So, you can say that IEnumerable<T> is a covariant on T.

Now check the definition of the Action<T> delegate in Visual Studio, as shown in Figure 4-5.

```
namespace System
{
    ...public delegate void Action<[NullableAttribute(2)]
    in T>(T obj);
}
```

Figure 4-5. *Partial screenshot of Action<T> delegate from Visual Studio 2019*

Alternatively, you can check the definition of the `IComparer<T>` interface in Visual Studio, as shown in Figure 4-6.

```
namespace System.Collections.Generic
{
    ...public interface IComparer<[NullableAttribute(2)]
    in T>
    {
        ...int Compare([AllowNull] T x, [AllowNull] T y);
    }
}
```

Figure 4-6. *Partial screenshot of IComparer<T> interface from Visual Studio 2019*

You can see that `in` is associated with the `Action` delegate and the `IComparer` interface. It simply means that you can assign `Action<BaseType>` to `Action<DerivedType>`. So, you can say that Action<T> is contravariant on T.

Similarly, since the type parameter is contravariant in the `IComparer` interface, you can use either the actual type you specified or any type that is more general (or less derived).

Q&A Session

4.12 In a Func delegate, I see the presence of both the `in` and out parameters. For example, in Func<in T, out TResult> ***or*** Func<in T1, in T2, out TResult>, **what should I interpret from these definitions?**

It simply tells you that `Func` delegates have covariant return types and contravariant parameter types.

4.13 What do you mean by "assignment compatibility"?

Here is an example where you can assign a more specific type (or a derived type) to a compatible less-specific type. For example, the value of an integer variable can be stored in an object variable, like this:

```
int i = 25;
object o = i;//Assignment Compatible
```

Covariance with Generic Delegate

Let's examine covariance with a generic delegate. In the following demonstration, I'm declaring a generic delegate with covariant return type, as follows.

```
delegate TResult CovDelegate<out TResult>();
```

In this example, Vehicle is the parent class, and Bus is the derived class, so you see the hierarchy. (I did not put any additional methods/code in these classes because they are not required for this demonstration.)

```
class Vehicle
{
    //Some code if needed
}
class Bus : Vehicle
{
    //Some code if needed
 }
```

In addition, you see the presence of the following two static methods: GetOneVehicle() and GetOneBus(). The first one returns a Vehicle object and the second one returns a Bus object.

```
private static Vehicle GetOneVehicle()
{
    Console.WriteLine("Creating one vehicle and returning it.");
        return new Vehicle();
}
private static Bus GetOneBus()
{
    Console.WriteLine("Creating one bus and returning the bus.");
```

The following segment of code is straightforward and easy to understand because they match the delegate signature.

```
CovDelegate<Vehicle> covVehicle = GetOneVehicle;
covVehicle();
CovDelegate<Bus> covBus = GetOneBus;
covBus();
```

Now comes the interesting part. Note the following assignment.

covVehicle = covBus;

This assignment doesn't raise any compilation errors because I'm using the delegate with a covariant return type. But it is important to note that if you do not make the delegate's return type covariant by using the out parameter, this assignment causes the following compile-time error.

```
Error CS0029  Cannot implicitly convert type
'CovarianceWithGenericDelegates.CovDelegate<CovarianceWithGenericDelegates.
Bus>' to 'CovarianceWithGenericDelegates.CovDelegate<CovarianceWithGeneric
Delegates.Vehicle>'
```

Demonstration 9

Go through the complete demonstration. Refer to the supporting comments to help you understand.

```
using System;

namespace CovarianceWithGenericDelegates
{
    //A generic delegate with covariant return type
    //(Notice the use of 'out' keyword)
    delegate TResult CovDelegate<out TResult>();

    //Here 'out' is not used(i.e. it is non-covariant)
    //delegate TResult CovDelegate<TResult>();

    class Vehicle
    {
```

```
        //Some code if needed
    }
    class Bus : Vehicle
    {
        //Some code if needed
    }
    class Program
    {
        static void Main(string[] args)
        {
            Console.WriteLine("***Testing covariance with a Generic
            Delegate.***");
            Console.WriteLine("Normal usage:");
            CovDelegate<Vehicle> covVehicle = GetOneVehicle;
            covVehicle();
            CovDelegate<Bus> covBus = GetOneBus;
            covBus();
            //Testing Covariance
            //covBus to covVehicle (i.e. more specific-> more general) is
            //allowed through covariance
            Console.WriteLine("Using covariance now.");
            //Following assignment is Ok, if you use 'out' in delegate
            //definition Otherwise, you'll receive compile-time error
            covVehicle = covBus;//Still ok
            covVehicle();
            Console.WriteLine("End covariance testing.\n");
            Console.ReadKey();
        }

        private static Vehicle GetOneVehicle()
        {
            Console.WriteLine("Creating one vehicle and returning it.");
            return new Vehicle();
        }
        private static Bus GetOneBus()
```

```
        {
            Console.WriteLine("Creating one bus and returning the bus.");
            return new Bus();
        }
    }
}
```

Output

This is the output.

```
***Testing covariance with a Generic Delegate.***
Normal usage:
Creating one vehicle and returning it.
Creating one bus and returning the bus.
Using covariance now.
Creating one bus and returning the bus.
End covariance testing.
```

Covariance with Generic Interfaces

Let's examine covariance with a generic interface. In this example, I use another built-in construct in C# called IEnumerable<T>. This is an interface that provides the foundation of the most important features in C#. IEnumerable<T> can be used in a foreach loop if you want to do something meaningful on each item in a collection and treat them one by one. Nearly every class in the .NET Framework that contains multiple elements implements this interface. For example, the commonly used List class implements this interface.

Demonstration 10

Like the previous demonstration, Vehicle is the parent class and Bus is the derived class in this example, but this time, I placed an instance method called ShowMe() in each of them. You've seen that in IEnumerable<T>, T is covariant, so this time, I can apply the following assignments.

```
IEnumerable<Vehicle> vehicleEnumerable= busEnumerable;
```

busEnumerable is an IEnumerable<Bus> object and may look like the following.

```
IEnumerable<Bus> busEnumerable=new List<Bus>();
```

In many real-life applications, it's a common practice to use methods that return IEnumerable<T>. This is useful when you do not want to disclose the actual concrete type to others and have the ability to loop through the items.

Now go through the complete demonstration, and refer to the supporting comments if you need to.

```
using System;
using System.Collections.Generic;

namespace CovarianceWithGenericInterface
{
    class Vehicle
    {
        public virtual void ShowMe()
        {
            Console.WriteLine("Vehicle.ShowMe().The hash code is :
            " + GetHashCode());
        }
    }
    class Bus : Vehicle
    {
        public override void ShowMe()
        {
            Console.WriteLine("Bus.ShowMe().Here the hash code is :
            " + GetHashCode());
        }
    }

    class Program
    {
        static void Main(string[] args)
        {
            //Covariance Example
```

```
Console.WriteLine("***Using Covariance with Generic
Interface.***\n");
Console.WriteLine("**Remember that T in IEnumerable<T> is
covariant");
//Some Parent objects
//Vehicle vehicle1 = new Vehicle();
//Vehicle vehicle2 = new Vehicle();
//Some Bus objects
Bus bus1 = new Bus();
Bus bus2 = new Bus();
//Creating a child List
//List<T> implements IEnumerable<T>
List<Bus> busList = new List<Bus>();
busList.Add(bus1);
busList.Add(bus2);
IEnumerable<Bus> busEnumerable = busList;
/*
 An object which was instantiated with a more derived type
 argument (Bus) is assigned to an object instantiated with a
 less derived type argument(Vehicle).Assignment compatibility
 is preserved here.
*/
IEnumerable<Vehicle> vehicleEnumerable = busEnumerable;
foreach (Vehicle vehicle in vehicleEnumerable)
{
    vehicle.ShowMe();
}

Console.ReadKey();
        }
    }
}
```

Output

This is the output.

```
***Using Covariance with Generic Interface.***

**Remember that T in IEnumerable<T> is covariant
Bus.ShowMe().Here the hash code is : 58225482
Bus.ShowMe().Here the hash code is : 54267293
```

Contravariance with Generic Delegates

Let's examine contravariance with a generic delegate. In this demonstration, I'm declaring a generic contravariant delegate, as follows.

```
delegate void ContraDelegate<in T>(T t);
```

Again, Vehicle is the parent class, and Bus is the derived class, and each of them contains a method called ShowMe(). You see the following code segment.

```
class Vehicle
{
    public virtual void ShowMe()
    {
        Console.WriteLine(" Vehicle.ShowMe()");
    }
}
class Bus : Vehicle
{
    public override void ShowMe()
    {
        Console.WriteLine(" Bus.ShowMe()");
    }
}
```

In addition to these classes, you see the presence of the following two static methods: ShowVehicleType() and ShowBusType(). (The first one invokes the ShowMe() from a Vehicle object and second one invokes ShowMe() from a Bus object.)

```
private static void ShowVehicleType(Vehicle vehicle)
{
    vehicle.ShowMe();
}
private static void ShowBusType(Bus bus)
{
    bus.ShowMe();
}
```

The following segment of code is straightforward and easy to understand because they match the delegate signature. (The output is also shown in the comments.)

```
ContraDelegate<Vehicle> contraVehicle = ShowVehicleType;
contraVehicle(obVehicle); // Vehicle.ShowMe()
ContraDelegate<Bus> contraBus = ShowBusType;
contraBus(obBus); // Bus.ShowMe()
```

Now comes the interesting part, which is opposite to covariance. Note the following assignment.

contraBus = contraVehicle;

This assignment doesn't raise any compilation errors because I'm using a contravariant delegate. ***But it is important to note that if you do not make the delegate contravariant by using the*** in ***parameter, this assignment causes the following compile-time error.***

```
Error CS0029 Cannot implicitly convert type
'ContravarianceWithGenericDelegates.ContraDelegate<ContravarianceWithGeneric
Delegates.Vehicle>' to 'ContravarianceWithGenericDelegates.ContraDelegate
<ContravarianceWithGenericDelegates.Bus>'
```

Demonstration 11

Now go through the complete demonstration, and refer to the supporting comments to help you understand.

```
using System;

namespace ContravarianceWithGenericDelegates
```

```csharp
{
    // A generic contravariant delegate
    delegate void ContraDelegate<in T>(T t);
    // A generic non-contravariant delegate
    //delegate void ContraDelegate<T>(T t);
    class Vehicle
    {
        public virtual void ShowMe()
        {
            Console.WriteLine(" Vehicle.ShowMe()");
        }
    }
    class Bus : Vehicle
    {
        public override void ShowMe()
        {
            Console.WriteLine(" Bus.ShowMe()");
        }
    }
    class Program
    {
        static void Main(string[] args)
        {
            Console.WriteLine("*** Testing Contra-variance with Generic
            Delegates.***");
            Vehicle obVehicle = new Vehicle();
            Bus obBus = new Bus();
            Console.WriteLine("Normal usage:");
            ContraDelegate<Vehicle> contraVehicle = ShowVehicleType;
            contraVehicle(obVehicle);
            ContraDelegate<Bus> contraBus = ShowBusType;
            contraBus(obBus);
            Console.WriteLine("Using contravariance now.");
            /*
            Using general type to derived type.
```

```
            Following assignment is Ok, if you use 'in' in delegate definition.
            Otherwise, you'll receive compile-time error.
            */
            contraBus = contraVehicle;//ok
            contraBus(obBus);
            Console.ReadKey();
        }

        private static void ShowVehicleType(Vehicle vehicle)
        {
            vehicle.ShowMe();
        }
        private static void ShowBusType(Bus bus)
        {
            bus.ShowMe();
        }
    }
}
```

Output

This is the output.

```
*** Testing Contra-variance with Generic Delegates.***
Normal usage:
 Vehicle.ShowMe()
 Bus.ShowMe()
Using contravariance now.
 Bus.ShowMe()
```

Contravariance with Generic Interface

Now you understand covariance and contravariance. You've seen the uses of covariance and contravariance with generic delegates, and an implementation of covariance using a generic interface. I'm leaving the remaining case as homework, where you need to write a complete program and implement the concept of contravariance using a generic interface.

I'm providing partial code segments that can help you implement it. If you want, you can verify your implementation using the following code segments as a reference. You can also refer to the associated comments for a better understanding.

Partial Implementation

Here is a generic contravariant interface.

```
// Contravariant interface
interface IContraInterface<in T>{ }
// Following interface is neither covariant nor contravariant
//interface IContraInterface< T> { }
class Implementor<T>: IContraInterface<T> { }
```

Here is an inheritance hierarchy.

```
class Vehicle
{
    // Some code if needed
}
class Bus : Vehicle
{
     // Some code if needed
}
```

Here is the key assignment.

```
IContraInterface<Vehicle> vehicleOb = new Implementor<Vehicle>();
IContraInterface<Bus> busOb = new Implementor<Bus>();
// Contravarince allows the following
// but you'll receive a compile-time error
// if you do not make the interface contravariant using 'in'
busOb = vehicleOb;
```

Q&A Session

4.14 When I use covariance, it looks as if I'm using a simple polymorphism technique. For example, in the previous demonstration, you used the following line.

```
IEnumerable<Vehicle> vehicleEnumerable = busEnumerable;
```

Is this correct?

Yes.

4.15 Can I override a generic method?

Yes. You need to follow the same rules that you apply for nongeneric methods. Let's look at demonstration 12.

Demonstration 12

In this demonstration, BaseClass<T> is the parent class. It has a method called MyMethod that accepts T as a parameter, and it's return type is also T. DerivedClass<T> derives from this parent class and overrides this method.

```
using System;

namespace MethodOverridingDemo
{
    class BaseClass<T>
    {
        public virtual T MyMethod(T param)
        {
            Console.WriteLine("Inside BaseClass.BaseMethod()");
            return param;
        }
    }
    class DerivedClass<T>: BaseClass<T>
    {
        public override T MyMethod(T param)
        {
            Console.WriteLine("Here I'm inside of DerivedClass.
            DerivedMethod()");
            return param;
        }
    }
    class Program
    {
        static void Main(string[] args)
```

```
        {
            Console.WriteLine("***Overriding a virtual method.***\n");
            BaseClass<int> intBase = new BaseClass<int>();
            // Invoking Parent class method
            Console.WriteLine($"Parent class method returns {intBase.
            MyMethod(25)}");//25
            // Now pointing to the child class method and invoking it.
            intBase = new DerivedClass<int>();
            Console.WriteLine($"Derived class method returns {intBase.
            MyMethod(25)}");//25
            // The following will cause compile-time error
            //intBase = new DerivedClass<double>(); // error
            Console.ReadKey();
        }
    }
}
```

Output

This is the output.

```
***Overriding a virtual method.***

Inside BaseClass.BaseMethod()
Parent class method returns 25
Here I'm inside of DerivedClass.DerivedMethod()
Derived class method returns 25
```

Analysis

You can see that by following a simple polymorphism, I'm using the parent class reference (intBase) to point to the child class object. There was no issue for this kind of coding because both cases dealt with int types only. But the following lines of code with comments are easy to understand because using intBase, you cannot point to an object that is dealing with different types (double in this case).

```
// The following will cause compile-time error
//intBase = new DerivedClass<double>(); // error
```

To print output messages, I used a string interpolation technique. I used it only for a change, but in cases like this, you need to use C# 6.0 or above; otherwise, you can use the traditional approach.

Q&A Session

4.16 Can I overload a generic method?

Yes. In this case, also you need to follow the same rules that you apply for nongeneric methods, but you have to be careful with methods that accept type parameters. In such cases, *the type difference is not considered on generic types; instead, it depends on the type argument that you substitute for a type parameter.*

4.17 You said that the type difference is not considered on generic types; instead, it depends on the type argument that you substitute for the type parameter. Can you please elaborate?

I meant that sometimes it may appear that you have followed the rule of overloading perfectly, but there is something more to consider when you overload a generic method that accepts type parameters.

You know that for overloading, the number and/or type parameters are different. So, if you have following two methods in your class, you can say that it's an example of overloading.

```
public void MyMethod2(int a, double b) { // some code };
public void MyMethod2(double b, int a) { // some code };
```

Now consider the following code segment, which involves generic type parameters.

```
class MyClass<T,U>
{
    public  void MyMethod(T param1, U param2)
    {
        Console.WriteLine("Inside MyMethod(T param1, U param2)");
    }
    public void MyMethod(U param1, T param2)
    {
        Console.WriteLine("Inside MyMethod(U param1, T param2)");
    }
}
```

It may appear that you have two overloaded versions of MyMethod, because the order of the generic type parameters differs. But there is potential ambiguity, which will be clear to you when you exercise the following code segments.

```
MyClass<int, double> object1 = new MyClass<int, double>();
object1.MyMethod(1, 2.3); // ok
MyClass<int, int> object2 = new MyClass<int, int>();
// Ambiguous call
object2.MyMethod(1, 2); // error
```

For this segment of code, you get the following compile-time error (for the line marked with // error).

```
CS0121 The call is ambiguous between the following methods or properties:
'MyClass<T, U>.MyMethod(T, U)' and 'MyClass<T, U>.MyMethod(U, T)'
```

Demonstration 13

This is the full demonstration.

```
using System;

namespace MethodOverloadingDemo
{
    class MyClass<T,U>
    {
        public  void MyMethod(T param1, U param2)
        {
            Console.WriteLine("Inside MyMethod(T param1, U param2)");
        }
        public void MyMethod(U param1, T param2)
        {
            Console.WriteLine("Inside MyMethod(U param1, T param2)");
        }
            public void MyMethod2(int a, double b)
        {
            Console.WriteLine("Inside MyMethod2(int a, double b).");
        }
```

```
    public void MyMethod2(double b, int a)
    {
        Console.WriteLine("MyMethod2(double b, int a) is called here.");
    }    }

class Program
{
    static void Main(string[] args)
    {
        Console.WriteLine("***Method overloading demo.***\n");
        MyClass<int, double> object1 = new MyClass<int, double>();
        object1.MyMethod(1, 2.3);//ok
        object1.MyMethod2(1, 2.3);//ok
        object1.MyMethod2(2.3, 1);//ok
        MyClass<int, int> object2 = new MyClass<int, int>();
        // Ambiguous call
        object2.MyMethod(1, 2); // error
        Console.ReadKey();
    }
}
}
```

Output

Again, you get the following compile-time error.

```
CS0121 The call is ambiguous between the following methods or properties:
'MyClass<T, U>.MyMethod(T, U)' and 'MyClass<T, U>.MyMethod(U, T)'
```

You can comment out the ambiguous call, as follows, and then compile and run the program.

```
//object2.MyMethod(1, 2);//error
```

This time, you get the following output.

```
***Method overloading demo.***

Inside MyMethod(T param1, U param2)
Inside MyMethod2(int a, double b).
MyMethod2(double b, int a) is called here.
```

153

Self-Referencing Generic Types

Sometimes you may need to compare two instances of a class. In a case like this, you have two options.

- Use the built-in constructs.

- Write your own comparison method.

When you are interested in using built-in constructs, you have multiple options. For example, you can use either the CompareTo method of IComparable<T> or the Equals method of IEquitable<T>. You may note that a nongeneric IComparable is also available in C#.

Here is information about CompareTo from Visual Studio.

```
//
// Summary:
//     Compares the current instance with another object of the same
//     type and returns an integer that indicates whether the current instance
//     precedes, follows, or occurs in the same position in the sort
//     order as the other object.
//
// Parameters:
//   other:
//     An object to compare with this instance.
//
// Returns:
//     A value that indicates the relative order of the objects being
//     compared. The return value has these meanings: Value Meaning Less
//     than zero This instance precedes other in the sort order. Zero
//     This instance occurs in the same position in the sort order as other.
//     Greater than zero This instance follows other in the sort order.
   int CompareTo([AllowNull] T other);
```

Here is information about Equals from Visual Studio.

```
//
// Summary:
```

```
//      Indicates whether the current object is equal to another object of
//      the same type.
//
// Parameters:
//   other:
//      An object to compare with this object.
//
// Returns:
//      true if the current object is equal to the other parameter;
//      otherwise, false.
    bool Equals([AllowNull] T other);
```

If your class implements any of these interfaces, you can use these methods and override them as you need. These interfaces are available in the System namespace, and they are implemented by built-in types like int, double, and string.

In many cases, however, you may want to write your own comparison method. I do this in demonstration 14.

A type can name itself as the concrete type when it closes the type argument.

Demonstration 14

In this demonstration, the Employee class implements IIdenticalEmployee<T>, which has an abstract method called CheckEqualityWith. Let's suppose that in your Employee class, you have employee IDs and department names. Once I instantiate objects from the Employee class, my task is to compare these objects.

For comparison purposes, I simply check whether the deptName and employeeID are the same for two employees. If they match, the employees are the same. (Using the word *same*, I mean only the content of these objects, not the reference to the heap.)

This is the comparison method.

```
public string CheckEqualityWith(Employee obj)
{
    if (obj == null)
    {
        return "Cannot Compare with a Null Object";
    }
```

```
    else
    {
        if (this.deptName == obj.deptName && this.employeeID == obj.
        employeeID)
        {
            return "Same Employee.";
        }
        else
        {
            return "Different Employees.";
        }
    }
}
```

Now go through the complete implementation and output.

```csharp
using System;

namespace SelfReferencingGenericTypeDemo
{
    interface IIdenticalEmployee<T>
    {
        string CheckEqualityWith(T obj);
    }
    class Employee : IIdenticalEmployee<Employee>
    {
            string deptName;
            int employeeID;
            public Employee(string deptName, int employeeId)
            {
                this.deptName = deptName;
                this.employeeID = employeeId;
            }
            public string CheckEqualityWith(Employee obj)
            {
```

```
            if (obj == null)
            {
                return "Cannot Compare with a null Object";
            }
            else
            {
                if (this.deptName == obj.deptName && this.employeeID ==
                obj.employeeID)
                {
                    return "Same Employee.";
                }
                else
                {
                    return "Different Employees.";
                }
            }
        }
    }
}
class Program
{
    static void Main(string[] args)
    {
        Console.WriteLine("**Self-referencing generic type
        demo.***\n");
        Console.WriteLine("***We are checking whether two employee
        objects are same or different.***");
        Console.WriteLine();
        Employee emp1 = new Employee("Chemistry", 1);
        Employee emp2 = new Employee("Maths", 2);
        Employee emp3 = new Employee("Comp. Sc.", 1);
        Employee emp4 = new Employee("Maths", 2);
        Employee emp5 = null;
        Console.WriteLine("Comparing emp1 and emp3 :{0}", emp1.
        CheckEqualityWith(emp3));
```

```
            Console.WriteLine("Comparing emp2 and emp4 :{0}", emp2.
            CheckEqualityWith(emp4));
            Console.WriteLine("Comparing emp2 and emp5 :{0}", emp2.
            CheckEqualityWith(emp5));
            Console.ReadKey();
        }
    }
}
```

Output

This is the output.

```
**Self-referencing generic type demo.***
***We are checking whether two employee objects are same or different.***

Comparing emp1 and emp3 :Different Employees.
Comparing emp2 and emp4 :Same Employee.
Comparing emp2 and emp5 :Cannot Compare with a null Object
```

Analysis

This example shows you that a type can name itself as a concrete type when it closes the type argument. It demonstrates how to use a ***self-referencing generic type.*** Again, by using the word *same* this example, I meant only the content of the objects, not the reference to the heap.

Q&A Session

4.18 Can you summarize the key usage of generics?

You can promote type-safety without creating lots of types that are very similar and particularly differ only by the types they use. As a result, you can avoid runtime errors and reduce costs due to boxing and unboxing.

4.19 How do static variables work in context of generic programming?

Static data is unique for each of the closed types. Consider the following program and output for your reference.

Demonstration 15

In this demonstration, let's focus on the count variable and see how it increments when the MyGenericClass<T> generic class is instantiated with different types.

```
using System;

namespace TestingStaticData
{
    class MyGenericClass<T>
    {
        public static int count;
        public void IncrementMe()
        {
            Console.WriteLine($"Incremented value is : {++count}");
        }
    }
    class Program
    {
        static void Main(string[] args)
        {
            Console.WriteLine("***Testing static in the context of generic
            programming.***");
            MyGenericClass<int> intOb = new MyGenericClass<int>();
            Console.WriteLine("\nUsing intOb now.");
            intOb.IncrementMe();//1
            intOb.IncrementMe();//2
            intOb.IncrementMe();//3

            Console.WriteLine("\nUsing strOb now.");
            MyGenericClass<string> strOb = new MyGenericClass<string>();
            strOb.IncrementMe();//1
            strOb.IncrementMe();//2
```

```
            Console.WriteLine("\nUsing doubleOb now.");
            MyGenericClass<double> doubleOb = new MyGenericClass<double>();
            doubleOb.IncrementMe();//1
            doubleOb.IncrementMe();//2

            MyGenericClass<int> intOb2 = new MyGenericClass<int>();
            Console.WriteLine("\nUsing intOb2 now.");
            intOb2.IncrementMe();//4
            intOb2.IncrementMe();//5

            Console.ReadKey();
        }
    }
}
```

Output

This is the output.

```
***Testing static in the context of generic programming.***

Using intOb now.
Incremented value is : 1
Incremented value is : 2
Incremented value is : 3

Using strOb now.
Incremented value is : 1
Incremented value is : 2

Using doubleOb now.
Incremented value is : 1
Incremented value is : 2

Using intOb2 now.
Incremented value is : 4
Incremented value is : 5
```

Q&A Session

4.20 What are the important restrictions in using generics?

Here are some important restrictions to note.

- Static data is unique for each of the closed types but *not* for different constructed types.

- You cannot use an external modifier in a generic method. So, following segment of code

```
using System;
using System.Runtime.InteropServices;
class GenericClassDemo2<T>
{
    [DllImport("avifil32.dll")] // error in generic method
    private static extern void AVIFileInit();
}
```

raises the following compile-time error:

Error CS7042   The DllImport attribute cannot be applied to a method that is generic or contained in a generic type.

- You cannot use a pointer type as type arguments. So, the last line in following code segment

```
class GenericClassDemo2<T>
{
    static unsafe void ShowMe()
    {
        int a = 10; // ok
        int* p; // ok
        p = &a; // ok

        T* myVar; // error
    }
}
```

raises the following compile-time error:

```
Error CS0208  Cannot take the address of, get the size of, or
declare a pointer to a managed type ('T')
```

- In Q&A Session question 4.9, you saw that if you have multiple constraints, the new() constraint must be placed at the end.

Final Words

I hope that this chapter demystified the key features of generic programming. At first, generic syntax may look little bit overwhelming, but practice and repeated use of these concepts will help you master them, and you'll be able to produce high-quality software using C#.

Now let's jump into the next chapter, where you'll learn about thread programming.

Summary

This chapter addressed the following key questions.

- What is a generic program? And why is it important?

- What are the advantages of generic programming over nongeneric programming?

- Why is the default keyword useful in the context of generics? And how can it be used in my program?

- How do you use built-in delegates—Func, Action, and Predicate—in a program?

- How do you impose constraints in generic programming?

- How do you use covariance and contravariance with generic delegates and interfaces?

- How do you overload a generic method? And why should you be careful?

- How do you override a generic method?

- How do you use a self-referencing generic type?

- How do static variables behave in a generic program?

- What are some of the key restrictions in generics?

CHAPTER 5

Thread Programming

In today's world, everyone is familiar with multitasking, which simply indicates that you can do multiple things in parallel. Consider a common scenario. For example, as I am writing this chapter using Microsoft Word on my laptop, I'm listening to a very calm piece of music in Windows Media Player. In much the same way, you can execute different methods in a C# application simultaneously. To implement this concept, you need to be familiar with multithreading.

In earlier days, computers had a single processor, but nowadays, the scenario has changed a lot. Most computers in today's world have multiple processors. For example, at the time of writing, I'm using a dual core system with four logical processors; yet in today's world, this is not considered a superfast computer, because there are machines with large numbers of processors (obviously those are expensive) and have much more computing power. Still, I can execute some of my work on another superfast computer if it is connected to my computer over a network. So, it is possible to use the computing power of other machines. But the fact is that unless you structure your code to run on multiple processors, you are not using the machine's full computing potential. In this chapter, you will become familiar with multithreading, and you will learn how to use it effectively. Let's start.

Foundations in Thread Programming

Most of the programs that you have seen so far had a single sequential flow of control (i.e., once the program started executing, it went through all statements sequentially until the end). As a result, at any particular moment, there is only one statement that is under execution. A thread is similar to a program. It has a single flow of control. It also has a body between the starting point and end point, and it executes the commands sequentially. Each program has at least one thread.

© Vaskaran Sarcar 2020
V. Sarcar, *Getting Started with Advanced C#*, https://doi.org/10.1007/978-1-4842-5934-4_5

In C#, you can have multiple flows of control in a program. In those cases, each flow of control is called a *thread,* and these threads can run in parallel. In a multithreaded environment, each thread has a unique flow of execution. It's a programming paradigm where a program is divided into multiple subprograms (or parts) that can be implemented in parallel. But, if the computer has only one processor, how can it perform multiple things in parallel? The processor switches among these subprograms (or segments of code) very fast, so it appears to the human eye that all of them are executing simultaneously.

In simple words, when the OS divides processor execution time among different applications, the scenario is multitasking, and when the OS divides the execution time among different threads within a single application, it is called multithreading. This is why multithreading is considered a special kind of multitasking.

In this context, it is important for you to review the differences between a process and a thread in any theoretical operating system book. For your reference, Table 5-1 highlights some key distinctions.

Table 5-1. *Comparisons Between a Process and a Thread*

Process	Thread
Unit of allocation.	Unit of execution.
Architectural construct.	Coding construct does not affect architecture.
Each process has one or more thread.	Each thread belongs to one process.
Interprocess communication (commonly known as IPC) is expensive due to context switching.	Interthread communication is cheap, can use process memory and may not need context switch.
Secure: one process cannot corrupt another process.	Not secure: a thread can write to the memory used by another thread.

Managing a multithreaded environment can be challenging, but you can complete tasks much faster and reduce overall idle time significantly. Generally, in an automated environment, a computer's input is much faster than the user's keyboard input. Or, when you transfer data over a network, the network transmission rate can be slower than the receiving computer's consumption rate. If you need to wait for each task to finish before you can start the next one, the overall idle time will be higher. A multithreaded environment is always a better choice in cases like these. C# can help you model a multithreaded environment efficiently.

Figure 5-1 demonstrates a common scenario in a multithreaded program, where the main thread creates two more threads—threadOne and threadTwo—and all threads are running concurrently.

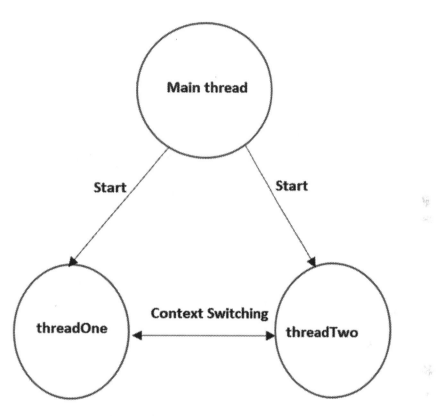

Figure 5-1. *In a multithreaded program, the main thread creates two more threads, and all of them are running concurrently*

POINTS TO REMEMBER

The core aim of multithreading is that you can execute independent segments of code in separate threads, so that you can complete a task faster.

In the .NET Framework, you can have both foreground and background threads. When you create a thread, it's a foreground thread by default. But you can convert a foreground thread to a background thread. The key difference is that when a foreground thread terminates, the associated background thread(s) are stopped too.

Q&A Session

5.1 In Figure 5-1, I'm seeing the term "context switching." What does it mean in this context?

In general, many threads can run in parallel on your computer. The computer allows one thread to run in one processor for a time, and then it can suddenly switch to a different one. This decision is made by different factors. Normally, all threads have equal priority and switching among them is performed nicely. Switching between threads is called *context switching*. It also enables you to store the state of the current thread (or process) so that you can resume execution from this point later.

5.2 What is the key advantage of a multithreaded environment over a single threaded environment?

In a single threaded environment, if the thread is blocked, the entire program is halted, which is not the case in a multithreaded environment. In addition, you can reduce overall idle time by making efficient use of the CPU. For example, when one part of a program is sending a large amount of data over a network, another part of the program can accept user input, and still another part of the program can validate this input and prepare the next block of data for sending.

5.3 I have a multicore system, but can multithreading still help me?

There was a time when most computers had a single core; concurrent threads shared the CPU cycles, but they could not run in parallel. Using the concept of multithreading, you can reduce overall idle time through efficient use of the CPU. But if you have multiple processors, you can run multiple threads concurrently. As a result, you can further enhance the speed of your program.

5.4 A multithreaded program can have multiple parts that run concurrently. Each of these parts are threads, and each thread can have a separate flow of execution. Is this correct?

Yes.

Coding Multithreaded Programs in C#

Before you write a multithreaded program in C#, the first thing to remember is to begin with

```
using System.Threading;
```

This namespace contains the Thread class, which has different methods. You will see some of these methods in the upcoming demonstrations. Now comes the next step. To run a method, let's say Method1(), in a separate thread, you need to write something like the following.

```
Thread threadOne = new Thread(Method1);
threadOne.Start();
```

Note the previous two lines. If you hover your mouse over the Thread type in Visual Studio, you see that the Thread class has four different constructors, as follows.

```
public Thread(ThreadStart start)
public Thread(ParameterizedThreadStart start)
public Thread(ThreadStart start, int maxStackSize)
public Thread(ParameterizedThreadStart start, int maxStackSize)
```

ThreadStart and ParameterizedThreadStart are delegates. Now let's investigate these delegates in detail. From the Visual Studio IDE, you get the following description for ThreadStart delegate.

```
//
// Summary:
// Represents the method that executes on a
//System.Threading.Thread.
[ComVisible(true)]
public delegate void ThreadStart();
```

Similarly, the Visual Studio IDE shows the following description for the ParameterizedThreadStart delegate.

```
//
// Summary:
// Represents the method that executes on a
//System.Threading.Thread.
//
// Parameters:
//   obj:
//     An object that contains data for the thread procedure.
   [ComVisible(false)]
   public delegate void ParameterizedThreadStart(object obj);
```

167

These descriptions show the following points.

- Both delegates have void return types.

- The ThreadStart delegate does not have a parameter, whereas ParameterizedThreadStart can accept an object parameter.

You'll experiment with both delegates shortly. But so far, you have learned to run a method in different threads; the methods should match either of the delegate signatures.

One last point: In demonstration 1 and demonstration 2, I have used the simplest version of Start() method which does not take any parameter. Later you'll also notice the use of another overloaded version of this method which can take an object parameter. So, based on your need, you can use any of the following methods:

```
public void Start();
public void Start(object? parameter);
```

Using the ThreadStart Delegate

Let's start with the ThreadStart delegate. Let's suppose that you have a method called Method1, as follows.

```
static void Method1()
{
    for (int i = 0; i < 10; i++)
    {
        Console.WriteLine("-ThreadOne from Method1() prints {0}", i);
    }}
```

Since Method1 doesn't accept any parameters, and it has a void return type, it matches with the ThreadStart delegate signature. In Chapter 1, you learned that if you write the following,

```
ThreadStart delegateObject = new ThreadStart(Method1);
```

it is equivalent to writing

```
ThreadStart delegateObject = Method1;
```

So, when you pass a `ThreadStart` delegate object inside a Thread constructor, you can write something like the following.

```
Thread threadOne = new Thread(new ThreadStart(Method1));
```

which is equivalent to writing

```
Thread threadOne = new Thread(Method1);
```

Lastly, it's worth noting the following points.

- In the upcoming example, `Method1()` is a static method. In this case, you can refer to the method without instantiating any object.

- Once you call the `Start()` method, the thread is created and starts executing.

- If you call the `Start()` method on a thread that is already running, you'll encounter a runtime error that says, *System.Threading. ThreadStateException*: *'Thread is running or terminated; it cannot restart.'*

Let's look at the last point again. Programmatically, a thread can have several states. The `Start` method can change the current instance's state to `ThreadState.Running`. In the Visual Studio2019 IDE, if you hover your mouse and go to the `ThreadState` definition, you see the enumeration shown in Figure 5-2, which describes different thread states.

```
namespace System.Threading
{
    ...public enum ThreadState
    {
        ...Running = 0,
        ...StopRequested = 1,
        ...SuspendRequested = 2,
        ...Background = 4,
        ...Unstarted = 8,
        ...Stopped = 16,
        ...WaitSleepJoin = 32,
        ...Suspended = 64,
        ...AbortRequested = 128,
        ...Aborted = 256
    }
}
```

Figure 5-2. *Different states of a thread in C#*

All of these are self-explanatory, but you may be interested in the one called WaitSleepJoin. A thread can enter this blocked state as a result of calling Sleep() or Join(), or requesting a lock; for example, when you call Wait(), Monitor.Enter(), and so forth with a proper argument. You'll learn about this shortly.

Demonstration 1

In the following demonstration, there are two static methods: Method1 and Method2. These methods match with the signature of the ThreadStart delegate. As discussed in the "Foundations in Thread Programming" section, I'm running them in separate threads.

| POINTS TO REMEMBER |

In this chapter, for some initial demonstrations, you see hard-coded lines in method bodies, such as

```
Console.WriteLine("-ThreadOne from Method1() prints {0}", i);
```

Or,

```
Console.WriteLine("--ThreadTwo from Method2() prints 2.0{0}", i);
```

Ideally, you should not hard-code thread details like this because in a multithreaded environment, Method1() can be executed in different threads. But if you set a thread name, then you can write something like the following.

```
Console.WriteLine("-{0} from Method1() prints {1}", Thread.CurrentThread.
Name, i);
```

Or, if you prefer to use string interpolation, you may write something like the following.

```
Console.WriteLine($"{Thread.CurrentThread.Name} from MyMethod() prints {i}");
```

Here, I go step by step. I have not introduced the Name property from the Thread class yet. For simplicity, I am executing Method1() using the threadOne object, Method2() using the threadTwo object, and so forth.

This is the complete demonstration.

```
using System;
using System.Threading;

namespace ThreadProgrammingEx1
{
    class Program
    {
        static void Main(string[] args)
        {
            Console.WriteLine("***Thread Demonstration-1****");
            Console.WriteLine("Main thread has started.");

            Thread threadOne = new Thread(Method1);
```

```csharp
            // Same as
            /* Thread threadOne = new Thread(new ThreadStart(Method1));*/

            Thread threadTwo = new Thread(Method2);
            // Same as
            /* Thread threadTwo = new Thread(new ThreadStart(Method2));*/

            Console.WriteLine("Starting threadOne shortly.");
            // threadOne starts
            threadOne.Start();
            Console.WriteLine("Starting threadTwo shortly.");
            // threadTwo starts
            threadTwo.Start();

            Console.WriteLine("Control comes at the end of Main()
            method.");
            Console.ReadKey();
        }
        static void Method1()
        {
            for (int i = 0; i < 10; i++)
            {
                Console.WriteLine("-ThreadOne from Method1() prints {0}", i);
            }
        }
        static void Method2()
        {
            for (int i = 0; i < 10; i++)
            {
                Console.WriteLine("--ThreadTwo from Method2() prints
                2.0{0}", i);
            }
        }
    }
}
```

This is one possible output.

```
***Thread Demonstration-1****
Main thread has started.
Starting threadOne shortly.
Starting threadTwo shortly.
-ThreadOne from Method1() prints 0
-ThreadOne from Method1() prints 1
-ThreadOne from Method1() prints 2
-ThreadOne from Method1() prints 3
-ThreadOne from Method1() prints 4
-ThreadOne from Method1() prints 5
-ThreadOne from Method1() prints 6
-ThreadOne from Method1() prints 7
-ThreadOne from Method1() prints 8
Control comes at the end of Main() method.
--ThreadTwo from Method2() prints 2.00
--ThreadTwo from Method2() prints 2.01
-ThreadOne from Method1() prints 9
--ThreadTwo from Method2() prints 2.02
--ThreadTwo from Method2() prints 2.03
--ThreadTwo from Method2() prints 2.04
--ThreadTwo from Method2() prints 2.05
--ThreadTwo from Method2() prints 2.06
--ThreadTwo from Method2() prints 2.07
--ThreadTwo from Method2() prints 2.08
--ThreadTwo from Method2() prints 2.09
```

This is another possible output.

```
***Thread Demonstration-1****
Main thread has started.
Starting threadOne shortly.
Starting threadTwo shortly.
-ThreadOne from Method1() prints 0
```

```
-ThreadOne from Method1() prints 1
-ThreadOne from Method1() prints 2
Control comes at the end of Main() method.
-ThreadOne from Method1() prints 3
-ThreadOne from Method1() prints 4
-ThreadOne from Method1() prints 5
-ThreadOne from Method1() prints 6
-ThreadOne from Method1() prints 7
-ThreadOne from Method1() prints 8
-ThreadOne from Method1() prints 9
--ThreadTwo from Method2() prints 2.00
--ThreadTwo from Method2() prints 2.01
--ThreadTwo from Method2() prints 2.02
--ThreadTwo from Method2() prints 2.03
--ThreadTwo from Method2() prints 2.04
--ThreadTwo from Method2() prints 2.05
--ThreadTwo from Method2() prints 2.06
--ThreadTwo from Method2() prints 2.07
--ThreadTwo from Method2() prints 2.08
--ThreadTwo from Method2() prints 2.09
```

Analysis

I presented two *possible* outputs; it may vary in your case. This is common in thread programming, because your operating system employs context switching as per the design. Later, you'll see that you can employ a special mechanism to control the execution order.

Demonstration 2

In demonstration 1, the original thread (for the Main() method) finishes before the spawned threads (for Method1 and Method2). But in real-world applications, you may not want the parent thread to finish before the child threads (though a program will continue to run until its foreground threads are alive).

In simple scenarios, you may use the Sleep(int millisecondsTimeout) method. It is a static method and commonly used. It causes the currently executing thread to pause for a specified period of time. The int parameter hints that you need to pass milliseconds as the argument. If you want the current thread to pause for 1 second, you pass 1000 as the argument to the Sleep method. But the Sleep method is not as effective as Join(), which is also defined in the Thread class. This is because the Join() method can help you block a thread until another thread finishes its execution. In the following demonstration, I use this method, and you see the following lines of code with supporting comments.

```
// Waiting for threadOne to finish
threadOne.Join();
// Waiting for threadtwo to finish
threadTwo.Join();
```

These statements are written inside the Main() method. Once the original thread passes through these statements, it waits for threadOne and threadTwo to finish their jobs and effectively join the execution of the child threads.

Now go through the complete demonstration and look at the output, followed by a short analysis.

```
using System;
using System.Threading;

namespace ThreadProgrammingEx2
{
    class Program
    {
        static void Main(string[] args)
        {
            Console.WriteLine("***Thread Demonstration-2****");
            Console.WriteLine("***Exploring Join() method.It helps to
            make a thread wait for another running thread to finish it's
            job.***");
            Console.WriteLine("Main thread has started.");

            Thread threadOne = new Thread(Method1);
            // Same as
            //Thread threadOne = new Thread(new ThreadStart(Method1));

            Thread threadTwo = new Thread(Method2);
```

```
        // Same as
        //Thread threadTwo = new Thread(new ThreadStart(Method2));

        Console.WriteLine("Starting threadOne shortly.");
        // threadOne starts
        threadOne.Start();
        Console.WriteLine("Starting threadTwo shortly.");
        // threadTwo starts
        threadTwo.Start();

        // Waiting for threadOne to finish
        threadOne.Join();
        // Waiting for threadtwo to finish
        threadTwo.Join();

        Console.WriteLine("Control comes at the end of Main()
        method.");
        Console.ReadKey();
    }
    static void Method1()
    {
        for (int i = 0; i < 10; i++)
        {
            Console.WriteLine("-ThreadOne from Method1() prints {0}", i);
        }
    }
    static void Method2()
    {
        for (int i = 0; i < 10; i++)
        {
            Console.WriteLine("--ThreadTwo from Method2() prints
            2.0{0}", i);
        }
    }
    }
}
```

This is one possible output.

```
***Thread Demonstration-2****
***Exploring Join() method.It helps to make a thread wait for another
running thread to finish it's job.***
Main thread has started.
Starting threadOne shortly.
Starting threadTwo shortly.
-ThreadOne from Method1() prints 0
-ThreadOne from Method1() prints 1
-ThreadOne from Method1() prints 2
-ThreadOne from Method1() prints 3
-ThreadOne from Method1() prints 4
--ThreadTwo from Method2() prints 2.00
--ThreadTwo from Method2() prints 2.01
--ThreadTwo from Method2() prints 2.02
--ThreadTwo from Method2() prints 2.03
--ThreadTwo from Method2() prints 2.04
--ThreadTwo from Method2() prints 2.05
--ThreadTwo from Method2() prints 2.06
--ThreadTwo from Method2() prints 2.07
--ThreadTwo from Method2() prints 2.08
--ThreadTwo from Method2() prints 2.09
-ThreadOne from Method1() prints 5
-ThreadOne from Method1() prints 6
-ThreadOne from Method1() prints 7
-ThreadOne from Method1() prints 8
-ThreadOne from Method1() prints 9
Control comes at the end of Main() method.
```

Analysis

In this demonstration, you saw the use of the Join() method inside the Main() method. The original thread remained alive until the other threads finished executing. So, the "Control comes at the end of Main() method." statement always appears at the end of output.

It's important to note that

- Both the Start and Join methods have different overloaded versions.

- You encounter a runtime error that says, *System.Threading. ThreadStateException: 'Thread has not been started.'* if you call Join() on a thread that hasn't started.

Q&A Session

5.5 How does Thread.Sleep() differ from Thread.Join()?

The Sleep() method has two variations.

```
public static void Sleep(int millisecondsTimeout)
and
public static void Sleep(TimeSpan timeout)
```

Using the Sleep() method, you can suspend the current thread for a specific amount of time.

```
Join() has three variations.
public void Join();
public bool Join(int millisecondsTimeout);
public bool Join(TimeSpan timeout);
```

The basic idea is that by using Join(), you can block the calling thread until the thread represented by this instance terminates. (Although you can specify a timeout limit inside the overloaded version of Join().)

With sleep(), if your specified time is unnecessarily big, the thread will be in suspended state, even if other threads have already finished their execution. But by using Join(), you can wait for other threads to finish, and then proceed immediately.

Another interesting difference is that Sleep() is a static method, and you call this method on the current thread. But Join() is an instance method, and when you write something like the following, from a caller's point of view, you pass an instance of some other thread (other than the calling thread) and wait for that thread to finish first.

```
// Waiting for threadOne to finish
threadOne.Join();
```

Using the ParameterizedThreadStart Delegate

You have seen the usage of the ThreadStart delegate. You were not able to deal with methods that can accept parameters, but methods with parameters are very common in programming. Next, you see the use of the ParameterizedThreadStart delegate. You already know that it can accept an object parameter, and it's return type is void. Since the parameter is an object, you can use it for any type—as long as you can apply the cast properly to the correct type.

Demonstration 3

In this demonstration, you have the following method.

```
static void Method3(Object number)
{
    int upperLimit = (int)number;
    for (int i = 0; i < upperLimit; i++)
    {
        Console.WriteLine("---ThreadThree from Method3() prints 3.0{0}", i);
    }
}
```

You can see that although the method has an object parameter, I'm casting it to an int, and then I use it to print the required data to the console window. In this demonstration, three methods are present: Method1, Method2, and Method3. Method1 and Method2 were in previous demonstrations. Method3 is newly added to demonstrate the usage of both ThreadStart delegate and ParameterizedThreadStart delegate together in the following example.

```csharp
using System;
using System.Threading;

namespace UsingParameterizedThreadStart_delegate
{
    class Program
    {
        static void Main(string[] args)
        {
            Console.WriteLine("***ParameterizedThreadStart delegate is used
            in this demonstration****");
            Console.WriteLine("Main thread has started.");

            Thread threadOne = new Thread(Method1);
            // Same as
            //Thread threadOne = new Thread(new ThreadStart(Method1));

            Thread threadTwo = new Thread(Method2);
            // Same as
            //Thread threadTwo = new Thread(new ThreadStart(Method2));

            Thread threadThree = new Thread(Method3);
            // Same as
            //Thread threadThree = new Thread(new ParameterizedThreadStart
            (Method3));

            Console.WriteLine("Starting threadOne shortly.");
            // threadOne starts
            threadOne.Start();
            Console.WriteLine("Starting threadTwo shortly.");
            // threadTwo starts
            threadTwo.Start();

            Console.WriteLine("Starting threadThree shortly.Here we use
            ParameterizedThreadStart delegate.");
            // threadThree starts
            threadThree.Start(15);

            // Waiting for threadOne to finish
```

```
            threadOne.Join();
            // Waiting for threadtwo to finish
            threadTwo.Join();
            // Waiting for threadthree to finish
            threadThree.Join();

            Console.WriteLine("Main() method ends now.");

            Console.ReadKey();
        }
        static void Method1()
        {
            for (int i = 0; i < 10; i++)
            {
                Console.WriteLine("-ThreadOne from Method1() prints {0}", i);
            }
        }
        static void Method2()
        {
            for (int i = 0; i < 10; i++)
            {
                Console.WriteLine("--ThreadTwo from Method2() prints
                2.0{0}", i);
            }
        }
```

```
/*
The following method has an object parameter
This method matches the ParameterizedThreadStart delegate signature;because
it has a single parameter of type Object and this method doesn't return a
value.
*/
        static void Method3(Object number)
        {
            int upperLimit = (int)number;
            for (int i = 0; i < upperLimit; i++)
            {
```

```
            Console.WriteLine("---ThreadThree from Method3() prints
            3.0{0}", i);
        }
      }
    }
}
```

Output

This is one possible output.

```
***ParameterizedThreadStart delegate is used in this demonstration****
Main thread has started.
Starting threadOne shortly.
Starting threadTwo shortly.
-ThreadOne from Method1() prints 0
-ThreadOne from Method1() prints 1
-ThreadOne from Method1() prints 2
-ThreadOne from Method1() prints 3
-ThreadOne from Method1() prints 4
Starting threadThree shortly.Here we use ParameterizedThreadStart delegate.
--ThreadTwo from Method2() prints 2.00
-ThreadOne from Method1() prints 5
--ThreadTwo from Method2() prints 2.01
-ThreadOne from Method1() prints 6
--ThreadTwo from Method2() prints 2.02
-ThreadOne from Method1() prints 7
--ThreadTwo from Method2() prints 2.03
-ThreadOne from Method1() prints 8
---ThreadThree from Method3() prints 3.00
--ThreadTwo from Method2() prints 2.04
-ThreadOne from Method1() prints 9
---ThreadThree from Method3() prints 3.01
--ThreadTwo from Method2() prints 2.05
---ThreadThree from Method3() prints 3.02
--ThreadTwo from Method2() prints 2.06
```

```
---ThreadThree from Method3() prints 3.03
---ThreadThree from Method3() prints 3.04
---ThreadThree from Method3() prints 3.05
---ThreadThree from Method3() prints 3.06
--ThreadTwo from Method2() prints 2.07
--ThreadTwo from Method2() prints 2.08
---ThreadThree from Method3() prints 3.07
--ThreadTwo from Method2() prints 2.09
---ThreadThree from Method3() prints 3.08
---ThreadThree from Method3() prints 3.09
---ThreadThree from Method3() prints 3.010
---ThreadThree from Method3() prints 3.011
---ThreadThree from Method3() prints 3.012
---ThreadThree from Method3() prints 3.013
---ThreadThree from Method3() prints 3.014
Main() method ends now.
```

Analysis

As in demonstration 2, the `Join()` method was used in this example. As a result, the line "`Main() method ends now.`" is at the end of the output. Also notice that this time I have used the following line: `threadThree.Start(15);` Here I have used the overloaded version of `Start()` method which can take an object parameter.

Q&A Session

5.6 I understand that by using the `ParameterizedThreadStart` delegate, I can use the methods that can accept an `object` parameter. But how can I use other methods that accept parameters other than object?

Since the parameter is an object, you can use it for nearly anything, and you may need to apply casting properly. For example, in demonstration 3, I passed an `int` to `Method3`'s argument, which is implicitly converted to an `object`, and later I applied casting to the object parameter to get back the required `int`.

5.7 Using the `ParameterizedThreadStart` delegate, can I deal with a method that accepts multiple parameters?

Yes, you can. Demonstration 4 shows you such a usage.

Demonstration 4

In this example, you see the following class, called Boundaries, which has a public constructor with two int parameters.

```
class Boundaries
{
    public int lowerLimit;
    public int upperLimit;
    public Boundaries( int lower, int upper)
    {
     lowerLimit = lower;
     upperLimit = upper;
    }
}
```

And there is a static method called Method4 that matches the signature of the ParameterizedThreadStart delegate. This method is defined as follows.

```
static void Method4(Object limits)
{
    Boundaries boundaries = (Boundaries)limits;
    int lowerLimit = boundaries.lowerLimit;
    int upperLimit = boundaries.upperLimit;
    for (int i = lowerLimit; i < upperLimit; i++)
    {
        Console.WriteLine("---ThreadFour from Method4() prints 4.0{0}", i);
    }
}
```

Inside Main are the following lines of code.

```
Thread threadFour = new Thread(Method4);
threadFour.Start(new Boundaries(0, 10));
```

You can see that I'm creating a Boundaries class object and passing 0 and 10 as arguments. In a similar way, you can pass as many arguments as you want to construct an object, and then pass it to a method that matches the ParameterizedThreadStart delegate.

```
using System;
using System.Threading;

namespace ThreadProgrammingEx4
{
    class Boundaries
    {
        public int lowerLimit;
        public int upperLimit;
        public Boundaries( int lower, int upper)
        {
            lowerLimit = lower;
            upperLimit = upper;
        }
    }
    class Program
    {
        static void Main(string[] args)
        {
            Console.WriteLine("***Thread Demonstration-4****");
            Console.WriteLine("Main thread has started.");

            Thread threadOne = new Thread(Method1);
            // Same as
            //Thread threadOne = new Thread(new ThreadStart(Method1));

            Thread threadTwo = new Thread(Method2);
            // Same as
            //Thread threadTwo = new Thread(new ThreadStart(Method2));

            Thread threadThree = new Thread(Method3);
            // Same as
            //Thread threadThree = new Thread(new ParameterizedThreadStart
            (Method3));

            Thread threadFour = new Thread(Method4);
            // Same as
```

```
    //Thread threadThree = new Thread(new ParameterizedThreadStart
    (Method4));

    Console.WriteLine("Starting threadOne shortly.");
    // threadOne starts
    threadOne.Start();
    Console.WriteLine("Starting threadTwo shortly.");
    // threadTwo starts
    threadTwo.Start();

    Console.WriteLine("Starting threadThree shortly.Here we use
    ParameterizedThreadStart delegate.");
    // threadThree starts
    threadThree.Start(15);

    Console.WriteLine("Starting threadFour shortly.Here we use
    ParameterizedThreadStart delegate.");
    // threadFour starts
    threadFour.Start(new Boundaries(0,10));

    // Waiting for threadOne to finish
    threadOne.Join();
    // Waiting for threadtwo to finish
    threadTwo.Join();
    // Waiting for threadthree to finish
    threadThree.Join();

    Console.WriteLine("Main() method ends now.");
    Console.ReadKey();
}
static void Method1()
{
    for (int i = 0; i < 10; i++)
    {
        Console.WriteLine("-ThreadOne from Method1() prints {0}", i);
    }
}
```

```
        static void Method2()
        {
            for (int i = 0; i < 10; i++)
            {
                Console.WriteLine("--ThreadTwo from Method2() prints
                2.0{0}", i);
            }
        }
```

```
/*
The following method has an object parameter
This method matches the ParameterizedThreadStart delegate signature;because
it has a single parameter of type Object and this method doesn't return a
value.
*/
```

```
        static void Method3(Object number)
        {
            int upperLimit = (int)number;
            for (int i = 0; i < upperLimit; i++)
            {
                Console.WriteLine("---ThreadThree from Method3() prints
                3.0{0}", i);
            }
        }
```

```
/*
The following method also has one parameter.This method matches the
ParameterizedThreadStart delegate signature; because it has a single
parameter of type Object and this method doesn't return a value.
*/
```

```
        static void Method4(Object limits)
        {
            Boundaries boundaries = (Boundaries)limits;
            int lowerLimit = boundaries.lowerLimit;
            int upperLimit = boundaries.upperLimit;
            for (int i = lowerLimit; i < upperLimit; i++)
```

```
            {
                Console.WriteLine("---ThreadFour from Method4() prints
4.0{0}", i);
            }
        }
    }
}
```

Output

This is one possible output.

```
***Thread Demonstration-4****
Main thread has started.
Starting threadOne shortly.
Starting threadTwo shortly.
-ThreadOne from Method1() prints 0
-ThreadOne from Method1() prints 1
Starting threadThree shortly.Here we use ParameterizedThreadStart delegate.
-ThreadOne from Method1() prints 2
-ThreadOne from Method1() prints 3
-ThreadOne from Method1() prints 4
-ThreadOne from Method1() prints 5
-ThreadOne from Method1() prints 6
-ThreadOne from Method1() prints 7
-ThreadOne from Method1() prints 8
-ThreadOne from Method1() prints 9
---ThreadThree from Method3() prints 3.00
---ThreadThree from Method3() prints 3.01
---ThreadThree from Method3() prints 3.02
---ThreadThree from Method3() prints 3.03
---ThreadThree from Method3() prints 3.04
---ThreadThree from Method3() prints 3.05
---ThreadThree from Method3() prints 3.06
--ThreadTwo from Method2() prints 2.00
--ThreadTwo from Method2() prints 2.01
```

```
--ThreadTwo from Method2() prints 2.02
--ThreadTwo from Method2() prints 2.03
--ThreadTwo from Method2() prints 2.04
--ThreadTwo from Method2() prints 2.05
--ThreadTwo from Method2() prints 2.06
--ThreadTwo from Method2() prints 2.07
--ThreadTwo from Method2() prints 2.08
--ThreadTwo from Method2() prints 2.09
---ThreadThree from Method3() prints 3.07
Starting threadFour shortly.Here we use ParameterizedThreadStart delegate.
---ThreadThree from Method3() prints 3.08
---ThreadThree from Method3() prints 3.09
---ThreadThree from Method3() prints 3.010
---ThreadThree from Method3() prints 3.011
---ThreadThree from Method3() prints 3.012
---ThreadThree from Method3() prints 3.013
---ThreadThree from Method3() prints 3.014
---ThreadFour from Method4() prints 4.00
---ThreadFour from Method4() prints 4.01
---ThreadFour from Method4() prints 4.02
---ThreadFour from Method4() prints 4.03
---ThreadFour from Method4() prints 4.04
---ThreadFour from Method4() prints 4.05
---ThreadFour from Method4() prints 4.06
---ThreadFour from Method4() prints 4.07
---ThreadFour from Method4() prints 4.08
Main() method ends now.
---ThreadFour from Method4() prints 4.09
```

Analysis

I have not used Join() for threadFour, so it is possible that the main thread finishes before threadFour finishes its job.

189

Q&A Session

5.8 The ParameterizedThreadStart delegate does not deal with methods that have non-void return types. But if I need to get the return information, how should I proceed?

You can deal with it in different ways. For example, in Chapter 6, you learn different techniques to implement asynchronous programming. In that chapter, you see a task-based asynchronous pattern demonstration in which there is a method that returns a string result. If you want to deal with a method that returns a different datatype, say an int, you can use a similar approach.

For now, you can use a lambda expression to get your intended result. Demonstration 5 shows such an example. (For variation, I used string interpolation to print console messages in this example.)

Demonstration 5

This demonstration is an example in which you can use lambda expressions to execute two different methods (with return type) that run in separate threads.

```csharp
using System;
using System.Threading;

namespace ThreadProgrammingEx5
{
    class Program
    {
        static void Main(string[] args)
        {
            Console.WriteLine("***Dealing methods with return types.These
            methods run in different threads.***");
            int myInt = 0;//Initial value
             Console.WriteLine($"Inside Main(),ManagedThreadId:{Thread.
             CurrentThread.ManagedThreadId}");
            Thread threadOne = new Thread(
                () => {
```

```csharp
        Console.WriteLine($"Method1() is executing
        in ManagedThreadId:{Thread.CurrentThread.
        ManagedThreadId}");
        // Do some activity/task
        myInt = 5;//An arbitrary value
    });

string myStr = "Failure"; // Initial value
Thread threadTwo = new Thread(
    () => {
        Console.WriteLine($"Method2() is executing
        in ManagedThreadId:{Thread.CurrentThread.
        ManagedThreadId}");
        // Do some activity/task
        myStr = "Success.";
    });

Console.WriteLine("Starting threadOne shortly.");
// threadOne starts
threadOne.Start();
Console.WriteLine("Starting threadTwo shortly.");
// threadTwo starts
threadTwo.Start();

// Waiting for threadOne to finish
threadOne.Join();
// Waiting for threadtwo to finish
threadTwo.Join();
Console.WriteLine($"Method1() returns {myInt}");
Console.WriteLine($"Method2() returns {myStr} ");
Console.WriteLine("Control comes at the end of Main()
method.");
Console.ReadKey();
        }
    }
}
```

Output

This is one possible output.

```
***Dealing methods with return types.These methods run in different
threads.***
Inside Main(),ManagedThreadId:1
Starting threadOne shortly.
Starting threadTwo shortly.
Method1() is executing in ManagedThreadId:3
Method2() is executing in ManagedThreadId:4
Method1() returns 5
Method2() returns Success.
Control comes at the end of Main() method.
```

Note   ManagedThreadId gets a unique identifier *only* for a particular managed thread. You may notice a different value when you run the application in your machine. Do not feel that since you have created *n* number of threads, you should see the thread IDs between 1 and *n* only. It's possible that there are other threads that are also running in the background.

Q&A Session

5.9 In this chapter, you are using the term *main thread*. What do you mean by it?

When you execute your program, one thread starts automatically. This is the main thread. The Main() method in these demonstrations are creating the main thread, which dies at the end of the Main() method. When I create other threads using the Thread class, I'm referring to them as the *child threads*. In this context, it is important to note that the Thread.CurrentThread property can help you get information about the thread; for example, you can use the following lines of code to get the name (which you can set earlier), ID, and priority of a thread.

```
Console.WriteLine("Inside Main,Thread Name is:{0}", Thread.CurrentThread.
Name);
Console.WriteLine("Inside Main,ManagedThreadId is:{0}", Thread.
CurrentThread.ManagedThreadId);
```

```
Console.WriteLine("Inside Main,Thread Priority is: {0}", Thread.
CurrentThread.Priority);
```

At the time of writing, a thread in C# can have the following priorities: `Lowest`, `BelowNormal`, `Normal`, `AboveNormal`, and `Highest`. Figure 5-3 displays a partial screenshot from Visual Studio that shows information about the `ThreadPriority` enumeration.

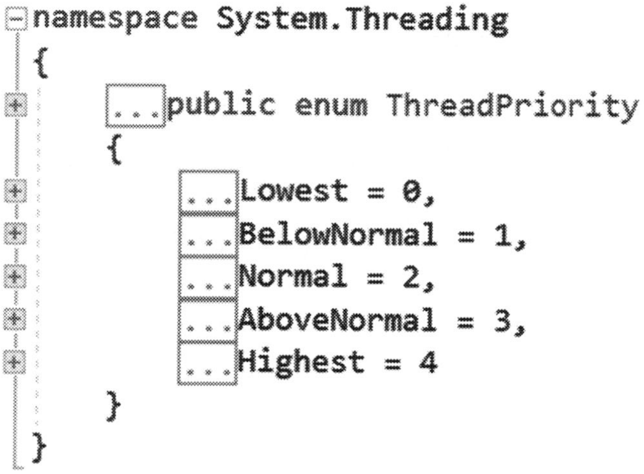

```
namespace System.Threading
{
    public enum ThreadPriority
    {
        Lowest = 0,
        BelowNormal = 1,
        Normal = 2,
        AboveNormal = 3,
        Highest = 4
    }
}
```

Figure 5-3. *Different thread priorities in C#*

Demonstration 6

This demonstration shows usage of the `Name`, `Priority`, and `ManagedThreadId` properties from the `Thread` class that we just discussed.

```
using System;
using System.Threading;

namespace UsingMainThread
{
    class Program
    {
        static void Main(string[] args)
        {
            Console.WriteLine("***Working on the main thread and a child
            Thread only.****");
```

```csharp
        Thread.CurrentThread.Name = "Main Thread";

        Thread threadOne = new Thread(Method1);
        threadOne.Name = "Child Thread-1";
        threadOne.Priority = ThreadPriority.AboveNormal;
        Console.WriteLine("Starting threadOne shortly.");
        // threadOne starts
        threadOne.Start();
        Console.WriteLine("Inside Main,Thread Name is:{0}", Thread.
        CurrentThread.Name);
        Console.WriteLine("Inside Main,ManagedThreadId is:{0}", Thread.
        CurrentThread.ManagedThreadId);
        Console.WriteLine("Inside Main,Thread Priority is: {0}",
        Thread.CurrentThread.Priority);
        Console.WriteLine("Control comes at the end of Main()
        method.");
        Console.ReadKey();
    }
    static void Method1()
    {
        Console.WriteLine("Inside Method1(),Thread Name is:{0}",
        Thread.CurrentThread.Name);
        Console.WriteLine("Inside Method1(),ManagedThreadId is:{0}",
        Thread.CurrentThread.ManagedThreadId);
        Console.WriteLine("Inside Method1(),Thread Priority is:{0}",
        Thread.CurrentThread.Priority);
        for (int i = 0; i < 5; i++)
        {
            Console.WriteLine("Using Method1(), printing the value
            {0}", i);
        }
    }
  }
}
```

Output

This is a possible output.

```
***Working on the main thread and a child Thread only.****
Starting threadOne shortly.
Inside Main,Thread Name is:Main Thread
Inside Main,ManagedThreadId is:1
Inside Method1(),Thread Name is:Child Thread-1
Inside Method1(),ManagedThreadId is:5
Inside Method1(),Thread Priority is:AboveNormal
Using Method1(), printing the value 0
Using Method1(), printing the value 1
Using Method1(), printing the value 2
Using Method1(), printing the value 3
Using Method1(), printing the value 4
Inside Main,Thread Priority is: Normal
Control comes at the end of Main() method.
```

Analysis

Although the child thread priority is higher than the main thread, it does not guarantee that the child thread will finish before the main thread. There are several other factors that may determine this output.

Q&A Session

5.10 "It does not guarantee that the child thread will finish before the main thread. There are several other factors that may determine this output". Can you please elaborate?

Conceptually, priority determines how frequently a thread can get CPU time. In theory, the higher-priority threads get more CPU time than lower-priority threads, and in preemptive scheduling, they can preempt the lower-priority threads. But, you need to consider many other factors. For example, it may happen that a high-priority thread is waiting to get a shared resource and is therefore blocked; and in such a situation, a low-priority thread can get a chance to complete its task.

Consider another case in which a low-priority thread is doing a very short task and a high-priority thread is doing a very long-running task. If the low-priority thread gets a chance to execute, it finishes before the high-priority thread.

Lastly, the way that task scheduling is implemented in an operating system also matters because CPU allocation depends on this too. This is why you shouldn't totally depend on priorities to predict an output.

5.11 How can I terminate a thread?

By using the Abort() method defined in the Thread class, you can terminate a thread.

Here is some sample code.

```
threadOne.Abort();
```

The Abort() method has two different overloaded versions, as follows.

```
public void Abort();
public void Abort(object stateInfo);
```

Foreground Thread vs. Background Thread

The Thread class has a property called IsBackground, which is described as follows.

```
//
// Summary:
//     Gets or sets a value indicating whether or not a thread is a
//     background thread.
//
// Returns:
//     true if this thread is or is to become a background thread;
//     otherwise, false.
//
// Exceptions:
//   T:System.Threading.ThreadStateException:
//     The thread is dead.
public bool IsBackground { get; set; }
```

By default, a thread is a foreground thread. You can convert a foreground thread to a background thread when you set the IsBackground property to true. The following segment of code can help you understand this better. (I made two Thread class objects: threadFour and threadFive. Later, I'll make a threadFive a background thread. I marked the expected output for this segment with comments).

```
Thread threadFour = new Thread(Method1);
Console.WriteLine("Is threadFour is a background thread?:{0} ",
threadFour.IsBackground); // False
Thread threadFive = new Thread(Method1);
threadFive.IsBackground = true;
Console.WriteLine("Is threadFive is a background thread?:{0} ",
threadFive.IsBackground); // True
```

If you want a complete demonstration, consider the following example.

Demonstration 7

In Main(), I created only one thread. I named it Child Thread-1 and set the IsBackground property to true. Now run this program and follow the output and corresponding discussions.

```
using System;
using System.Threading;

namespace TestingBackgroundThreads
{
    class Program
    {
        static void Main(string[] args)
        {
            Console.WriteLine("***Comparing a foreground threads with a
            background thread****");
            Thread.CurrentThread.Name = "Main Thread";
            Console.WriteLine($"{Thread.CurrentThread.Name} has started.");
            Thread childThread = new Thread(MyMethod);
            childThread.Name = "Child Thread-1";
```

```
            Console.WriteLine("Starting Child Thread-1 shortly.");
            // threadOne starts
            childThread.Start();
            childThread.IsBackground = true;
            Console.WriteLine("Control comes at the end of Main()
            method.");
            //Console.ReadKey();
        }
        static void MyMethod()
        {
            Console.WriteLine($"{Thread.CurrentThread.Name} enters into
            MyMethod()");
            for (int i = 0; i < 10; i++)
            {
                Console.WriteLine($"{Thread.CurrentThread.Name} from
                MyMethod() prints {i}");
                //Taking a small sleep
                Thread.Sleep(100);
            }
            Console.WriteLine($"{Thread.CurrentThread.Name} exits from
            MyMethod()");
        }
    }
}
```

Output

This is a possible output.

```
***Comparing a forground threads with a background thread****
Main Thread has started.
Starting Child Thread-1 shortly.
Control comes at the end of Main() method.
Child Thread-1 enters into MyMethod()
Child Thread-1 from MyMethod() prints 0
```

But if you comment out the following line in the preceding example as follows,

```
//childThread.IsBackground = true;
```

you may get the following output.

```
***Comparing a forground threads with a background thread****
Main Thread has started.
Starting Child Thread-1 shortly.
Control comes at the end of Main() method.
Child Thread-1 enters into MyMethod()
Child Thread-1 from MyMethod() prints 0
Child Thread-1 from MyMethod() prints 1
Child Thread-1 from MyMethod() prints 2
Child Thread-1 from MyMethod() prints 3
Child Thread-1 from MyMethod() prints 4
Child Thread-1 from MyMethod() prints 5
Child Thread-1 from MyMethod() prints 6
Child Thread-1 from MyMethod() prints 7
Child Thread-1 from MyMethod() prints 8
Child Thread-1 from MyMethod() prints 9
Child Thread-1 exits from MyMethod()
```

This tells you that the child thread (a.k.a. worker thread) was able to complete its task; when you do not make it a background thread, it can continue its task after the main thread finishes its execution.

Additional Note

I also commented the following line when I set IsBackground property to true.

```
//Console.ReadKey();
```

This is because I didn't want to wait for user input. I wanted the child thread to terminate immediately once the main thread dies.

> **Note**   In many contexts (particularly in UI applications), you see the term *worker thread*. It describes another thread that is different from the current thread. Technically, it is a thread that runs in the background, although no one claims that this is the true definition. Microsoft writes, "A worker thread is commonly used to handle background tasks that the user should not have to wait for to continue using your application. Tasks such as recalculation and background printing are good examples of worker threads." (See `https://docs.microsoft.`
> `com/en-us/cpp/parallel/multithreading-creating-worker-`
> `threads?view=vs-2019`).   In the context of C#, Microsoft says, "By default, a .NET program is started with a single thread, often called the primary thread. However, it can create additional threads to execute code in parallel or concurrently with the primary thread. These threads are often called worker threads." (See `https://docs.microsoft.com/en-us/dotnet/standard/threading/`
> `threads-and-threading`).

Thread Safety

Sometimes multiple threads need to access shared resources. Controlling these situations is tricky; for example, consider when one thread is trying to read the data from a file and another thread is still writing or updating in the same file. If you cannot manage the correct order, you may get surprising results. The concept of synchronization is useful in these situations.

A Non-Synchronized Version

To understand the need for a synchronized method, let's start with a program where the concept is not implemented. In the following demonstration, a class called SharedResource contains a public method called SharedMethod(). Let's assume that inside this method, there are resources that can be shared among multiple threads. For simplicity, I put some simple statements to indicate the entry and exit of a thread. To see the effect precisely, I put a simple Sleep statement inside the method body. It increases the probability to switch the execution to another thread.

I created two child threads inside the Main method: Child Thread-1 and Child Thread-2. Note the following lines of code in the demonstration.

```
SharedResource sharedObject = new SharedResource();
Thread threadOne = new Thread(sharedObject.SharedMethod);
threadOne.Name = "Child Thread-1";
Thread threadTwo = new Thread(sharedObject.SharedMethod);
threadTwo.Name = "Child Thread-2";
```

Once you run this non-synchronized version of the program, you may notice the following lines in your possible output.

Child Thread-1 has entered in the shared location.
Child Thread-2 has entered in the shared location.
Child Thread-1 exits.
Child Thread-2 exits.

From this output segment you can see that Child Thread-1 has entered the shared location first. But before it finishes its execution, Child Thread-2 has also entered the shared location.

When you deal with shared resources (or shared location), you need to be extremely careful, and so if any thread is working there, you may want to restrict any other thread from entering that location.

Demonstration 8

This complete example describes the situation.

```
using System;
using System.Threading;

namespace ExploringTheNeedofSynchronizationInDotNetCore
{
    class Program
    {
        static void Main(string[] args)
        {
            Console.WriteLine("***Exploring Thread Synchronization.****");
```

```
            Console.WriteLine("***We are beginning with a non-synchronized
            version.****");
            Thread.CurrentThread.Name = "Main Thread";
            Console.WriteLine("Main thread has started already.");

            SharedResource sharedObject = new SharedResource();
            Thread threadOne = new Thread(sharedObject.SharedMethod);
            threadOne.Name = "Child Thread-1";

            Thread threadTwo = new Thread(sharedObject.SharedMethod);
            threadTwo.Name = "Child Thread-2";
            // Child Thread-1 starts.
            threadOne.Start();
            // Child Thread-2 starts.
            threadTwo.Start();
            // Waiting for Child Thread-1 to finish.
            threadOne.Join();
            // Waiting for Child Thread-2 to finish.
            threadTwo.Join();
            Console.WriteLine("The {0} exits now.", Thread.CurrentThread.Name);
            Console.ReadKey();
        }
    }
    class SharedResource
    {
        public void SharedMethod()
        {
            Console.Write(Thread.CurrentThread.Name + " has entered in the
            shared location. \n");
            Thread.Sleep(3000);
            Console.Write(Thread.CurrentThread.Name + " exits.\n");
        }
    }
}
```

Output

This is a complete possible output.

```
***Exploring Thread Synchronization.****
***We are beginning with a non-synchronized version.****
Main thread has started already.
Child Thread-1 has entered in the shared location.
Child Thread-2 has entered in the shared location.
Child Thread-1 exits.
Child Thread-2 exits.
The Main Thread exits now.
```

Note   This output may vary in each time you run it in your system. To get the same output, you may need to execute the application multiple times.

A Synchronized Version

I believe that you understand the need for a synchronized version now. So, let's implement the concept of synchronization and update the previous demonstration.

Demonstration 9

In this demonstration, you see the use of a lock. This locking mechanism typically prevents accidental modification of shared resources due to simultaneous access to multiple threads in a shared location; when you successfully implement this, you can say that your application is thread safe.

First, let me explain some common terms. These terms are frequently used in a similar context. The segment of code that you want to guard against simultaneous access from multiple threads is called a **critical section**. At any given moment, you allow only one thread to work in the critical section. This principle is known as **mutual exclusion**. The mechanism to enforce this principle is often called a **mutex**.

When a thread obtains a lock, it can enter the critical section. Once its job is done, it exits from this location and releases the lock. Now, another thread can obtain the lock and proceed. But if a thread wants to enter the critical section and sees that the lock is currently held by another thread, it cannot enter. The thread needs to suspend the activity until the lock is released.

How do you create a lock? It is very simple, and often done with a private instance variable in the same object/class, as follows.

```
private object myLock = new object(); // You can use any object.
```

As the comment says, you can make the lock as you wish. For example, if you deal with a static method, you could even write something like the following.

```
private static StringBuilder strLock = new StringBuilder();
```

To implement thread safety in the previous demonstration, you can modify the SharedResource class as follows. (Note the newly introduced lines in bold.) I also made some changes inside the Main method to indicate that it is a synchronized version. So, I'm replacing the following line in from previous demonstration

```
Console.WriteLine("***We are beginning with a non-synchronized
version.****");
```

with the following lines in the upcoming demonstration.

```
Console.WriteLine("***Here we have a synchronized version.We are using the
concept of lock.****");
```

```
class SharedResource
{
    private object myLock = new object();
    public void SharedMethod()
    {
        lock (myLock)
        {
            Console.Write(Thread.CurrentThread.Name + " has entered in the
            shared location. \n");
            Thread.Sleep(3000);
            Console.Write(Thread.CurrentThread.Name + " exits.\n");
        }
```

```
    }
}
```

Output

This time, you get this output.

```
***Exploring Thread Synchronization.****
***Here we have a synchronized version.We are using the concept of
lock.****
Main thread has started already.
Child Thread-1 has entered in the shared location.
Child Thread-1 exits.
Child Thread-2 has entered in the shared location.
Child Thread-2 exits.
The Main Thread exits now.
```

You need to remember that when you use the lock statement as follows, myLock is an expression of a reference type.

```
lock(myLock){ // Some code},
```

For example, in this example, myLock is an Object instance, which is nothing but a reference type. But, instead of using a reference type, if you use a value type in this context as follows,

```
private int myLock = new int();//not correct
```

you'll get the following error.

```
Error CS0185 'int' is not a reference type as required by the lock statement
```

An Alternative Approach Using the Monitor Class

In the Monitor class, the members implement synchronization. Since you've seen the use of locks, it's worth noting that it internally wraps Monitor's Entry and Exit methods. So, you can replace the following code segment

```
lock (myLock)
{
```

```
    Console.Write(Thread.CurrentThread.Name + " has entered in the shared
    location. \n");
    Thread.Sleep(3000);
    Console.Write(Thread.CurrentThread.Name + " exits.\n");
}
```

with an equivalent code segment using Monitor's Entry and Exit methods, like the following.

```
// lock internally wraps Monitor's Entry and Exit method in a  try...
// finally block.
try
{
    Monitor.Enter(myLock);
    Console.Write(Thread.CurrentThread.Name + " has entered in the shared
    location. \n");
    Thread.Sleep(3000);
    Console.Write(Thread.CurrentThread.Name + " exits.\n");
}
finally
{
    Monitor.Exit(myLock);
}
```

In addition to these methods, the Monitor class has additional methods that can send notifications. For example, in this class, you can see the Wait, Pulse, and PulseAll methods with different overloaded versions. The following are simple descriptions of these methods.

- Wait(): Using this method, a thread can wait for other threads to notify.

- Pulse(): Using this method, a thread can send notifications to another thread.

- PulseAll(): Using this method, a thread can notify all other threads within a process.

Apart from these methods, there is another interesting method with overloaded versions called TryEnter.

This is the simplest form of this method with a description from Visual Studio.

```
//
// Summary:
//      Attempts to acquire an exclusive lock on the specified object.
//
// Parameters:
//   obj:
//      The object on which to acquire the lock.
//
// Returns:
//      true if the current thread acquires the lock; otherwise, false.
//
// Exceptions:
//   T:System.ArgumentNullException:
//      The obj parameter is null.
public static bool TryEnter(object obj);
```

The TryEnter method returns the boolean value true if the calling thread can obtain a lock on the desired object; otherwise, it will return false. Using a different overloaded version of this method, you can specify a time limit, in which you attempt to get an exclusive lock on the desired object.

Deadlock

Deadlock is a situation or condition where at least two processes or threads are waiting for each other to complete or release control, so that each one can finish its job. This may result in none of them being able to start (and they go to a hang state.) You may often hear about these real-life examples.

You can't get a job without experience; you can't get experience without a job.

Or,

After a fight between two close friends, each of them expects the other to initiate the friendship again.

POINTS TO REMEMBER

Without synchronization, you may see surprising output (for example, some corrupted data), but with improper use of synchronization, you can encounter a deadlock.

Types of Deadlock

Theoretically, there are different types of deadlock.

- **Resource deadlock**. Suppose two processes (P1 and P2) hold two resources (R1 and R2, respectively). P1 asks for resource R2 and P2 asks for resource R1 to complete their jobs. The OS generally deals with this type of deadlock.

- **Synchronization deadlock**. Suppose process P1 is waiting to perform an action (a1) only after P2 completes a specific action (a2), and P2 is waiting to complete action a2 only after P1 completes a1.

- **Communication deadlock**. Similar to the prior scenarios, you can replace the concept of actions/resources by messages (i.e., two processes waiting to receive a message from each other to proceed further).

In this chapter, we are focusing on the multithreaded environment, so let's discuss deadlock that is caused by multiple threads in C# applications only.

Demonstration 10

The following program can cause a deadlock. There are two locks used in this program. These locks are called myFirstLock and mySecondLock, respectively. For demonstration purposes, the wrong design is shown in this example; you see Child Thread-1 try to obtain myFirstLock, and then mySecondLock and Child Thread-2 try to get the locks in the reverse order. So, when both threads lock their first lock at the same time, they encounter with a deadlocked situation.

Again, the following is an incorrect implementation used only for demonstration purposes.

```
using System;
using System.Threading;

namespace DeadlockDemoInDotNetCore
{
    class Program
    {
        static void Main(string[] args)
        {
            Console.WriteLine("***Exploring Deadlock with an incorrect
            design of application.****");

            Thread.CurrentThread.Name = "Main Thread";
            Console.WriteLine("Main thread has started already.");

            SharedResource sharedObject = new SharedResource();
            Thread threadOne = new Thread(sharedObject.SharedMethodOne);
            threadOne.Name = "Child Thread-1";

            Thread threadTwo = new Thread(sharedObject.SharedMethodTwo);
            threadTwo.Name = "Child Thread-2";
            // Child Thread-1 starts.
            threadOne.Start();
            // Child Thread-2 starts.
            threadTwo.Start();
            // Waiting for Child Thread-1 to finish.
            threadOne.Join();
            // Waiting for Child Thread-2 to finish.
            threadTwo.Join();
            Console.WriteLine("The {0} exits now.", Thread.CurrentThread.Name);
            Console.ReadKey();
        }

    }
```

```csharp
class SharedResource
{
    private object myFirstLock = new object();
    private object mySecondLock = new object();
    public void SharedMethodOne()
    {
        lock (myFirstLock)
        {
            Console.Write(Thread.CurrentThread.Name + " has entered
            into first part of SharedMethodOne. \n");
            Thread.Sleep(1000);
            Console.Write(Thread.CurrentThread.Name + " exits
            SharedMethodOne--first part.\n");

            lock (mySecondLock)
            {
                Console.Write(Thread.CurrentThread.Name + " has entered
                into last part of SharedMethodOne. \n");
                Thread.Sleep(1000);

                Console.Write(Thread.CurrentThread.Name + " exits
                SharedMethodOne--last part.\n");
            }
        }
    }
    public void SharedMethodTwo()
    {
        lock (mySecondLock)
        {
            Console.Write(Thread.CurrentThread.Name + " has entered
            into first part of SharedMethodTwo. \n");
            Thread.Sleep(1000);

            Console.Write(Thread.CurrentThread.Name + " exits
            SharedMethodTwo--first part.\n");

            lock (myFirstLock)
            {
```

```
                        Console.Write(Thread.CurrentThread.Name + " has entered
                        into last part of SharedMethodTwo. \n");
                        Thread.Sleep(1000);
                        Console.Write(Thread.CurrentThread.Name + " exits
                        SharedMethodTwo--last part.\n");
                    }
                }
            }
        }
    }
}
```

Output

When your program hangs, you see only the following lines in your output.

```
***Exploring Deadlock with an incorrect design of application.****
Main thread has started already.
Child Thread-1 has entered into first part of SharedMethodOne.
Child Thread-2 has entered into first part of SharedMethodTwo.
Child Thread-1 exits SharedMethodOne--first part.
Child Thread-2 exits SharedMethodTwo--first part.
```

Note   You may not encounter deadlock in your first run, but keep executing the program; there will eventually be a case in which you see deadlock.

Investigating the Deadlocked State in Visual Studio

In this hang state, go to **Debug ➤ Break All**. Then go to **Debug ➤ Window ➤ Thread**.

You see a screen that looks like Figure 5-4. Notice that you can see the status of the Main thread and the child threads. Let's open all the windows (see Figures 5-4, 5-5, and 5-6).

Figure 5-4 is the Main thread window.

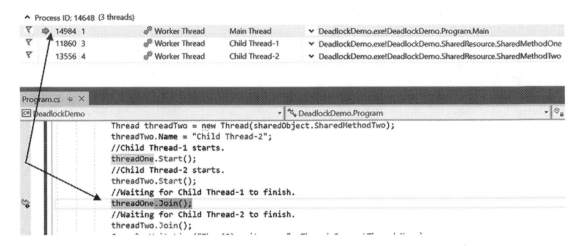

Figure 5-4. *Main Thread window in a deadlocked state*

Figure 5-5 is the Child Thread-1 window.

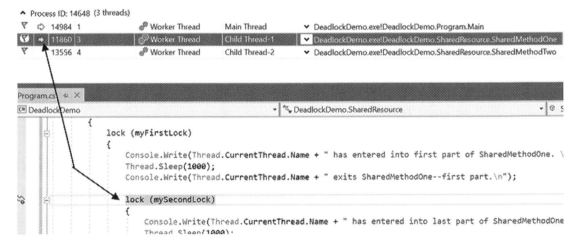

Figure 5-5. *Child Thread-1 window in a deadlocked state*

Figure 5-6 is the Child Thread-2 window.

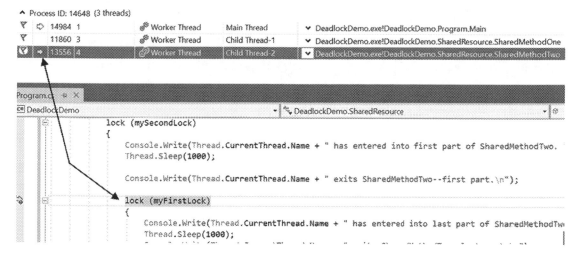

Figure 5-6. *Child Thread-2 window in deadlocked state*

If you split the window into vertical and horizontal sections, you can see them all at once, as shown in Figure 5-7.

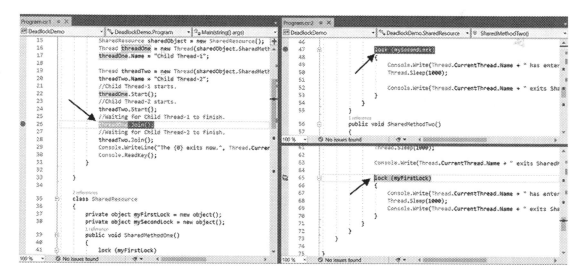

Figure 5-7. *Main Thread, Child Thread-1, Child-Thread-2 windows at a glance in deadlocked state*

Note   To split a window vertically, you can go to **Window ➤ New Window** to create a clone of the tab. Note the tabs named Program.cs:1 and Program2.cs:2. Right-click on any of them, and then choose **New Vertical Tab Group**. Similarly, to split the windows horizontally, select **New Horizontal Tab Group**. In Figure 5-7, I divided the windows vertically and then I divided one of them horizontally.

You should clearly be able to see that threads are stuck on the lock statements in child threads. And as a side effect, the Main thread is also stuck on threadOne.Join().

During an execution of a multithreaded program, if Visual Studio shows you a hang state, you can investigate the cause in a similar way. It is also important to note that deadlock can occur in many different situations, but the focus of this section is on locks.

That's the basics of thread programming. Like any advanced topic, in-depth discussions need many more pages. Still, you should now have a fair idea about the fundamentals.

Final Words

Now you probably understand why you started with the following line of code.

```
using System.Threading;
```

It is because this namespace has the Thread class, which is the foundation for thread programming. Thread is a sealed class, which has lots of members, including properties, methods, constructors, and destructors. So far, you have seen the following.

- Use of the following two constructors:

```
public Thread(ThreadStart start);
public Thread(ParameterizedThreadStart start);
```

- Use of the following properties:

```
public bool IsBackground { get; set; }
public static Thread CurrentThread { get; }
public string Name { get; set; }
public int ManagedThreadId { get; }
```

- Use of the following methods:

```
public void Start();
public void Join();
public void Abort();
```

There are many other members that are also useful. I recommend that you have a look at them. If you're using the Visual Studio IDE, you can simply right-click the Thread class, and then select **Go to Definition (F2)** to see their definitions.

It's also worth noting that some members of Thread class became deprecated, (for example, Suspend and Resume). Microsoft recommends that you use other methods for your application instead of those methods. For example, in the Suspend method definition, you see the following.

```
[Obsolete("Thread.Suspend has been deprecated.  Please use other classes
in System.Threading, such as Monitor, Mutex, Event, and Semaphore, to
synchronize Threads or protect resources.  http://go.microsoft.com/
fwlink/?linkid=14202", false)]
[SecuritySafeCritical]
public void Suspend();
```

This also tells you that Monitor, Mutex, Event, and Semaphore are important classes when you implement synchronization in your program. A more detailed description of these classes is beyond the scope of this book.

Lastly, you use multithreading when you want concurrent execution rather than sequential execution, and you may think that creating threads enhances the performance of an application. But this may not always be true! You should limit the number of threads in your application to avoid too much context switching among the threads. The overhead due to context switching can degrade the overall performance of your application.

These are the basics of thread programming in C#. Multithreading is a complex topic, and there are several facets in it. An entire book could be dedicated to this topic. I believe that this chapter should give you a clear idea about the fundamentals, however. In next chapter, asynchronous programming is discussed, and you learn some interesting concepts in a similar context.

Summary

This chapter addressed the following key questions.

- What is a thread, and how is it different from a process?

- How do you create threads?

- How do you use different Thread class constructors?

- Using the `ParameterizedThreadStart` delegate, how do you use a method that accepts multiple parameters?

- How do you use important `Thread` class members?

- How do you distinguish a foreground thread from a background thread?

- What is synchronization, and why is it needed?

- How do you implement thread safety in C# using lock statements?

- How can you implement an alternative approach to lock statements using Monitor's `Entry` and `Exit` methods?

- What is a deadlock, and how can you detect deadlock in your system?

CHAPTER 6

Asynchronous Programming

Asynchronous programming is tough and challenging but interesting. It is also known as *asynchrony*. The overall concept did not evolve in one day; it took time. The async and await keywords first appeared in C# 5.0 to make it easier. Prior to that, different programmers implemented the concept using various techniques. Each technique has its own pros and cons. The goal of this chapter is to introduce you to asynchronous programming and to go through some common implementation methods.

Overview

Let's first discuss what asynchronous programming is. In simple terms, you take a code segment in your application and run it on a separate thread. What is the key benefit? The simple answer is that you can free the original thread and let it continue to do its remaining tasks, and in a separate thread, you perform a different task. This mechanism helps you develop modern-day applications; for example, when you implement a highly responsive user interface, these concepts are very useful.

© Vaskaran Sarcar 2020
V. Sarcar, *Getting Started with Advanced C#*, https://doi.org/10.1007/978-1-4842-5934-4_6

| **POINTS TO REMEMBER** |

Broadly, you notice three different patterns in asynchronous programming.

- **IAsyncResult Pattern:** This is also known as *Asynchronous Programming Model (APM)*. In this pattern, you see the `IAsyncResult` interface to support the asynchronous behavior. In a synchronous model, if you have a synchronous method called XXX(), in the asynchronous version, you see the use of `BeginXXX()` and `EndXXX()` methods for the corresponding synchronous method. For example, in the synchronous version, if the `Read()` method supports read operations, in asynchronous programming, you see the `BeginRead()` and `EndRead()` methods support the corresponding read operations asynchronously. Using this concept, you see the `BeginInvoke` and `EndInvoke` methods in demonstrations 5, 6, and 7. This pattern is not recommended for new development, however.

- **Event-based Asynchronous Pattern:** This pattern came with .NET Framework 2.0. It is based on an event mechanism. Here you see the method name with the `Async` suffix, one or multiple events, and `EventArg` derived types. This pattern is not recommended for new development.

- **Task-based Asynchronous Pattern:** This first appeared in .NET Framework 4. It's the recommended practice for asynchronous programming nowadays. In C#, you often see the `async` and `await` keywords in this pattern.

To better understand asynchronous programming, let's start our discussion with its counterpart: *synchronous programming*. A synchronous approach is straightforward, and the code paths are easy to understand; but you need to wait for the result from a particular segment of code, and until then, you just sit idle. Consider some typical cases; for example, when you know that a segment of code is trying to open a web page that may take time to load, or when a segment of code is exercising a long-running algorithm and so forth. If you follow the synchronous approach, when you perform a long-running operation, you must sit idle because you cannot do anything useful.

This is why, to support modern-day demands and build highly responsive applications, the need for asynchronous programming is growing.

Using a Synchronous Approach

Demonstration 1 executes a simple program. Let's start with a synchronous approach. There are two simple methods: Method1() and Method2(). Inside the Main() method, these methods are called synchronously (i.e., Method1() is called first and then Method2() is called.) I used simple sleep statements so that the jobs performed by these methods take a significant amount of time to complete. Once you run the application and note the output, you see that only after Method1() finishes its execution, does Method2() start its execution. The Main() method cannot complete until these methods finish their execution.

Note   Throughout this chapter, you see these methods with slight variations. I tried to maintain similar methods (or operations) so that you can compare different techniques of asynchronous programming. For demonstration purposes, Method1() takes more time to finish because it performs a lengthy operation (I forced a relatively long sleep inside it). Method2() performs a small task, so I placed a short sleep inside it. Also, to keep it simple, I used short names.

Demonstration 1

This is the complete demonstration.

```
using System;
using System.Threading;

namespace SynchronousProgrammingExample
{
    class Program
    {
        static void Main(string[] args)
        {
            Console.WriteLine("***Demonstration-1.A Synchronous Program
            Demo.***");
            Method1();
            Method2();
            Console.WriteLine("End Main().");
```

219

```
        Console.ReadKey();
    }
    // Method1
    private static void Method1()
    {
        Console.WriteLine("Method1() has started.");
        // Some big task
        Thread.Sleep(1000);
        Console.WriteLine("Method1() has finished.");
    }
    // Method2
    private static void Method2()
    {
        Console.WriteLine("Method2() has started.");
        // Some small task
        Thread.Sleep(100);
        Console.WriteLine("Method2() has finished.");
    }
  }
}
```

Output

This is the output.

```
***Demonstration-1.A Synchronous Program Demo.***
Method1() has started.
Method1() has finished.
Method2() has started.
Method2() has finished.
End Main().
```

Using Thread Class

If you look closely at the methods in demonstration 1, you find that they were not dependent on each other. If you can execute them in parallel, the response time of your application is improved, and you can reduce the overall execution time. Let's find some better approaches.

You learned about threads in Chapter 5, so you can implement the concepts of multithreading. Demonstration 2 shows you an obvious solution using threads. I kept the commented codes for your reference. This demonstration focuses on substituting `Method1()` inside a new thread.

Demonstration 2

```
using System;
using System.Threading;

namespace UsingThreadClass
{
    class Program
    {
        static void Main(string[] args)
        {
            Console.WriteLine("***Asynchronous Programming
            Demonstration-1.***");
            //Method1();
            // Old approach.Creating a separate thread for the following
            // task(i.e Method1.)
            Thread newThread = new Thread(()=>
            {
                Console.WriteLine("Method1() has started on a separate
                thread.");
                // Some big task
                Thread.Sleep(1000);
                Console.WriteLine("Method1() has finished.");
            }
            );
            newThread.Start();
            Thread.Sleep(10);
            Method2();
            Console.WriteLine("End Main().");
            Console.ReadKey();
        }
```

```
// Method1
//private static void Method1()
//{
//    Console.WriteLine("Method1() has started.");
//    // Some big task
//    Thread.Sleep(1000);
//    Console.WriteLine("Method1() has finished.");
//}

private static void Method2()
{
    Console.WriteLine("Method2() has started.");
    // Some small task
    Thread.Sleep(100);
    Console.WriteLine("Method2() has finished.");
}
}
}
```

Output

This is one possible output.

```
***Asynchronous Programming Demonstration-1.***
Method1() has started on a separate thread.
Method2() has started.
Method2() has finished.
End Main().
Method1() has finished.
```

Analysis

Note that although Method1() was invoked early, Method2 did not need to wait for Method1() to finish execution. Also, since Method2() is doing very little (sleep time is 100 milliseconds), it was able to finish before Method1() finished its execution. Also note that since the main thread was not blocked, it was able to continue its execution.

Q&A Session

6.1 Why did you use a sleep statement prior to the execution of Method2() inside Main?

Good catch. It was not necessary, but in some cases, you may notice that even though you try to start Method1() to execute on a separate thread before Method2() in the current thread, that doesn't happen, and as a result, you may notice the following output.

```
***Asynchronous Programming Demonstration-1.***
Method2() has started.
Method1() has started in a separate thread.
Method2() has finished.
End Main().
Method1() has finished.
```

This simple sleep statement can help you increase the probability of starting Method1() prior to Method2() in this example.

Using the ThreadPool Class

Creating threads directly in a real-world application is normally discouraged. The following are some of the chief reasons behind this.

- Maintaining too many threads incur tough and costly operations.

- A large amount of time is wasted on context switching rather than doing the real work.

To avoid directly creating threads, C# gives you the facility to use the built-in ThreadPool class. With this class, you can use the existing threads, which can be reused to serve your purpose. The ThreadPool class is very effective in maintaining the optimal number of threads in your application. If needed, you can execute some of your task asynchronously using this facility.

ThreadPool is a static class that contains static methods, and some of them also have an overloaded version. Figure 6-1 is a partial screenshot from Visual Studio IDE that shows the methods in the ThreadPool class.

```
namespace System.Threading
{
    ...public static class ThreadPool
    {
        ...public static bool BindHandle(SafeHandle osHandle);
        ...public static bool BindHandle(IntPtr osHandle);
        ...public static void GetAvailableThreads(out int workerThreads, out int completionPortThreads);
        ...public static void GetMaxThreads(out int workerThreads, out int completionPortThreads);
        ...public static void GetMinThreads(out int workerThreads, out int completionPortThreads);
        ...public static bool QueueUserWorkItem(WaitCallback callBack);
        ...public static bool QueueUserWorkItem(WaitCallback callBack, object state);
        ...public static RegisteredWaitHandle RegisterWaitForSingleObject(WaitHandle waitObject, WaitOrT:
        ...public static RegisteredWaitHandle RegisterWaitForSingleObject(WaitHandle waitObject, WaitOrT:
        ...public static RegisteredWaitHandle RegisterWaitForSingleObject(WaitHandle waitObject, WaitOrT:
        ...public static RegisteredWaitHandle RegisterWaitForSingleObject(WaitHandle waitObject, WaitOrT:
        ...public static bool SetMaxThreads(int workerThreads, int completionPortThreads);
        ...public static bool SetMinThreads(int workerThreads, int completionPortThreads);
        ...public static bool UnsafeQueueNativeOverlapped(NativeOverlapped* overlapped);
        ...public static bool UnsafeQueueUserWorkItem(WaitCallback callBack, object state);
        ...public static RegisteredWaitHandle UnsafeRegisterWaitForSingleObject(WaitHandle waitObject, Wa
        ...public static RegisteredWaitHandle UnsafeRegisterWaitForSingleObject(WaitHandle waitObject, Wa
        ...public static RegisteredWaitHandle UnsafeRegisterWaitForSingleObject(WaitHandle waitObject, Wa
        ...public static RegisteredWaitHandle UnsafeRegisterWaitForSingleObject(WaitHandle waitObject, Wa
    }
}
```

Figure 6-1. *A screenshot of the ThreadPool class from Visual Studio 2019 IDE*

In this section, our focus is on the QueueUserWorkItem method. In Figure 6-1, note that this method has two overloaded versions. To learn more about this method, let's expand the method description in Visual Studio. For example, once you expand the first overloaded version of this method, you see the following.

```
//
// Summary:
//     Queues a method for execution. The method executes when a thread
//     pool thread becomes available.
//
// Parameters:
//   callBack:
//     A System.Threading.WaitCallback that represents the method to be
//     executed.
//
// Returns:
//     true if the method is successfully queued; System.
//     NotSupportedException is thrown
//     if the work item could not be queued.
```

```
//
// Exceptions:
//   T:System.ArgumentNullException:
//     callBack is null.
//
//   T:System.NotSupportedException:
//     The common language runtime (CLR) is hosted, and the host does not
//     support this action.
[SecuritySafeCritical]
public static bool QueueUserWorkItem(WaitCallback callBack);
```

If you further investigate on the method parameter, you find that WaitCallBack is a delegate with the following description.

```
//
// Summary:
//     Represents a callback method to be executed by a thread pool thread.
//
// Parameters:
//   state:
//     An object containing information to be used by the callback method.
[ComVisible(true)]
public delegate void WaitCallback(object state);
```

The second overloaded version of QueueUserWorkItem can take an object parameter called state. It is as follows.

```
public static bool QueueUserWorkItem(WaitCallback callBack, object state);
```

If you look at the details, you see that you can pass valuable data to your method through this parameter. In demonstration 3, I use both overloaded versions, and I introduce Method3, in which I pass an object parameter.

Demonstration 3

To use the QueueUserWorkItem method effectively, you need a method that matches the WaitCallBack delegate signature. In the following demonstration, I queue two methods in ThreadPool. In demonstration 2, Method2 does not accept any parameter. If you pass it to QueueUserWorkItem, you get the following compilation error.

```
No overload for 'Method2' matches delegate 'WaitCallback'
```

Let's modify Method2 with a dummy Object parameter, as follows (I kept the comments for your reference).

```
/* The following method's signature should match the delegate
WaitCallback.*/
private static void Method2(Object state)
{
    Console.WriteLine("--Method2() has started.");
    // Some small task
    Thread.Sleep(100);
    Console.WriteLine("--Method2() has finished.");
}
```

Next, let's introduce Method3, which uses the Object parameter. Method3 is described as follows.

```
static void Method3(Object number)
{
    Console.WriteLine("---Method3() has started.");
    int upperLimit = (int)number;
    for (int i = 0; i < upperLimit; i++)
    {
        Console.WriteLine("---Method3() prints 3.0{0}", i);
    }
     Thread.Sleep(100);
     Console.WriteLine("---Method3() has finished.");
}
```

Now go through the following demonstration and the corresponding output.

```
using System;
using System.Threading;

namespace UsingThreadPool
{
    class Program
```

```csharp
{
    static void Main(string[] args)
    {
        Console.WriteLine("***Asynchronous Programming Demonstration.***");
        Console.WriteLine("***Using ThreadPool.***");

        // Using Threadpool
        // Not passing any parameter for Method2
        ThreadPool.QueueUserWorkItem(new WaitCallback(Method2));
        // Passing 10 as the parameter for Method3
        ThreadPool.QueueUserWorkItem(new WaitCallback(Method3), 10);
        Method1();

        Console.WriteLine("End Main().");
        Console.ReadKey();
    }

    private static void Method1()
    {
        Console.WriteLine("-Method1() has started.");
        // Some big task
        Thread.Sleep(1000);
        Console.WriteLine("-Method1() has finished.");
    }

    /* The following method's signature should match the delegate WaitCallback.
    It is as follows:
    public delegate void WaitCallback(object state)
    */
    //private static void Method2()//Compilation error
    private static void Method2(Object state)
    {
        Console.WriteLine("--Method2() has started.");
        // Some small task
        Thread.Sleep(100);
        Console.WriteLine("--Method2() has finished.");
    }
```

```
        /*
The following method has a parameter.This method's signature matches the
WaitCallBack  delegate signature.Notice that this method also matches
the ParameterizedThreadStart delegate signature; because it has a single
parameter of type Object and this method doesn't return a value.
        */
        static void Method3(Object number)
        {
          Console.WriteLine("---Method3() has started.");
          int upperLimit = (int)number;
          for (int i = 0; i < upperLimit; i++)
          {
              Console.WriteLine("---Method3() prints 3.0{0}", i);
          }
          Thread.Sleep(100);
          Console.WriteLine("---Method3() has finished.");
        }
    }
}
```

Output

This is a possible output.

```
***Asynchronous Programming Demonstration.***
***Using ThreadPool.***
-Method1() has started.
---Method3() has started.
---Method3() prints 3.00
---Method3() prints 3.01
---Method3() prints 3.02
---Method3() prints 3.03
--Method2() has started.
---Method3() prints 3.04
---Method3() prints 3.05
```

```
---Method3() prints 3.06
---Method3() prints 3.07
---Method3() prints 3.08
---Method3() prints 3.09
--Method2() has finished.
---Method3() has finished.
-Method1() has finished.
End Main().
```

Q&A Session

6.2 Following the simple delegate instantiation technique, if I use the following line:

```
ThreadPool.QueueUserWorkItem(Method2);
```

instead of this line:
```
ThreadPool.QueueUserWorkItem(new WaitCallback(Method2));
```

will the application compile and run?
Yes, but since you are learning to use the WaitCallback delegate now, I kept it for your reference.

Using Lambda Expressions with ThreadPool

If you like lambda expressions, you can use it in a similar context. For example, in demonstration 3, you can replace Method3 using a lambda expression, as follows.

```
// Using lambda Expression
// Here the method needs a parameter(input).
// Passing 10 as the parameter for Method3
ThreadPool.QueueUserWorkItem((number) =>
{
    Console.WriteLine("---Method3() has started.");
    int upperLimit = (int)number;
    for (int i = 0; i < upperLimit; i++)
    {
        Console.WriteLine("---Method3() prints 3.0{0}", i);
```

```
        }
        Thread.Sleep(100);
        Console.WriteLine("---Method3() has finished.");
    }, 10
);
```

In demonstration 3, you can comment out the following line and replace Method3 with the lambda expression shown earlier.

```
ThreadPool.QueueUserWorkItem(new WaitCallback(Method3), 10);
```

If you execute the program again, you get a similar output. Demonstration 4 is the full implementation for your reference.

Demonstration 4

```
using System;
using System.Threading;

namespace UsingThreadPoolWithLambdaExpression
{
    class Program
    {
        static void Main(string[] args)
        {
            Console.WriteLine("***Asynchronous Programming
            Demonstration.***");
            Console.WriteLine("***Using ThreadPool with Lambda
            Expression.***");

            // Using Threadpool
            // Not passing any parameter for Method2
            ThreadPool.QueueUserWorkItem(Method2);
            //  Using lambda Expression
            // Here the method needs a parameter(input).
            // Passing 10 as the parameter for Method3
```

```csharp
        ThreadPool.QueueUserWorkItem( (number) =>
        {
            Console.WriteLine("--Method3() has started.");
            int upperLimit = (int)number;
            for (int i = 0; i < upperLimit; i++)
            {
                Console.WriteLine("---Method3() prints 3.0{0}", i);
            }
            Thread.Sleep(100);
            Console.WriteLine("--Method3() has finished.");
        }, 10

    );

    Method1();
    Console.WriteLine("End Main().");
    Console.ReadKey();
}

private static void Method1()
{
    Console.WriteLine("-Method1() has started.");
    // Some task
    Thread.Sleep(500);
    Console.WriteLine("-Method1() has finished.");
}

/* The following method's signature should match the delegate
WaitCallback.
It is as follows:
public delegate void WaitCallback(object state)
*/
//private static void Method2()//Compilation error
private static void Method2(Object state)
{
    Console.WriteLine("--Method2() has started.");
```

```
            // Some task
            Thread.Sleep(100);
            Console.WriteLine("--Method2() has finished.");
        }
    }
}
```

Output

This is a possible output.

```
***Asynchronous Programming Demonstration.***
***Using ThreadPool with Lambda Expression.***
-Method1() has started.
--Method3() has started.
---Method3() prints 3.00
--Method2() has started.
---Method3() prints 3.01
---Method3() prints 3.02
---Method3() prints 3.03
---Method3() prints 3.04
---Method3() prints 3.05
---Method3() prints 3.06
---Method3() prints 3.07
---Method3() prints 3.08
---Method3() prints 3.09
--Method2() has finished.
--Method3() has finished.
-Method1() has finished.
End Main().
```

Note   This time, you saw the use of lambda expressions in the ThreadPool
class. In demonstration 2, you saw the use of lambda expressions with the Thread
class.

Using the IAsyncResult Pattern

The IAsyncResult interface helps you implement asynchronous behavior. Let's recollect what I told you earlier. In a synchronous model, if there is a synchronous method called XXX, in the asynchronous version, the BeginXXX and EndXXX methods are the corresponding synchronous methods. Let's take a closer look.

Polling Using Asynchronous Delegates

So far, you have seen many different uses of delegates. In this section, you get to know another usage, which teaches that by using delegates, you can invoke methods asynchronously. Polling is a mechanism that repeatedly checks a condition. In demonstration 5, let's check whether a delegate instance completes its task or not.

Demonstration 5

There are two methods called Method1 and Method2. Let's again assume that Method1 takes more time to complete its task than Method2. To make it simple, Sleep() statements pass inside these methods. In this example, Method1 receives an argument that sleeps for 3000 milliseconds, and Method2 sleeps for 100 milliseconds.

Now look at the important segment of the codes. First, a delegate instance is created to match the Method1 signature. Method1 is as follows.

```
// Method1
private static void Method1(int sleepTimeInMilliSec)
{
    Console.WriteLine("Method1() has started.");
    Console.WriteLine("Inside Method1(),Thread id {0} .",
    Thread.CurrentThread.ManagedThreadId);
    // Some big task
    Thread.Sleep(sleepTimeInMilliSec);
    Console.WriteLine("\nMethod1() has finished.");
}
```

To match the signature, declare Method1Delegate as follows.

```
public delegate void Method1Delegate(int sleepTimeinMilliSec);
```

233

Later, instantiate it as follows.

```
Method1Delegate method1Del = Method1;
```

Everything is straightforward so far. Now we come to the most important line of the code, which is as follows.

```
IAsyncResult asyncResult = method1Del.BeginInvoke(3000, null, null);
```

Do you remember that in the context of the delegate, you can use the Invoke() method? But the last time, the code was following a synchronous path. Now that we are exploring asynchronous programming, you see the use of the BeginInvoke and EndInvoke methods. When the C# compiler sees the delegate keyword, it supplies these methods for your dynamically generated class.

The BeginInvoke method's return type is IAsyncResult. If you hover your mouse on BeginInvoke or note its structure, you see that although Method1 accepts only one parameter, the BeginInvoke method always takes two additional parameters—one of type AsyncCallback and one of type object. I discuss them shortly.

In this example, I use the first argument only and pass 3000 milliseconds as Method1's argument. But for the last two parameters of BeginInvoke, I pass null.

The result of BeginInvoke is important. I hold the result in an IAsyncResult object. The IAsyncResult has the following read-only properties.

```
public interface IAsyncResult
{
    bool IsCompleted { get; }
    WaitHandle AsyncWaitHandle { get; }
    object AsyncState { get; }
    bool CompletedSynchronously { get; }
 }
```

For now, my focus is on the isCompleted property. If you expand these definitions further, you see that isCompleted is defined as follows.

```
//
// Summary:
//     Gets a value that indicates whether the asynchronous operation has
//     completed.
```

```
//
// Returns:
//     true if the operation is complete; otherwise, false.
bool IsCompleted { get; }
```

It's clear that you can use this property to verify whether the delegate has completed its work.

In the following example, I check whether the delegate in the other thread has completed its work. If the work is not completed, I print asterisks (*) in the console window and force the main thread to take a short sleep. This is why you see the following segment of code in this demonstration.

```
while (!asyncResult.IsCompleted)
{
    // Keep working in main thread
    Console.Write("*");
    Thread.Sleep(5);
}
```

Lastly, the EndInvoke method accepts an argument of type IAsyncResult. I passed asyncResult as an argument in this method.

Now go through the complete demonstration.

```
using System;
using System.Threading;

namespace PollingDemo
{
    class Program
    {
        public delegate void Method1Delegate(int sleepTimeinMilliSec);
        static void Main(string[] args)
        {
            Console.WriteLine("***Polling Demo.***");
            Console.WriteLine("Inside Main(),Thread id {0} .",
            Thread.CurrentThread.ManagedThreadId);
            // Synchronous call
            //Method1(3000);
```

```
        Method1Delegate method1Del = Method1;
        IAsyncResult asyncResult = method1Del.BeginInvoke(3000, null, null);
        Method2();
        while (!asyncResult.IsCompleted)
        {
            // Keep working in main thread
            Console.Write("*");
            Thread.Sleep(5);
        }

        method1Del.EndInvoke(asyncResult);
        Console.ReadKey();
    }
    // Method1
    private static void Method1(int sleepTimeInMilliSec)
    {
        Console.WriteLine("Method1() has started.");
        Console.WriteLine("Inside Method1(),Thread id {0} .",
        Thread.CurrentThread.ManagedThreadId);
        // Some big task
        Thread.Sleep(sleepTimeInMilliSec);
        Console.WriteLine("\nMethod1() has finished.");

    }
    // Method2
    private static void Method2()
    {
        Console.WriteLine("Method2() has started.");
        Console.WriteLine("Inside Method2(),Thread id {0} .",
        Thread.CurrentThread.ManagedThreadId);
        // Some small task
        Thread.Sleep(100);
        Console.WriteLine("Method2() has finished.");
    }

  }
}
```

Output

This is one possible output.

```
***Polling Demo.***
Inside Main(),Thread id 1 .
Method2() has started.
Inside Method2(),Thread id 1 .
Method1() has started.
Inside Method1(),Thread id 3 .
Method2() has finished.
************************************************************************
************************************************************************
************************************************************************
************************************************************************
************************************************************************
************************************************************************
Method1() has finished.
```

Q&A Session

6.3 In a previous case, Method1 took one parameter and BeginInvoke **took three parameters. If** Method1 **accepts n number of parameters, then** BeginInvoke **will have** n+2 **parameters.**

Yes, the initial set of parameters is based on your methods, but for the last two parameters, one is of type AsyncCallback and the final one is of type object.

POINTS TO REMEMBER

- This type of example was run in .NET Framework 4.7.2. If you execute the program in .NET Core 3.0, you get an exception saying, "System. PlatformNotSupportedException: Operation is not supported on this platform." One of the primary reasons for this is that async delegate implementation depends on remoting features that are not present in .NET Core. A discussion on this is at https://github.com/dotnet/runtime/issues/16312.

- If you do not want to examine and print asterisks (∗) in the console window, you can simply call the EndInvoke() method of the delegate type once your main thread completes its execution. The EndInvoke() method waits until the delegate completes its work.

- If you don't explicitly examine whether the delegate finishes its execution or not, or you simply forget to call EndInvoke(), the thread of the delegate is stopped after the main thread dies. For example, if you comment out the following segment of code from the prior example,

```
//while (!asyncResult.IsCompleted)
//{
//    Keep working in main thread
//    Console.Write("*");
//    Thread.Sleep(5);
//}
//method1Del.EndInvoke(asyncResult);
//Console.ReadKey();
```

  and run the application again, you may not see the "Method1() has finished." Statement.

- BeginInvoke helps the calling thread get the result of asynchronous method invocation at a later time by using EndInvoke.

Using the AsyncWaitHandle Property of IAsyncResult

Now I'll show you an alternative approach using another property, AsyncWaitHandle, which is also available in IAsyncResult. If you see the contents of IAsyncResult, you find that AsyncWaitHandle returns WaitHandle, which has the following description.

```
//
// Summary:
//     Gets a System.Threading.WaitHandle that is used to wait for an
//     asynchronous operation to complete.
//
// Returns:
//     A System.Threading.WaitHandle that is used to wait for an
//     asynchronous operation to complete.
WaitHandle AsyncWaitHandle { get; }
```

The Visual Studio IDE confirms that WaitHandle is an abstract class that waits for exclusive access to shared resources. Inside WaitHandle, you see the WaitOne() method with five different overloaded versions.

```
public virtual bool WaitOne(int millisecondsTimeout);
public virtual bool WaitOne(int millisecondsTimeout, bool exitContext);
public virtual bool WaitOne(TimeSpan timeout);
public virtual bool WaitOne(TimeSpan timeout, bool exitContext);
public virtual bool WaitOne();
```

By using WaitHandle, you can wait for a delegate thread to finish its work. In demonstration 6, the first overloaded version is used, and an optional timeout value in milliseconds is provided. If the wait is successful, the control exits from the while loop; but if timeout occurs, WaitOne() returns false, and the while loop continues and prints asterisks (*) in the console.

Demonstration 6

```
using System;
using System.Threading;

namespace UsingWaitHandle
{
    class Program
    {
        public delegate void Method1Delegate(int sleepTimeinMilliSec);
        static void Main(string[] args)
        {
            Console.WriteLine("***Polling and WaitHandle Demo.***");
            Console.WriteLine("Inside Main(),Thread id {0} .",
            Thread.CurrentThread.ManagedThreadId);
            // Synchronous call
            //Method1(3000);
            // Asynchrous call using a delegate
            Method1Delegate method1Del = Method1;
```

```csharp
        IAsyncResult asyncResult = method1Del.BeginInvoke(3000, null, null);
        Method2();
        // while (!asyncResult.IsCompleted)
        while (true)
        {
            // Keep working in main thread
            Console.Write("*");
            /* There are 5 different overload method for WaitOne().
               Following method blocks the current thread until the
               current System.Threading.WaitHandle receives a signal,
               using a 32-bit signed integer to specify the time
               interval in milliseconds.
            */
            if (asyncResult.AsyncWaitHandle.WaitOne(10))
            {
                Console.Write("\nResult is available now.");
                break;
            }
        }
        method1Del.EndInvoke(asyncResult);
        Console.WriteLine("\nExiting Main().");
        Console.ReadKey();
    }
    // Method1
    private static void Method1(int sleepTimeInMilliSec)
    {
        Console.WriteLine("Method1() has started.");
        // It will have a different thread id
        Console.WriteLine("Inside Method1(),Thread id {0} .",
        Thread.CurrentThread.ManagedThreadId);
        // Some big task
        Thread.Sleep(sleepTimeInMilliSec);
        Console.WriteLine("\nMethod1() has finished.");
```

```
        }
        // Method2
        private static void Method2()
        {
            Console.WriteLine("Method2() has started.");
            // Main thread id and this thread id will be same
            Console.WriteLine("Inside Method2(),Thread id {0} .",
            Thread.CurrentThread.ManagedThreadId);
            // Some small task
            Thread.Sleep(100);
            Console.WriteLine("Method2() has finished.");
        }
    }
}
```

Output

This is one possible output.

```
***Polling and WaitHandle Demo.***
Inside Main(),Thread id 1 .
Method2() has started.
Inside Method2(),Thread id 1 .
Method1() has started.
Inside Method1(),Thread id 3 .
Method2() has finished.
************************************************************************
************************************************************************
*********
Method1() has finished.
*
Result is available now.
Exiting Main().
```

Analysis

If you compare this demonstration with the previous one, you notice that here you wait for the asynchronous operation to complete in a different manner. Instead of using IsCompleted property, this time you used the AsyncWaitHandle property of IAsyncResult.

Using Asynchronous Callback

Let's revisit the BeginInvoke method from the previous two demonstrations.

```
// Asynchrous call using a delegate
Method1Delegate method1Del = Method1;
IAsyncResult asyncResult = method1Del.BeginInvoke(3000, null, null);
```

This means two null values were passed for the last two method arguments. If you hover your mouse over the line of these prior demonstrations, you notice that BeginInvoke is expecting an IAsyncCallback delegate as the second parameter and an object for the third parameter in this case.

Let's investigate the IAsyncCallback delegate. Visual Studio IDE says that this delegate is defined in the System namespace; it has the following description.

```
//
// Summary:
//    References a method to be called when a corresponding asynchronous
//    operation completes.
//
// Parameters:
//   ar:
//     The result of the asynchronous operation.
  [ComVisible(true)]
  public delegate void AsyncCallback(IAsyncResult ar);
```

You can use a callback method to execute something useful (for example, housekeeping works). The AsyncCallback delegate has a void return type, and it accepts an IAsyncResult parameter. Let's define a method that can match this delegate signature and call this method once the Method1Del instance finishes its execution.

Here is a sample method, which is used in an upcoming demonstration.

```
// Method3: It's a callback method.
// This method will be invoked when Method1Delegate completes its work.
private static void Method3(IAsyncResult asyncResult)
{
    if (asyncResult != null) // if null you can throw some exception
    {
        Console.WriteLine("\nMethod3() has started.");
        Console.WriteLine("Inside Method3(),Thread id {0} .",
        Thread.CurrentThread.ManagedThreadId);
        // Do some housekeeping work/ clean-up operation
        Thread.Sleep(100);
        Console.WriteLine("Method3() has finished.");
    }
}
```

Demonstration 7

Now go through the complete implementation.

```
using System;
using System.Threading;

namespace UsingAsynchronousCallback
{
    class Program
    {
        public delegate void Method1Delegate(int sleepTimeinMilliSec);
        static void Main(string[] args)
        {
            Console.WriteLine("***Using Asynchronous Callback.***");
            Console.WriteLine("Inside Main(),Thread id {0} .",
            Thread.CurrentThread.ManagedThreadId);
            // Synchronous call
            //Method1(3000);
            // Asynchrous call using a delegate
            Method1Delegate method1Del = Method1;
```

```csharp
        IAsyncResult asyncResult = method1Del.BeginInvoke(3000,
        Method3, null);

        Method2();
        while (!asyncResult.IsCompleted)
        {
                // Keep working in main thread
                Console.Write("*");
                Thread.Sleep(5);
        }

        method1Del.EndInvoke(asyncResult);
        Console.WriteLine("Exit Main().");
        Console.ReadKey();
    }
    // Method1
    private static void Method1(int sleepTimeInMilliSec)
    {
        Console.WriteLine("Method1() has started.");
        Console.WriteLine("Inside Method1(),Thread id {0} .",
        Thread.CurrentThread.ManagedThreadId);
        // Some big task
        Thread.Sleep(sleepTimeInMilliSec);
        Console.WriteLine("\nMethod1() has finished.");

    }
    // Method2
    private static void Method2()
    {
        Console.WriteLine("Method2() has started.");
        Console.WriteLine("Inside Method2(),Thread id {0} .",
        Thread.CurrentThread.ManagedThreadId);
        //Some small task
        Thread.Sleep(100);
        Console.WriteLine("Method2() has finished.");
    }
```

```
    /* Method3: It's a callback method.This method will be invoked when
       Method1Delegate completes its work.*/
    private static void Method3(IAsyncResult asyncResult)
    {
        if (asyncResult != null)//if null you can throw some exception
        {
            Console.WriteLine("\nMethod3() has started.");
            Console.WriteLine("Inside Method3(),Thread id {0} .",
            Thread.CurrentThread.ManagedThreadId);
            // Do some housekeeping work/ clean-up operation
            Thread.Sleep(100);
            Console.WriteLine("Method3() has finished.");
        }
    }
  }
}
```

Output

This is a possible output.

```
***Using Asynchronous Callback.***
Inside Main(),Thread id 1 .
Method2() has started.
Inside Method2(),Thread id 1 .
Method1() has started.
Inside Method1(),Thread id·3 .
Method2() has finished.
**********************************************************************
**********************************************************************
**********************************************************************
**********************************************************************
**********************************************************************
*******************************************
Method1() has finished.

Method3() has started.
```

```
Inside Method3(),Thread id 3 .
Exit Main().
Method3() has finished.
```

Analysis

Note that Method3 started its work only after Method1() finished its execution. Also note that the thread ID of Method1() and Method3() are the same. This is because Method3() was invoked from the thread in which Method1() was running.

Q&A Session

6.4 What is a callback method?

Normally, it is a method that is invoked only after a specific operation is completed. You often see the usage of this kind of method in asynchronous programming, where you do not know the exact finishing time of an operation but want to start some specific task once the prior task is over. For example, in the previous example, Method3 can perform some clean-up work if Method1() allocates resources during its execution.

6.5 I see that Method3() was not invoked from the main thread. Is this expected?

Yes. Here you are using a callback method. In this example, Method3() is the callback method, which can start its execution only after Method1() completes its work. So, it makes sense that you call Method3() from the same thread in which Method1() is running.

6.6 Can I use a lambda expression in this example?

Good catch. To get a similar output, in the previous demonstration, instead of creating a new method, Method3(), and using the following line,

```
IAsyncResult asyncResult = method1Del.BeginInvoke(3000, Method3, null);
```

you could replace it using a lambda expression as follows.

```
IAsyncResult asyncResult = method1Del.BeginInvoke(3000,
 (result) =>
{
    if (result != null)//if null you can throw some exception
    {
        Console.WriteLine("\nMethod3() has started.");
```

246

```
        Console.WriteLine("Inside Method3(),Thread id {0} .",
        Thread.CurrentThread.ManagedThreadId);
        // Do some housekeeping work/ clean-up operation
        Thread.Sleep(100);
        Console.WriteLine("Method3() has finished.");
    }
  },
null);
```

6.7 When you used the callback method, Method3, inside the BeginInvoke **method, instead of passing an object as the final parameter, you pass a null value. Is there any specific reason for this?**

No, I did not use that parameter in these demonstrations. Since it is an object parameter, you can literally pass anything meaningful to you. When you use a callback method, you can pass the delegate instance. It can help your callback method analyze the result of the asynchronous method.

But for simplicity, let's modify the previous demonstration and pass a string message as the last argument inside BeginInvoke. Let's assume that you are modifying the existing line of code,

```
IAsyncResult asyncResult = method1Del.BeginInvoke(3000,Method3, null);
```

with the following one.

IAsyncResult asyncResult = method1Del.BeginInvoke(3000, Method3, "Method1Delegate, thank you for using me.");

To accommodate this change, let's modify the Method3() method too.The newly added lines are shown in bold.

```
private static void Method3(IAsyncResult asyncResult)
{
    if (asyncResult != null) // if null you can throw some exception
    {
        Console.WriteLine("\nMethod3() has started.");
        Console.WriteLine("Inside Method3(),Thread id {0} .",
        Thread.CurrentThread.ManagedThreadId);
        // Do some housekeeping work/ clean-up operation
```

```
        Thread.Sleep(100);
        // For Q&A
        string msg = (string)asyncResult.AsyncState;
        Console.WriteLine("Method3() says : '{0}'",msg);
        Console.WriteLine("Method3() has finished.");
    }
}
```

If you run the program again, this time you may see the following output.

```
***Using Asynchronous Callback.***
Inside Main(),Thread id 1 .
Method2() has started.
Inside Method2(),Thread id 1 .
Method1() has started.
Inside Method1(),Thread id 3 .
Method2() has finished.
***********************************************************************
***********************************************************************
************************************************************************
************************************************************************
************************************************************************
************************************************************************
Method1() has finished.

Method3() has started.
Inside Method3(),Thread id 3 .
Exit Main().
Method3() says : 'Method1Delegate, thank you for using me.'
Method3() has finished.
```

POINTS TO REMEMBER

You have seen the implementation of polling, wait handles, and asynchronous callbacks using delegates. This programming model is also in other places in the .NET Framework; for example, BeginGetResponse, BeginGetRequestStream of the HttpWebRequest class, or BeginExecuteNonQuery(), BeginExecuteReader(), BeginExecuteXmlReader() of the SqlCommand class. These methods have overloads too.

Using an Event-based Asynchronous Pattern (EAP)

In this section, you see the usage of EAP. Event-based patterns often seem tough to understand at first. Based on the complexity of your application, this pattern can take various forms.

Here are some key characteristics of this pattern.

- In general, an asynchronous method is an exact replica of its synchronous version, but when you call it, it starts on a separate thread and then returns immediately. This mechanism allows calling a thread to continue while the intended operations run in the background. Examples of these operations can be a long-running process, such as loading a large image, downloading a large file, connecting and establishing a connection to a database, and so forth. EAP is helpful in these contexts. For example, once the long-running download operation is completed, an event can be raised to notify the information. The subscribers of the event can act based on this notification immediately.

- You can execute multiple operations simultaneously and receive a notification when each of them completes.

- Using this pattern, you take advantage of multithreading, but at the same time, you hide the overall complexity.

- In simplest case, your method name will have an *Async* suffix to tell others that you are using an asynchronous version of the method. At the same time, you have a corresponding event with a *Completed* suffix. In an ideal case, you should have a corresponding cancel method, and it should support displaying the progress bar/report. The method that supports a cancel operation can also be named *MethodNameAsyncCancel* (or simply *CancelAsync*).

- Components like SoundPlayer, PictureBox, WebClient, and BackgroundWorker are commonly known representatives of this pattern.

Demonstration 8 is a simple application for WebClient. Let's start.

Demonstration 8

At the beginning of the program, you see that I needed to include some specific namespaces. I used the comments to say why these were necessary for this demonstration.

In this case study, I want to download a file into my local system. But instead of using an actual URL from the Internet, I'm storing the source file in my local system. This can give you two major benefits.

- You do not need an Internet connection to run this application.

- Since you're not using an Internet connection, the download operation will be relatively faster.

Now look at the following block of code, which you will see in the complete example.

```
WebClient webClient = new WebClient();
// File location
Uri myLocation = new Uri(@"C:\TestData\testfile_original.txt");
// Target location for download
string targetLocation = @"C:\TestData\downloaded_file.txt";
webClient.DownloadFileAsync(myLocation, targetLocation);
webClient.DownloadFileCompleted += new AsyncCompletedEventHandler(Completed);
```

So far, things are straightforward and simple. But I'm drawing your attention to the following lines of code.

```
webClient.DownloadFileAsync(myLocation, targetLocation);
webClient.DownloadFileCompleted += new
AsyncCompletedEventHandler(Completed);
```

You can see that in the first line, I use a method defined in WebClient called DownloadFileAsync. In Visual Studio, the method description tells us the following.

```
// Summary:
//     Downloads, to a local file, the resource with the specified URI.
//     This method does not block the calling thread.
//
```

```
// Parameters:
//   address:
//     The URI of the resource to download.
//
//   fileName:
//     The name of the file to be placed on the local computer.
//
// Exceptions:
//   T:System.ArgumentNullException:
//     The address parameter is null. -or- The fileName parameter is null.
//
//   T:System.Net.WebException:
//     The URI formed by combining System.Net.WebClient.BaseAddress and
//     address is invalid.
//     -or- An error occurred while downloading the resource.
//
//   T:System.InvalidOperationException:
//     The local file specified by fileName is in use by another thread.
public void DownloadFileAsync(Uri address, string fileName);
```

From the method summary, you understand that when you use this method, the calling thread is not blocked. (Actually, DownloadFileAsync is the asynchronous version of the DownloadFile method, which is also defined in WebClient.)

Now come to next line of code.

```
webClient.DownloadFileCompleted += new AsyncCompletedEventHandler(Completed);
```

Visual Studio describes the DownloadFileCompleted event as follows.

```
/ Summary:
//     Occurs when an asynchronous file download operation completes.
public event AsyncCompletedEventHandler DownloadFileCompleted;
```

It describes AsyncCompletedEventHandler as follows.

```
// Summary:
//     Represents the method that will handle the MethodNameCompleted event
//     of an asynchronous operation.
```

```
//
// Parameters:
//    sender:
//       The source of the event.
//
//    e:
//       An System.ComponentModel.AsyncCompletedEventArgs that contains the
//       event data.
public delegate void AsyncCompletedEventHandler(object sender,
AsyncCompletedEventArgs e);
```

You can subscribe to the DownloadFileCompleted event to show a notification that the download operation is finished. To do that, the following method is used.

```
private static void DownloadCompleted(object sender,
AsyncCompletedEventArgs e)
{
    Console.WriteLine("Successfully downloaded the file now.");
}
```

Note   The DownloadCompleted method matches the signature of the AsyncCompletedEventHandler delegate.

Since you've mastered the concept of delegates and events, you know that you could replace this line of code

```
webClient.DownloadFileCompleted += new AsyncCompletedEventHandler(Download
Completed);
```

with the following line of code.

```
webClient.DownloadFileCompleted += DownloadCompleted;
```

I kept the long version for a better readability.

Now go through the complete example and output.

```csharp
using System;
// For AsyncCompletedEventHandler delegate
using System.ComponentModel;
using System.Net; // For WebClient
using System.Threading; // For Thread.Sleep() method

namespace UsingWebClient
{
    class Program
    {
        static void Main(string[] args)
        {
            Console.WriteLine("***Demonstration-.Event Based Asynchronous
            Program Demo.***");
            // Method1();
            #region The lenghty operation(download)
            Console.WriteLine("Starting a download operation.");
            WebClient webClient = new WebClient();
            // File location
            Uri myLocation = new Uri(@"C:\TestData\OriginalFile.txt");
            // Target location for download
            string targetLocation = @"C:\TestData\DownloadedFile.txt";
            webClient.DownloadFileAsync(myLocation, targetLocation);
            webClient.DownloadFileCompleted += new AsyncCompletedEvent
            Handler(Completed);
            #endregion
            Method2();
            Console.WriteLine("End Main()...");
            Console.ReadKey();
        }
        // Method2
        private static void Method2()
        {
            Console.WriteLine("Method2() has started.");
            // Some small task
            // Thread.Sleep(10);
```

```
            Console.WriteLine("Method2() has finished.");
        }

        private static void Completed(object sender,
        AsyncCompletedEventArgs e)
        {
            Console.WriteLine("Successfully downloaded the file now.");
        }
    }
}
```

Output

This is a possible output.

```
***Demonstration-.Event Based Asynchronous Program Demo.***
Starting a download operation.
Method2() has started.
Method2() has finished.
End Main()...
Successfully downloaded the file now.
```

Analysis

You can see that the download operation started prior to Method2() starting its execution. Still, Method2() completed its job before the download operation completed. If you are interested in seeing the content of Original.txt, it is as follows.

```
Dear Reader,
This is my test file.It is originally stored at C:\TestData in my system.
```

You can test a similar file and its contents for a quick verification on your end.

Additional Note

You can make this example even better when you introduce a progress bar. You can use a Windows Form App to get built-in support for a progress bar. Let's ignore Method2, and focus on the asynchronous download operation. You can make a basic form, as shown in Figure 6-2, that contains three simple buttons and one progress bar. (You need to drag and drop these controls on your form first. I assume that you know these activities).

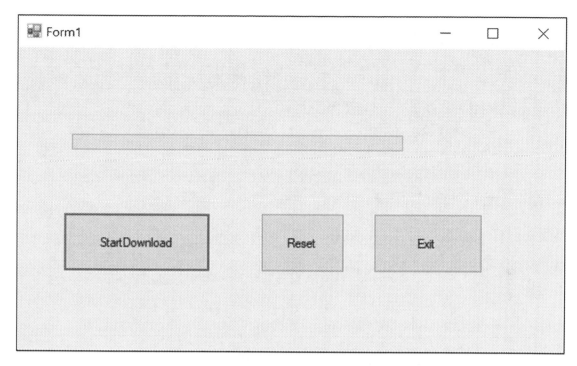

Figure 6-2. *A simple UI application to demonstrate event-based asynchrony*

The following segment of code is self-explanatory.

```
using System;
using System.ComponentModel;
using System.Net;
using System.Threading;
using System.Windows.Forms;

namespace UsingWebClientWithWinForm
{
    public partial class Form1 : Form
    {
        public Form1()
        {
            InitializeComponent();
        }

        private void StartDownload_Click(object sender, EventArgs e)
```

```csharp
        {
          WebClient webClient = new WebClient();
          Uri myLocation = new Uri(@"C:\TestData\testfile_original.txt");
          string targetLocation = @"C:\TestData\downloaded_file.txt";
          webClient.DownloadFileAsync(myLocation, targetLocation);
          webClient.DownloadFileCompleted += new AsyncCompletedEvent
          Handler(DownloadCompleted);
          webClient.DownloadProgressChanged += new DownloadProgressChanged
          EventHandler(ProgressChanged);
          Thread.Sleep(3000);
          MessageBox.Show("Method1() has finished.");
        }
        private void DownloadCompleted(object sender, AsyncCompletedEventArgs e)
        {
            MessageBox.Show("Successfully downloaded the file now.");
        }
        private void ProgressChanged(object sender,
        DownloadProgressChangedEventArgs e)
        {
            progressBar.Value = e.ProgressPercentage;
        }

        private void ResetButton_Click(object sender, EventArgs e)
        {
            progressBar.Value = 0;
        }

        private void ExitButton_Click(object sender, EventArgs e)
        {
            this.Close();
        }
        }
}
```

Output

Once you click the StartDownload button, you get the output shown in Figure 6-3.

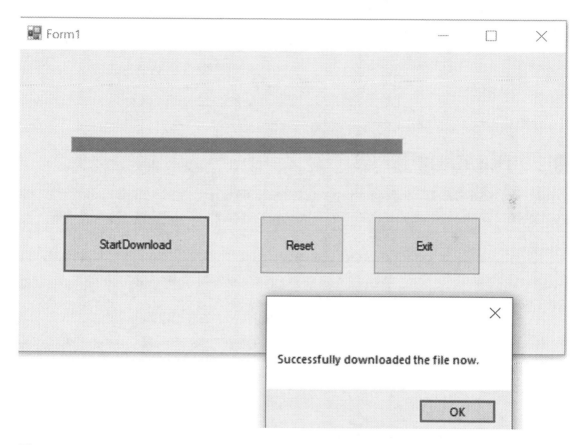

Figure 6-3. *A runtime screenshot when the UI application is running*

Q&A Session

6.8 What are the pros and cons associated with an event-based asynchronous program?

Here are some common pros and cons associated with this approach.

Pros

- You can invoke a long-running method and get a return immediately. When the method completes, you get a notification.

Cons

- Since you have segregated the code, it's often difficult to understand, debug, and maintain.

- A major problem can occur when you subscribe an event but later forget to unsubscribe from it. This mistake can lead to memory leaks in your application, and the impact can be severe; for example, your system can hang or be unresponsive, and you may need to reboot your system often.

Understanding Tasks

To understand a Task-based Asynchronous Pattern, the first thing to know is that a *task* is simply a unit of work that you want to perform. You can complete this work in the same thread or in a different thread. By using tasks, you have a better control of threads; for example, you can perform continuation work once a task is finished. A parent task can create child task(s), so you can organize the hierarchy. This kind of hierarchy is important when you cascade your messages; for example, in your application, you may decide that once a parent task is cancelled, the child task(s) should be cancelled too.

You can create tasks in different ways. In the following demonstration, I create three tasks in three different ways. Note the following segment of code with supporting comments.

```
#region Different ways to create and execute task
// Using constructor
Task taskOne = new Task(MyMethod);
taskOne.Start();
// Using task factory
TaskFactory taskFactory = new TaskFactory();
// StartNew Method creates and starts a task.
// It has different overloaded version.
Task taskTwo = taskFactory.StartNew(MyMethod);
// Using task factory via a task
Task taskThree = Task.Factory.StartNew(MyMethod);
#endregion
```

You can see that all three tasks are doing the same operation. Each of them is executing the MyMethod(), which is described as follows.

```
private static void MyMethod()
{
    Console.WriteLine("Task.id={0} with Thread id {1} has started.",
    Task.CurrentId, Thread.CurrentThread.ManagedThreadId);
    // Some task
    Thread.Sleep(100);
    Console.WriteLine("MyMethod for Task.id={0} and Thread id {1} is
    completed.", Task.CurrentId,  Thread.CurrentThread.ManagedThreadId);
    }
```

You can see that inside MyMethod(), to distinguish the tasks and threads, their corresponding IDs are printed in the console.

One last thing. You can see that the method name is passed as an argument inside the StartNew() method. This method has 16 overloaded versions at the time of writing, and I'm using the one that is defined as follows.

```
//
// Summary:
//     Creates and starts a task.
//
// Parameters:
//   action:
//     The action delegate to execute asynchronously.
//
// Returns:
//     The started task.
//
// Exceptions:
//   T:System.ArgumentNullException:
//     The action argument is null.
public Task StartNew(Action action);
```

Since MyMethod() matches the signature of the Action delegate in this case, there was no problem using this method with StartNew.

Demonstration 9

Now go through the complete demonstration and output.

```
using System;
using System.Threading;
using System.Threading.Tasks;

namespace CreatingTasks
{
    class Program
    {
     static void Main(string[] args)
     {
            Console.WriteLine("***Using different ways to create
            tasks.****");
            Console.WriteLine("Inside Main().Thread ID:{0}",
            Thread.CurrentThread.ManagedThreadId);

            #region Different ways to create and execute task
            // Using constructor
            Task taskOne = new Task(MyMethod);
            taskOne.Start();
            // Using task factory
            TaskFactory taskFactory = new TaskFactory();
            // StartNew Method creates and starts a task.
            // It has different overloaded version.
            Task taskTwo = taskFactory.StartNew(MyMethod);
            // Using task factory via a task
            Task taskThree = Task.Factory.StartNew(MyMethod);
            #endregion
            Console.ReadKey();
        }

        private static void MyMethod()
        {
            Console.WriteLine("Task.id={0} with Thread id {1}
            has started.", Task.CurrentId, Thread.CurrentThread.
            ManagedThreadId);
```

```
        Thread.Sleep(100);
        Console.WriteLine("MyMethod for Task.id={0} and Thread id
        {1} is completed.", Task.CurrentId, Thread.CurrentThread.
        ManagedThreadId);
      }
    }
}
```

Output

This is a possible output.

```
***Using different ways to create tasks.****
Inside Main().Thread ID:1
Task.id=2 with Thread id 6 has started.
Task.id=1 with Thread id 5 has started.
Task.id=3 with Thread id 4 has started.
MyMethod for Task.id=1 and Thread id 5 is completed.
MyMethod for Task.id=3 and Thread id 4 is completed.
MyMethod for Task.id=2 and Thread id 6 is completed.
```

Q&A Session

6.9 StartNew() **can be used only for methods that match the Action delegate signature. Is this correct?**

No. I used it in one of the StartNew overloads that accepts a parameter, which is the name of a method that matches an Action delegate signature. But, there are other overloaded versions of StartNew; for example, consider the following.

```
public Task<TResult> StartNew<[NullableAttribute(2)]TResult>
(Func<TResult> function, TaskCreationOptions creationOptions);
Or,
public Task<TResult> StartNew<[NullableAttribute(2)]TResult>
(Func<TResult> function, CancellationToken cancellationToken);
```

6.10 In a previous Q&A, I saw the use of TaskCreationOptions. **What does it mean?**

It is an enum. You can set a task's behavior by using it. The following describes this enum and includes the different options that you have.

```
public enum TaskCreationOptions
{
        None = 0,
        PreferFairness = 1,
        LongRunning = 2,
        AttachedToParent = 4,
        DenyChildAttach = 8,
        HideScheduler = 16,
        RunContinuationsAsynchronously = 64,
}
```

In an upcoming demonstration, you see the use of an important enum called TaskContinuationOptions, which also helps set a task behavior.

Using a Task-based Asynchronous Pattern (TAP)

TAP first appeared in C# 4.0. It was the foundation of async/await, which appeared in C# 5.0. TAP introduced the Task class and its generic variant, Task<TResult>. Task is used when the return value of an asynchronous chunk of code is not a concern, but when you want the return value to proceed further, you should use the Task<TResult> generic version. You already had an overview of tasks. Let's use this concept to implement TAP using Method1() and Method2().

Demonstration 10

This is a complete demonstration.

```
using System;
using System.Threading;
using System.Threading.Tasks;

namespace UsingTAP
{
    class Program
    {
        static void Main(string[] args)
```

```csharp
{
    Console.WriteLine("***Using Task-based Asynchronous
    Pattern.****");
    Console.WriteLine("Inside Main().Thread ID:{0}",
    Thread.CurrentThread.ManagedThreadId);
    Task taskForMethod1 = new Task(Method1);
    taskForMethod1.Start();
    Method2();
    Console.ReadKey();
}

private static void Method1()
{
    Console.WriteLine("Method1() has started.");
    Console.WriteLine("Inside Method1(),Thread id {0} .",
    Thread.CurrentThread.ManagedThreadId);
    // Some big task
    Thread.Sleep(3000);
    Console.WriteLine("Method1() has completed its job now.");
}

private static void Method2()
{
    Console.WriteLine("Method2() has started.");
    Console.WriteLine("Inside Method2(),Thread id {0} .",
    Thread.CurrentThread.ManagedThreadId);
    Thread.Sleep(100);
    Console.WriteLine("Method2() is completed.");
}
}
}
```

Output

This is a possible output.

```
***Using Task-based Asynchronous Pattern.****
Inside Main().Thread ID:1
Method2() has started.
Inside Method2(),Thread id 1 .
Method1() has started.
Inside Method1(),Thread id 4 .
Method2() is completed.
Method1() has completed its job now.
```

You have just seen a sample demo of a task-based asynchronous pattern. I did not care about the return value of Method1. But let's say that you want to see whether Method1 executed successfully or not. For simplicity, I'm using a string message to indicate a successful completion. And this time you'll see a generic variant of Task which is Task<string>. For lambda expression lovers, I modified Method1 with a lambda expression in this example. To fulfill the key requirement, I adjusted the return type. This time I'm adding another method called Method3(). For a comparison purpose, initially this method will be commented out and the program will be executed and output will be analyzed. Later I'll uncomment it, and create a task hierarchy using the method. Once this is done, the program will be executed again, and you will notice that Method3() executes when Method1() completes its job. I have kept the comments for a better understanding.

Now go through the upcoming demonstration.

Demonstration 11

This is a complete demonstration.

```
using System;
using System.Threading;
using System.Threading.Tasks;
```

```csharp
namespace UsingTAPDemo2
{
    class Program
    {
        static void Main(string[] args)
        {
            Console.WriteLine("***Using Task-based Asynchronous Pattern.
            Using lambda expression into it.****");
            Console.WriteLine("Inside Main().Thread ID:{0}",
            Thread.CurrentThread.ManagedThreadId);
            // Task taskForMethod1 = new Task(Method1);
            // taskForMethod1.Start();
            Task<string> taskForMethod1 = Method1();
            // Wait for task to complete.It'll be no more
            //asynchonous now.
            // taskForMethod1.Wait();
            // Continue the task
            // The taskForMethod3 will continue once taskForMethod1 is
            // finished
            // Task taskForMethod3 = taskForMethod1.ContinueWith(Method3,
                TaskContinuationOptions.OnlyOnRanToCompletion);
            Method2();
            Console.WriteLine("Task for Method1 was a : {0}",
            taskForMethod1.Result);
            Console.ReadKey();
        }
        // Using lambda expression
        private static Task<string> Method1()
        {
            return Task.Run(() =>
            {
                string result = "Failure";
                try
                {
```

```csharp
                Console.WriteLine("Inside Method1(),Task.id={0}",
                Task.CurrentId);
                Console.WriteLine("Method1() has started.");
                Console.WriteLine("Inside Method1(),Thread id {0} .",
                Thread.CurrentThread.ManagedThreadId);
                //Some big task
                Thread.Sleep(3000);
                Console.WriteLine("Method1() has completed its job
                now.");
                result = "Success";
            }
            catch (Exception ex)
            {
                Console.WriteLine("Exception caught:{0}", ex.Message);
            }
            return result;
        }
        );
    }

    private static void Method2()
    {
        Console.WriteLine("Method2() has started.");
        Console.WriteLine("Inside Method2(),Thread id {0} .",
        Thread.CurrentThread.ManagedThreadId);
        Thread.Sleep(100);
        Console.WriteLine("Method2() is completed.");
    }
    private static void Method3(Task task)
    {
        Console.WriteLine("Method3 starts now.");
        Console.WriteLine("Task.id is:{0} with Thread id is :{1} ",
        Task.CurrentId, Thread.CurrentThread.ManagedThreadId);
        Thread.Sleep(20);
```

```
        Console.WriteLine("Method3 for Task.id {0} and Thread id
        {1} is completed.", Task.CurrentId, Thread.CurrentThread.
        ManagedThreadId);
      }
    }
}
```

Output

```
***Using Task-based Asynchronous Pattern.Using lambda expression into it.****
Inside Main().Thread ID:1
Method2() has started.
Inside Method2(),Thread id 1 .
Inside Method1(),Task.id=1
Method1() has started.
Inside Method1(),Thread id 4 .
Method2() is completed.
Method1() has completed its job now.
Task for Method1 was a : Success
```

Analysis

Did you notice that I did not use the Start() method for taskForMethod1? Instead, I used the Run() method from the Task class to execute Method1(). Why did I do that? Well, inside Task class, Run is a static method. The method summary in Visual Studio tells us the following about this Run method: "Queues the specified work to run on the thread pool and returns a System.Threading.Tasks.Task`1 object that represents that work." At the time of writing, this method has eight overloaded versions, as follows.

```
public static Task Run(Action action);
public static Task Run(Action action, CancellationToken cancellationToken);
public static Task<TResult> Run<TResult>(Func<TResult> function);
public static Task<TResult> Run<TResult>(Func<TResult> function,
CancellationToken cancellationToken);
public static Task Run(Func<Task> function);
public static Task Run(Func<Task> function, CancellationToken cancellationToken);
```

```
public static Task<TResult> Run<TResult>(Func<Task<TResult>> function);
public static Task<TResult> Run<TResult>(Func<Task<TResult>> function,
CancellationToken cancellationToken);
```

Now check another important point in this example. If you uncomment the following line

```
// Task taskForMethod3 = taskForMethod1.ContinueWith(Method3,
TaskContinuationOptions.OnlyOnRanToCompletion);
```

and run the application again, you can get an output similar to the following.

```
***Using Task-based Asynchronous Pattern.Using lambda expression into it.****
Inside Main().Thread ID:1
Method2() has started.
Inside Method1(),Task.id=1
Method1() has started.
Inside Method1(),Thread id 4 .
Inside Method2(),Thread id 1 .
Method2() is completed.
Method1() has completed its job now.
Task for Method1 was a : Success
Method3 starts now.
Task.id is:2 with Thread id is :5
Method3 for Task.id 2 and Thread id 5 is completed.
```

The ContinueWith() method helps continue a task. You may also note the following part.

TaskContinuationOptions.OnlyOnRanToCompletion

It simply states that the task will continue when taskForMethod1 completes its job. Similarly, you can opt for other options by using the TaskContinuationOptions enum, which has the following description.

```
public enum TaskContinuationOptions
{
    None = 0,
    PreferFairness = 1,
    LongRunning = 2,
    AttachedToParent = 4,
```

```
    DenyChildAttach = 8,
    HideScheduler = 16,
    LazyCancellation = 32,
    RunContinuationsAsynchronously = 64,
    NotOnRanToCompletion = 65536,
    NotOnFaulted = 131072,
    OnlyOnCanceled = 196608,
    NotOnCanceled = 262144,
    OnlyOnFaulted = 327680,
    OnlyOnRanToCompletion = 393216,
    ExecuteSynchronously = 524288
}
```

Q&A Session

6.11 Can I assign multiple tasks at a time?

Yes, you can. In the previously modified example, let's suppose that you have a method called Method4 with the following description.

```
private static void Method4(Task task)
{
    Console.WriteLine("Method4 starts now.");
    Console.WriteLine("Task.id is:{0} with Thread id is :{1} ",
    Task.CurrentId, Thread.CurrentThread.ManagedThreadId);
            Thread.Sleep(10);
    Console.WriteLine("Method4 for Task.id {0} and Thread id {1} is
    completed.", Task.CurrentId, Thread.CurrentThread.ManagedThreadId);
}
```

You can write the following lines.

```
Task<string> taskForMethod1 = Method1();
Task taskForMethod3 = taskForMethod1.ContinueWith(Method3,
TaskContinuationOptions.OnlyOnRanToCompletion);
 taskForMethod3 = taskForMethod1.ContinueWith(Method4,
TaskContinuationOptions.OnlyOnRanToCompletion);
```

This means that once taskForMethod1 completes the task, you see the continuation work with taskForMethod3, which executes both Method3 and Method4.

It is also important to note that continuation work can have continuation work. For example, let's suppose that you want the following.

- Once taskForMethod1 finishes, then to continue with taskForMethod3.

- Once taskForMethod3 finishes, then only to continue with taskForMethod4

You can write something similar to the following.

```
// Method1 starts
Task<string> taskForMethod1 = Method1();
// Task taskForMethod3 starts after Task taskForMethod1
Task taskForMethod3 = taskForMethod1.ContinueWith(Method3,
TaskContinuationOptions.OnlyOnRanToCompletion);
// Task taskForMethod4 starts after Task taskForMethod3
Task taskForMethod4 = taskForMethod3.ContinueWith(Method4,
TaskContinuationOptions.OnlyOnRanToCompletion);
```

Using the async and await Keywords

The use of async and await keywords makes the TAP pattern super flexible. This chapter has used two methods, in which the first method is a long-running method and takes more time to complete than the second method. I continue the case studies with the same Method1() and Method2() methods.

In the upcoming demonstration, I use async and await keywords. I start with a non-lambda version, but in the *analysis section*, I give the lambda expression *variant of the code.* First, let's look at Method1() again.

```
private static void Method1()
{
    Console.WriteLine("Method1() has started.");
    Console.WriteLine("Inside Method1(),Thread id {0} .", Thread.
    CurrentThread.ManagedThreadId);
```

```
    // Some big task
    Thread.Sleep(3000);
    Console.WriteLine("Method1() has completed its job now.");
}
```

When you use lambda expressions and an `async`/`await` pair, your code may look like the following.

```
// Using lambda expression
private static async Task ExecuteMethod1()
{
    await Task.Run(() =>
    {
        Console.WriteLine("Method1() has started.");
        Console.WriteLine("Inside Method1(),Thread id {0} .",
        Thread.CurrentThread.ManagedThreadId);
        // Some big task
        Thread.Sleep(3000);
        Console.WriteLine("Method1() has completed its job now.");
        }
        );
    }
```

Have you noticed that the synchronous version and the asynchronous version are very similar? But many of the earlier solutions to implement asynchronous programming were not like this. (I also believe that they were complex.)

What does await do? When you analyze the code, you find that once you get an `await`, the calling thread jumps out of the method and continues with something else. In the upcoming demonstration, `Task.Run is used;` it causes the asynchronous call to continue on a separate thread. *It should be noted, however, that this* does not mean that the continuation work should be done on a new thread, *because* you may not *always be concerned* about different threads; *for example, when your call is waiting to establish a connection over a network to download something.*

In the non-lambda version, I use the following block of code.

```
private static async Task ExecuteTaskOne()
{
    await Task.Run(Method1);
}
```

Inside `Main()`, instead of calling `Method1()`, `ExecuteTaskOne()` executes `Method1()` asynchronously. I passed `Method1` inside the Run method. I used the shortest overloaded version of the Run method here. Since `Method1` matches the signature of an `Action` delegate (remember that this delegate encapsulates any method with no parameter and `void` return type), you can pass it as an argument in the Run method of the `Task` class.

Demonstration 12

This is the complete demonstration.

```
using System;
using System.Threading;
using System.Threading.Tasks;

namespace UsingAsyncAwaitDemo
{
    class Program
    {
        static void Main(string[] args)
        {
            Console.WriteLine("***Exploring task-based asynchronous
            pattern(TAP) using async and await.****");
            Console.WriteLine("Inside Main().Thread ID:{0}",
            Thread.CurrentThread.ManagedThreadId);
            /*
             * This call is not awaited.So,the current method
             * continues before the call is completed.
             */
            ExecuteTaskOne();//Async call,this call is not awaited
            Method2();
```

```csharp
            Console.ReadKey();
        }
        private static async Task ExecuteTaskOne()
        {
            await Task.Run(Method1);
        }
        private static void Method1()
        {
            Console.WriteLine("Method1() has started.");
            Console.WriteLine("Inside Method1(),Thread id {0} .",
            Thread.CurrentThread.ManagedThreadId);
            // Some big task
            Thread.Sleep(3000);
            Console.WriteLine("Method1() has completed its job now.");
        }

        private static void Method2()
        {
            Console.WriteLine("Method2() has started.");
            Console.WriteLine("Inside Method2(),Thread id {0} .",
            Thread.CurrentThread.ManagedThreadId);
            Thread.Sleep(100);
            Console.WriteLine("Method2() is completed.");
        }
    }
}
```

Output

This is a possible output.

```
***Exploring task-based asynchronous pattern(TAP) using async and
await.****
Inside Main().Thread ID:1
Method1() has started.
Inside Method1(),Thread id 4 .
```

```
Method2() has started.
Inside Method2(),Thread id 1 .
Method2() is completed.
Method1() has completed its job now.
```

Analysis

You can see that Method1() started earlier but Method2()'s execution was not blocked for that. Also note that Method2() ran inside a main thread, whereas Method1() executed in a different thread.

Like previous cases, if you like lambda expressions, you could replace the following code segment:

```
private static async Task ExecuteTaskOne()
{
        await Task.Run(Method1);
}

private static void Method1()
{
        Console.WriteLine("Method1() has started.");
        Console.WriteLine("Inside Method1(),Thread id {0} .",
        Thread.CurrentThread.ManagedThreadId);
        // Some big task
        Thread.Sleep(3000);
        Console.WriteLine("Method1() has completed its job now.");
}
```

with this one:

```
// Using lambda expression
private static async Task ExecuteMethod1()
{
    await Task.Run(() =>
    {
            Console.WriteLine("Method1() has started.");
            Console.WriteLine("Inside Method1(),Thread id {0} .",
            Thread.CurrentThread.ManagedThreadId);
```

```
        // Some big task
        Thread.Sleep(3000);
        Console.WriteLine("Method1() has completed its job now.");
    }
    );
}
```

In demonstration 12, instead of calling ExecuteTaskOne(), you can directly call the ExecuteMethod1() method to get similar output.

In the previous example, you see a warning message for the following line: ExecuteMethod1(); which states the following.

```
Warning  CS4014  Because this call is not awaited, execution of the current
method continues before the call is completed. Consider applying the
'await' operator to the result of the call.
```

If you hover your mouse on this, you get two suggestions. First one suggests you to apply discard as follows:

```
_ = ExecuteMethod1(); // applying discard
```

Note   The discards are supported in C #7.0 onward. They are temporary, dummy, and unused variables in an application. Since these variables may not be in allocated storage, they can reduce memory allocation. These variables can enhance better readability and maintainability. Use an underscore (_) to indicate a discarded variable in your application.

The following uses the second suggestion and inserts await prior to the line.

```
await ExecuteMethod1();
```

The compiler raises another error in that case.

Error CS4033 The 'await' operator can only be used within an async method. Consider marking this method with the 'async' modifier and changing its return type to 'Task'.

To remove this error, you need to make the containing method async (i.e., start with the following line as follows:

```
static async Task Main(string[] args)
```

After applying the async/await pair, the Main() method may look like the following.

```
class Program
{
    // static void Main(string[] args)
    static async Task Main(string[] args)
    {
        Console.WriteLine("***Exploring task-based asynchronous
        pattern(TAP) using async and await.****");
        Console.WriteLine("Inside Main().Thread ID:{0}",
        Thread.CurrentThread.ManagedThreadId);
        await ExecuteMethod1();
        // remaining code
```

This overall discussion reminds you to apply async/await together and place them properly.

I finish the chapter with another demonstration, in which I slightly modify the calling sequence of the application. I use Method3(), which is similar to Method2(). This method is called from ExecuteTaskOne(), which has the following structure.

```
private static async Task ExecuteTaskOne()
{
    Console.WriteLine("Inside ExecuteTaskOne(), prior to await() call.");
    int value=await Task.Run(Method1);
    Console.WriteLine("Inside ExecuteTaskOne(), after await() call.");
    // Method3 will be called if Method1 executes successfully
    if (value != -1)
    {
        Method3();
    }
}
```

This segment of code simply says that I want to grab the return value from Method1(), and based on that value, I decide whether I call Method3() or not. This time, Method1()'s return type is not void; instead, it is returning an int (0 for successful completion; otherwise, –1). This method is restructured with a try-catch block like the following.

```
private static int Method1()
{
    int flag = 0;
    try
    {
        Console.WriteLine("Method1() has started.");
        Console.WriteLine("Inside Method1(),Thread id {0} .",
        Thread.CurrentThread.ManagedThreadId);
        // Some big task
        Thread.Sleep(3000);
        Console.WriteLine("Method1() has completed its job now.");
 }
 catch (Exception e)
 {
        Console.WriteLine("Caught Exception {0}", e);
        flag = -1;
 }
 return flag;
}
```

Now go through the following example.

Demonstration 13

This is the complete demonstration.

```
using System;
using System.Threading;
using System.Threading.Tasks;

namespace UsingAsyncAwaitDemo3
{
```

```csharp
class Program
{
    static void Main(string[] args)
    {
        Console.WriteLine("***Exploring task-based asynchronous
        pattern(TAP) using async and await.****");
        Console.WriteLine("***This is a modified example with three
        methods.***");
        Console.WriteLine("Inside Main().Thread ID:{0}",
        Thread.CurrentThread.ManagedThreadId);
        /*
         * This call is not awaited.So,the current method
         * continues before the call is completed.
         */
        _=ExecuteTaskOne();//Async call,this call is not awaited
        Method2();
        Console.ReadKey();
    }

    private static async Task ExecuteTaskOne()
    {
        Console.WriteLine("Inside ExecuteTaskOne(), prior to await()
        call.");
        int value=await Task.Run(Method1);
        Console.WriteLine("Inside ExecuteTaskOne(), after await()
        call.");
        // Method3 will be called if Method1 executes successfully
        if (value != -1)
        {
            Method3();
        }
    }

    private static int Method1()
    {
        int flag = 0;
        try
```

```csharp
        {
            Console.WriteLine("Method1() has started.");
            Console.WriteLine("Inside Method1(),Thread id {0} .",
            Thread.CurrentThread.ManagedThreadId);
            //Some big task
            Thread.Sleep(3000);
            Console.WriteLine("Method1() has completed its job now.");
        }
        catch (Exception e)
        {
            Console.WriteLine("Caught Exception {0}", e);
            flag = -1;
        }
        return flag;
    }
    private static void Method2()
    {
        Console.WriteLine("Method2() has started.");
        Console.WriteLine("Inside Method2(),Thread id {0} .",
        Thread.CurrentThread.ManagedThreadId);
        Thread.Sleep(100);
        Console.WriteLine("Method2() is completed.");
    }
private static void Method3()
{
    Console.WriteLine("Method3() has started.");
        Console.WriteLine("Inside Method3(),Thread id {0} .",
        Thread.CurrentThread.ManagedThreadId);
        Thread.Sleep(100);
        Console.WriteLine("Method3() is completed.");
    }
}
}
```

Output

```
***Exploring task-based asynchronous pattern(TAP) using async and await.****
***This is a modified example with three methods.***
Inside Main().Thread ID:1
Inside ExecuteTaskOne(), prior to await() call.
Method1() has started.
Inside Method1(),Thread id 4 .
Method2() has started.
Inside Method2(),Thread id 1 .
Method2() is completed.
Method1() has completed its job now.
Inside ExecuteTaskOne(), after await() call.
Method3() has started.
Inside Method3(),Thread id 4 .
Method3() is completed.
```

Analysis

Note the output closely. You can see that Method3() needs to wait for Method1()'s completion, but Method2() could finish its execution before Method1() ends its execution. Here Method3() can continue if the returned value from Method1() is not equal to –1. This scenario is similar to the case in which you saw the ContinueWith() method in demonstration11.

Most importantly, note the following line of code once more.

```
int value=await Task.Run(Method1);
```

It simply divides the code segment into two parts: *prior call to await* and *post call to await*. This syntax is similar to any synchronous call, but by using await (inside an async method), you apply a suspension point and use the power of asynchronous programming.

I finish this chapter with some interesting notes from Microsoft. They are handy as you further explore the async/await keywords. Remember the following points.

- The await operator cannot be present in the body of a lock statement.

- You may see multiple `awaits` inside the body of an `async` method. The absence of `await` inside an `async` method will not raise any compile-time error. Instead, you get a warning, and the method executes in a synchronous fashion. Note the following warning in a similar context: `Warning CS1998 This async method lacks 'await' operators and will run synchronously. Consider using the 'await' operator to await non-blocking API calls, or 'await Task.Run(...)' to do CPU-bound work on a background thread.`

Final Words

Another big chapter! Hopefully, I was able to demystify the different approaches to asynchronous programming. Although the `IAsyncResult` pattern and `event-based asynchrony` are no longer recommended for future developments, I discussed them in this chapter to help you understand legacy code and show you the evolution of asynchronous programs. Undoubtedly, you'll find it useful in the future.

Now you are ready to jump into the vast ocean of asynchronous programming and explore the remaining corner cases, which can't be mastered without self-practice. So, keep pressing on.

You have seen many applications based on delegates, events, and lambda expressions so far! Now let's move into the final chapter, which is on database programming. It is a little different but very useful and interesting.

Summary

This chapter addressed the following key questions.

- What is an asynchronous program? How is it different from a synchronous program?

- How do you write an asynchronous program using the `Thread` class?

- What is a thread pool? How do you write an asynchronous program using the `ThreadPool` class?

- How do you use lambda expressions inside an asynchronous program?

- How do you write asynchronous programs following an Event-based Asynchronous Pattern?

- What is a task? How can you use the `Task` class in your program?

- How do you write asynchronous programs following a Task-based Asynchronous Pattern?

- How do you write an asynchronous program using the `async/await` keywords?

- How do you use discards in your application?

- What are some important restrictions when you use the `async/await` keywords in your program?

CHAPTER 7

Database Programming

C# client applications can talk to a database using ADO.NET. Collectively, it is a set of classes (often called a *framework*) that can help you connect a datasource, such as an XML file or a database. Using these classes (and the corresponding methods), you can manipulate the required data. It is another big topic, but I limit the discussion to how a simple C# application can talk to a RDBMS (relational database management system) using SQL queries.

When I talk about RDBMS, there are multiple choices. For example, Oracle, Microsoft SQL Server, and MySQL are some of the key players. In fact, in many books, ADO.NET is discussed with Microsoft SQL Server. In this chapter, MySQL is the preferred relational database. But the good news is that the underlying approach doesn't change much when you choose a different option (for example, Microsoft SQL Server).

There are alternative approaches for talking to a database. For example, instead of using ADO.NET, a developer can chose Entity Framework (EF), which is based on object-relational mapping (ORM). So, instead of directly writing SQL queries, they deal with classes (or objects) and use LINQ queries. Although a detailed discussion is beyond the scope of this chapter, it may be useful to know that since EF is built on top of ADO.NET, it isn't faster than using ADO.NET (but it can make your code development faster and neatly organized). Also, when you troubleshoot data access issues, understanding the core responsibilities of ADO.NET can make programming easier.

To experience database programming, you need to be familiar with the following concepts.

- What a database is and how it helps you store or organize data

- How a database is connected

- How a C# application talks to a database (i.e, how you establish a connection to a database, and how you insert, update, or delete a record in a database)

© Vaskaran Sarcar 2020
V. Sarcar, *Getting Started with Advanced C#*, https://doi.org/10.1007/978-1-4842-5934-4_7

Figure 7-1 presents a simplified view of the overall process of a client application (a C# program) and a database connecting using ADO.NET.

Note   You can store data in various ways; for example, you use a database, you may store the data in text files, and so forth. In this chapter, I use the terms *data store* and *database* interchangeably.

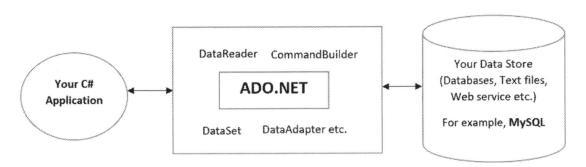

Figure 7-1.   Connecting a C# application to a database through ADO.NET

If you are new to database programming, you may need to learn the key terms, which are covered briefly in this chapter. I recommend that you go over these definitions repeatedly to better understand them. Gradually, these terms will become clearer to you.

Database and DBMS

A *database* is an organized collection of data. For example, depending on its type, a database can be a collection related files (or, tables). A *table* can be a collection of related records where each *record* can be a collection of related fields. A *field* is the smallest piece of meaningful information in a file (or, table).

A *database management system* (DBMS) creates and manages databases effectively. Oracle Database, SQL Server, MySQL, and MS Access are popular DBMS packages.

In general, a collection of databases, DBMS, and corresponding applications can form a database system.

Types of DBMS

There are different types of DBMS, including the following.

- Hierarchical DBMS (HDBMS)

- Network DBMS (NDBMS)

- Relational DBMS (RDBMS)

- Object-oriented database (OODB)

- Distributed DBMS (DDBMS)

Each has its own pros and cons. Selecting a database depends on your needs. Rather than choosing a SQL data structure (which is suitable for a RDBMS), you may prefer NoSQL (a nonrelational structure suitable for a DDBMS). In this chapter, you see the usage of a RDBMS and simple SQL statements only.

RDBMS

In a RDBMS, data is stored in rows and columns, which is similar to tables. You may see common terms, such as *relation*, *tuple*, and *attribute*. When you use SQL, formal relational model terms—*relations*, *tuples*, and *attributes*—are used for tables, rows, and columns, respectively.

Each row of a table contains a record. Each column contains fields. The table shown in Figure 7-2 marks all the records and attributes.

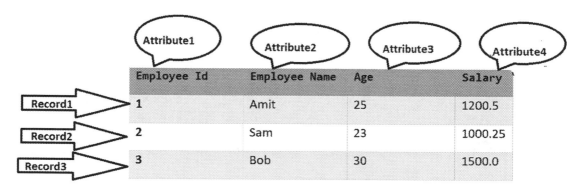

Figure 7-2. *A sample table is marked with records and attributes*

You can process different records of a relation based on a mathematical formulation known as *relational algebra*. Since the entire database can be processed using it, relational algebra is the theoretical foundation for relational databases and SQL.

Oracle Database, MySQL, Microsoft SQL Server, and IBM DB2 are common examples of RDBMS; in this chapter, I use MySQL to demonstrate the examples.

Note   Appendix A includes the steps to install MySQL in a Win10 machine.

SQL

SQL stands for Structured Query Language. It is a very popular and widely used RDBMS language. It is an English-like language and considered a fourth-generation language. Create data, update data, read data, and delete data are the most common operations with SQL.

POINTS TO REMEMBER

- C#, Java, C++, and C are examples of general-purpose languages. Each is commonly categorized as a third-generation language (3GL), whereas SQL is known as 4GL. In 3GL, the focus is on "How do I solve a problem?" but in 4GL, the focus is on "What results do I want?" but instead of supplying the means, you have freedom to let your computer/machine to decide how to obtain it. Although an advance 3GL can combine some of the important aspects of 4GL.

- It is important to note that SQL does not differentiate between uppercase and lowercase character sets, but most often it is necessary to use uppercase keywords.

- Simple SQL statements are used in various programs in this chapter. If you are new to SQL, I recommend that you do exersices with simple SQL statements in your preferred database to get a better idea before you further proceed.

I assume that you have installed MySQL on your local computer. If it is not installed yet, go to https://dev.mysql.com/downloads/installer/ to download the installer and learn relevant information. You can also refer to Appendix A, which includes the steps to install MySQL in a Win10 machine.

When I wrote a similar chapter on a different technology for another book, mysql-installer-community-8.0.16.0 was the latest version. But as I went forward, updates kept coming, and I kept updating. Finally, I settled on 8.0.19.

Installing the database is a first step. Then you need a vendor-specific connector. I used MySQL, and the .NET Framework. I searched for a connector suitable for me. I went to `https://dev.mysql.com/downloads/connector/net/`, as shown in Figure 7-3.

Connector/NET 8.0.19

Select Operating System:

| Microsoft Windows | ▼ |

Recommended Download:

MySQL Installer
for Windows

All MySQL Products. For All Windows Platforms.
In One Package.

Starting with MySQL 5.6 the MySQL installer package replaces the standalone MSI packages.

Windows (x86, 32 & 64-bit), MySQL Installer MSI   Go to Download Page >

Other Downloads:

| Windows (x86, 32-bit), MSI Installer | 8.0.19 | 3.2M | Download |

(mysql-connector-net-8.0.19.msi)   MD5: 963929710291e727ded35e4a589ee91b | Signature

Figure 7-3. *Download the connector*

Once you have downloaded the zipped file, extract it to get the connector. It is highly recommended that you visit the official website (`https://dev.mysql.com/doc/connector-net/en/connector-net-versions.html`) to learn more about .NET connectors. I can't resist mentioning the following interesting points.

- There are several versions of MySQL Connector/NET available.

- The official website says that MySQL Connector/NET 8.0 is a continuation of Connector/NET 7.0, and currently named to synchronize the first digit of the version number with the (highest) MySQL server version it supports.

- MySQL Connector/NET 8.0 is highly recommended for use with MySQL Server 8.0, 5.7, and 5.6. Based on your system configuration, you may need to upgrade and use the proper version of the connector. It's worth looking at the table on the website, as shown in Figure 7-4, before you proceed.

Connector/NET Version	ADO.NET Version	.NET Version Required	MySQL Server	Supported?
8.0	2.x+	• C/NET 8.0.18+: .NET Core 3.0 for VS 2019 (version 16.3 or higher) • C/NET 8.0.17+: .NET Core 2.2 for VS 2017 (version 15.0.9 or higher), .NET Core 2.1 for VS 2017 (version 15.0.7 or higher) • C/NET 8.0.10+: .NET Core 2.0 for VS 2017 (version 15.0.3 or higher) • C/NET 8.0.8+: .NET Framework 4.5.x for VS 2013 / 2015 / 2017	8.0, 5.7, 5.6	Yes
6.10	2.x+	• C/NET 6.10.9+: .NET Core 2.2 for VS 2017 (version 15.0.9 or higher), .NET Core 2.1 for VS 2017 (version 15.0.7 or higher) • C/NET 6.10.5+: .NET Core 2.0 for VS 2017 (version 15.0.3 or higher)	8.0, 5.7, 5.6	Upgrade to 8.0

Figure 7-4. *Connector/NET requirement for related products (Source: https://dev.mysql.com/doc/connector-net/en/connector-net-versions.html)*

- The version of Visual Studio installed on my computer is 16.3.9. The MySQL version is 8.0.18. I used .NET Core 3.0 for many of the examples in this book. So, it makes sense to use connector version 8.0 and higher.

- Once installed, you need to add a MySql.Data.dll reference to your project. On my machine, I used C:\Program Files (x86)\MySQL\ MySQL Connector Net 8.0.19\Assemblies\v4.5.2. Once you do this, to verify the information, open the Properties window. Note the arrow in Figure 7-5. It is an ADO.NET driver for MySQL for .NET Framework and .NET Core.

MySql.Data Reference Properties

(Name)	MySql.Data
Aliases	global
Copy Local	True
Culture	
Description	ADO.Net driver for MySQL for .Net Framework and .Net Core
Embed Interop Types	False
File Type	Assembly
Identity	MySql.Data
Path	C:\Program Files (x86)\MySQL\MySQL Connector Net 8.0.19\A
Resolved	True
Runtime Version	v4.0.30319
Specific Version	False
Strong Name	True

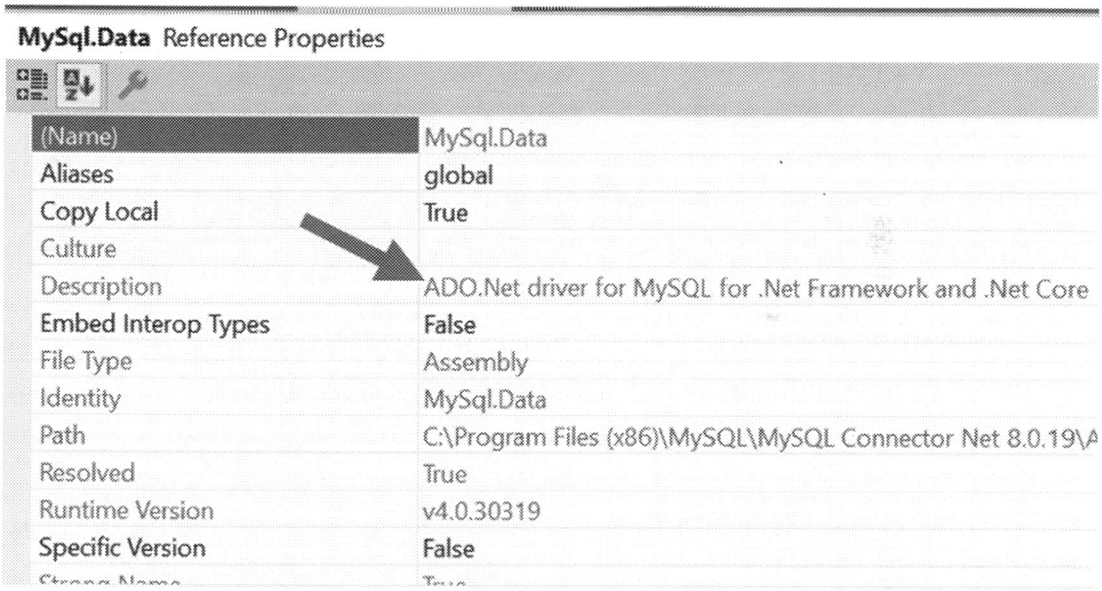

Figure 7-5. *MySql.Data is the ADO.NET for MySQL for .NET Framework and .NET Core*

- If you use .NET Core, you may need to install a MySql.Data package before you proceed. You can use Visual Studio to add the package. Or, you can go to Tools ➤ NuGet Package Manager ➤ Package Manger Console and type the following command (the version may differ in your case):

```
PM> Install-Package MySql.Data -Version 8.0.19
```

Once you do it properly, you see a screen similar to Figure 7-6.

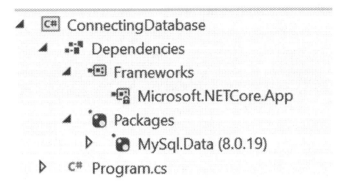

Figure 7-6. MySql.Data is added successfully in the .NET Core application

A Brief Discussion of ADO.NET

Since I'm going to use ADO.NET in upcoming demonstrations, let's have a quick discussion about it. First, it is an object-oriented framework and very flexible. In traditional approaches, you must open a connection to connect a database, and then exercise simple SQL queries. Your application is always connected to the database. As a result, even if you do not use the data store, expensive database resources are used, which reduce the overall performance and efficiency of your application.

To overcome this, ADO.NET also supports *disconnected data architecture*, which says that when you need to run a SQL query, you connect to the database, get the result, and disconnect the connection immediately. To hold these results, you use a local buffer, called a DataSet. But keep in mind that ADO.NET can support the traditional connection-oriented services too, and there you use a DataReader. In this chapter, I show you both a traditional connection-oriented implementation and its counterpart disconnected data architecture implementation.

Note   ADO stands for ActiveX Data Objects. But Microsoft's COM-based data access model (ADO) is different from ADO.NET. Yes, there are some similarities (for example, Command and Connection objects) but they are largely different. Many ADO.NET types do not have a direct equivalent in ADO (e.g., DataAdapter). ADO has a small number of datatypes that support the COM standard; whereas ADO. NET is made for .NET applications that connect databases, and it supports a large number of datatypes.

Understanding the Code

In C#, there are lots of classes, interfaces, methods, and properties involved in database programming. A detailed description of each of them is not essential at this level. (Honestly, if you start with the detailed descriptions of all these terms, it may bore you. They are remembered with practice.) So, let's focus on the part that is necessary to understand in the upcoming demonstrations.

In the first two demonstrations, I use a connection-oriented architecture. In this approach, your codebase explicitly connects to the data store, and once the data processing is done, it disconnects from the data store. You commonly see the use of Connection objects, Command objects, and DataReader objects.

In the third demonstration, you see the use of disconnected data architecture. In this approach, you first see a DataSet object, which can store the tables, the relationships, and the constraints (that are applied on the tables). Once you obtain this object, you can use it to traverse or manipulate the data and use it as a client-side copy (i.e., local copy). A user can make changes to the local copies and apply the changes to the actual database later. This approach speeds up data processing. It reduces network traffic and improves the overall performance of the application.

In ADO.NET, you do not see single sets of objects to connect different DBMSes; instead, there are various data providers. These providers are optimized to connect a specific DBMS, such as Oracle, MySQL, and Microsoft SQL Server. For example, Microsoft provides specialized and optimized classes for SQL Server databases. These classes start with *Sql* and are contained in System.Data.SqlClient.

Similarly, in our case, the class names start with *MySql*; for example, MySqlConnection, MySqlCommandBuilder, and MySqlDataReader. To use these classes in my program, the following namespace is needed.

```
using MySql.Data.MySqlClient;
```

You can correctly assume that each provider gives you a set of types in a namespace. To use these types in your program, you need to include the corresponding namespace and install the correct NuGet package (you learned the steps to install a MySql.Data package in your program). At this stage, it doesn't matter which database management system you choose. In general, to support the core functionalities of database programming, each provider offers similar classes and interfaces. You get a better idea of this when you see the demonstrations.

First, let me introduce you to some common types of objects that are frequently used in database programming, summarized as follows.

- `Connection` object: Connects and disconnects a data store.

- `Command` object: Represents SQL queries and stores procedures. (Stored procedures are discussed later.)

- `DataReader` object: Reads data from a database in a connected architecture.

- `DataAdapter` object: Connects to a database, fetches records from it, and fills a local buffer (`DataSet`). In a disconnected architecture, its role is vital.

- `Parameter` object: Represents parameters in a parameterized query.

Although the specific names of the core classes for each provider differ, since the classes are inherited from the same base classes and implement identical interfaces, you can assume how to work with a vendor-specific database. For example, since I'm using a MySQL database, you see the use of `MySqlConnection`, `MySqlDataReader`, and `MySqlCommand` in my programs.

Similarly, other vendors provide names that follow a general naming convention. Each provider prefixes the name of the related DBMS with their constructs. So, if you connect to a SQL server, you may see the use of `SqlConnection`, `SqlDataReader`, `SqlCommand`, and so forth, in a similar context.

It is interesting to note that there is no class named `Connection`. The same holds true for other objects, such as `Command` objects, `DataAdapter` objects, and so forth. So, in these contexts, you only see the vendor-specific names (for example, `MySqlConnection`, `MySqlCommandBuilder`, `MySqlDataReader`, etc.).

Let's start coding. In the upcoming demonstration, you see the following lines of code.

```
static MySqlConnection mySqlConnection = null;
static MySqlCommand mySqlCommand = null;
static MySqlDataReader mySqlDataReader = null;
```

Let's focus on these three elements: `MySqlConnection`, `MySqlCommand`, and `MySqlDataReader`. I used "static" variables, but this is not required. To share the common copies and to avoid repeated initialization in different methods, I made them static in these programs.

Note   There are partial/full screenshots from Visual Studio IDE for your immediate reference. I explain the important characteristics.

MySqlConnection

MySqlConnection is a sealed class that inherits DbConnection. Figure 7-7 is a partial screenshot from Visual Studio IDE for the MySqlConnection class.

```
namespace MySql.Data.MySqlClient
{
    ...public sealed class MySqlConnection : DbConnection, ICloneable
    {
        ...public MySqlConnection();
        ...public MySqlConnection(string connectionString);

        ~MySqlConnection();
```

Figure 7-7. *Partial screenshot of MySqlConnection class from Visual Studio 2019*

If you go deep, you see that DbConnection derives from IDbConnection. Figure 7-8 is a partial screenshot from Visual Studio IDE for the DbConnection class.

```
namespace System.Data.Common
{
    //
    // Summary:
    //     Represents a connection to a database.
    public abstract class DbConnection : Component, IDbConnection, IDisposable
    {
        ...protected DbConnection();
```

Figure 7-8. *Partial screenshot of DbConnection class from Visual Studio 2019*

IDbConnection is contained in the System.Data namespace, and it has the methods shown in Figure 7-9.

```
namespace System.Data
{
    //
    // Summary:
    //     Represents an open connection to a data source, and is implemented by .NET Framework
    //     data providers that access relational databases.
    public interface IDbConnection : IDisposable
    {
        string ConnectionString { get; set; }
        int ConnectionTimeout { get; }
        string Database { get; }
        ConnectionState State { get; }

        IDbTransaction BeginTransaction();
        IDbTransaction BeginTransaction(IsolationLevel il);
        void ChangeDatabase(string databaseName);
        void Close();
        IDbCommand CreateCommand();
        void Open();
    }
}
```

Figure 7-9. *Partial screenshot of IDbConnection interface from Visual Studio 2019*

These interface members configure a connection to a specific data store. You can always expand the method description to see information about the method. But at a high level, you can see that a data provider type needs to override the abstract class methods or implement the interface methods. MySqlConnection is doing this.

MySqlCommand

MySqlCommand is a sealed class that inherits from DbCommand. Figure 7-10 is a partial screenshot from Visual Studio IDE for the MySqlCommand class.

```
namespace MySql.Data.MySqlClient
{
    public sealed class MySqlCommand : DbCommand, IDisposable, ICloneable
    {
        public MySqlCommand();
        public MySqlCommand(string cmdText);
        public MySqlCommand(string cmdText, MySqlConnection connection);
        public MySqlCommand(string cmdText, MySqlConnection connection, MySqlTransaction transaction);

        ~MySqlCommand();
```

Figure 7-10. *Partial screenshot of MySqlCommand class from Visual Studio 2019*

DbCommand is an abstract class that provides a base class for database-specific classes that represent various commands. It contains a method called ExecuteReader() with the following description.

```
//
// Summary:
//      Executes the System.Data.Common.DbCommand.CommandText against the
//      System.Data.Common.DbCommand.Connection,
//      and returns an System.Data.Common.DbDataReader.
//
// Returns:
//      A System.Data.Common.DbDataReader object.
public DbDataReader ExecuteReader();
```

The MySqlCommand class overrides this method. In demonstration 1, you see the usage of this class in the following segment of code.

```
mySqlCommand = new MySqlCommand(sqlQuery,mySqlConnection);
mySqlDataReader = mySqlCommand.ExecuteReader();
```

From this segment, you can see that I'm making a MySqlCommand object using the following line.

```
mySqlCommand = new MySqlCommand(sqlQuery,mySqlConnection);
```

In the partial screenshot of the MySqlCommand class, there are four overloaded constructor versions available. In this code segment, I used the following version.

```
// Summary:
//      Initializes a new instance of the MySql.Data.MySqlClient.
//      MySqlCommand class with the text of the query and a MySql.Data.
//      MySqlClient.MySqlConnection.
//(Other details omitted)
public MySqlCommand(string cmdText, MySqlConnection connection);
```

Then I used the ExecuteReader() method to build a MySqlDataReader object.

MySqlDataReader

MySqlDataReader is a sealed class that extends DbDataReader, IDataReader,
IDataRecord, and IDisposable. Figure 7-11 is a partial screenshot from VS2019; it shows
information about MySqlDataReader.

```
public sealed class MySqlDataReader : DbDataReader, IDataReader, IDataRecord, IDisposable
{
    ~MySqlDataReader();
```

Figure 7-11. *Partial screenshot of MySqlDataReader class from Visual
Studio 2019*

The class members help you read a forward-only stream of rows from a MySQL
database. In other words, once you get an object of MySqlDataReader, you can iterate
over the results in a read-only and forward-only manner. The word *forward-only* means
that once you point to record 2, you cannot go back to record 1, and so on.

Figure 7-12 shows a summary of IDataReader.

```
//
// Summary:
//     Provides a means of reading one or more forward-only streams of result sets obtained
//     by executing a command at a data source, and is implemented by .NET Framework
//     data providers that access relational databases.
public interface IDataReader : IDataRecord, IDisposable
{
    ...  int Depth { get; }
    ...  bool IsClosed { get; }
    ...  int RecordsAffected { get; }

    ...  void Close();
    ...  DataTable GetSchemaTable();
    ...  bool NextResult();
    ...  bool Read();
}
```

Figure 7-12. *Partial screenshot of IDataReader interface from Visual Studio 2019*

You can see that IDataReader extends the IDataRecord interface, which contains
many methods. The interface definition tells us that these methods can access the
column values within each row of a DataReader. You can also extract a strongly typed
value from a stream.

In demonstration 1, you see the Close() and Read() methods. The Close() method closes the DataReader object and the Read() method helps the DataReader object advance to the next record, if possible.

IRecord methods are not used in the upcoming demonstrations, but I'm including a Visual Studio screenshot that can help you in future implementations. Figure 7-13 shows the summary of the IDataRecord interface.

```
//
// Summary:
//     Provides access to the column values within each row for a DataReader, and is
//     implemented by .NET Framework data providers that access relational databases.
[DefaultMember("Item")]
public interface IDataRecord
{
    object this[string name] { get; }
    object this[int i] { get; }

    int FieldCount { get; }

    bool GetBoolean(int i);
    byte GetByte(int i);
    long GetBytes(int i, long fieldOffset, byte[] buffer, int bufferoffset, int length);
    char GetChar(int i);
    long GetChars(int i, long fieldoffset, char[] buffer, int bufferoffset, int length);
    IDataReader GetData(int i);
    string GetDataTypeName(int i);
    DateTime GetDateTime(int i);
    decimal GetDecimal(int i);
    double GetDouble(int i);
    Type GetFieldType(int i);
    float GetFloat(int i);
    Guid GetGuid(int i);
    short GetInt16(int i);
    int GetInt32(int i);
    long GetInt64(int i);
    string GetName(int i);
    int GetOrdinal(string name);
    string GetString(int i);
    object GetValue(int i);
    int GetValues(object[] values);
    bool IsDBNull(int i);
```

Figure 7-13. Partial screenshot of IDataRecord interface from Visual Studio 2019

Implementing Connection-Oriented Architecture

Now you are ready to implement a connection-oriented model. To connect to a MySQL database using a C# application, you need to have a `MySqlConnection` object and a connection string. A connection string may contain several key-value pairs, separated by semicolons. In each key/value pair, the option name and its corresponding value are joined by an equals sign. In the next demonstration, you see the following line of code.

```
connectMe = "server=localhost;database=test;username=root;password=admin";
mySqlConnection = new MySqlConnection(connectMe);
```

mySqlConnection is an instance of `MySqlConnection`. This line simply states that I'm going to use a MySqlConnection object, which is configured to connect to a MySQL server at the `localhost` (the server). The database name is *test*, the username is *root*, and the password is *admin*.

In demonstration 1, inside `Main()`, you see the presence of the following three methods.

```
// Open the database connection i.e. connect to a MySQL database.
ConnectToMySqlDatabase();
// Display details of Employee table.
DisplayRecordsFromEmployeeTable();
// Close the database connection.
CloseDatabaseConnection();
```

From the names of these methods and supporting comments, it's easy to assume that I'm opening a connection to the MySQL database using a C# application, then I'm retrieving information from a table called Employee, and finally, I'm closing the connection. In this example, all the methods are surrounded by `try-catch` blocks. It's a recommended practice. Once you encounter an exception, this structure can help you analyze the situation better.

The `Open()` and `Close()` methods are used to open and close a connection in this program. The details of the `Open()` method in the `MySqlConnection` class show the following.

```
public override void Open();
```

This simply says that the vendor has overridden the Open() method of DbConnection, in which Open() was declared as an abstract method, as follows.

```
//
// Summary:
//     When overridden in a derived class, opens a database connection with
//     the settings specified by the System.Data.Common.DbConnection.
//     ConnectionString.public abstract void Open();
```

The Close() method is also overridden in the MySqlConnection class, but it closes a database connection.

Inside the DisplayRecordsFromEmployeeTable() method, you see the MySqlCommand object and the ExecuteReader() method.

mySqlDataReader.Close(); closes the DataReader object when it finishes reading all the records in the Employee table.

In many cases, you see a Windows Forms application for similar programs. When you use Windows Forms (WPF, ASP.NET, UWP, etc.), you get a better layout, and you can beautify the work by using various controls. But those beautifications are not of interest in this chapter. For almost all the programs in this book, I used console applications, and I maintain the same here.

Demonstration 1

This is the complete demonstration.

```
using System;
using MySql.Data.MySqlClient;

namespace ConnectingDatabase
{
    class Program
    {
        static string connectMe = String.Empty;
        static MySqlConnection mySqlConnection = null;
        static MySqlCommand mySqlCommand = null;
        static MySqlDataReader mySqlDataReader = null;
        static void Main(string[] args)
```

```
{
    Console.WriteLine("***Demonstration-1.Connecting and retrieving
    details from a MySQL database table.***");
    try
    {
        /* Open the database connection i.e. connect to a  MySQL
        database.*/
        ConnectToMySqlDatabase();
        // Display details of Employee table.
        DisplayRecordsFromEmployeeTable();
        // Close the database connection.
        CloseDatabaseConnection();
    }
    catch (Exception ex)
    {
        Console.WriteLine("Caught exception.Here is the problem
        details.");
        Console.WriteLine(ex.Message);
    }
    Console.ReadKey();
}

private static void DisplayRecordsFromEmployeeTable()
{
    try
    {
        string sqlQuery = "select * from Employee ;";
        mySqlCommand = new MySqlCommand(sqlQuery,mySqlConnection);
        mySqlDataReader = mySqlCommand.ExecuteReader();
        Console.WriteLine("EmployeeId\t" + "EmployeeName\t" +
        "Age\t" + "Salary");
        Console.WriteLine("_____");
        while (mySqlDataReader.Read())
        {
            Console.WriteLine(mySqlDataReader["EmpId"]
            + "\t\t" + mySqlDataReader["Name"] +
```

```
                "\t\t" + mySqlDataReader["Age"] + "\t" +
                mySqlDataReader["Salary"]);
            }
            mySqlDataReader.Close();
        }
        catch (MySqlException ex)
        {
            Console.WriteLine("Cannot show the records.Here is the
            problem details.");
            Console.WriteLine(ex.Message);
        }
    }

    private static void ConnectToMySqlDatabase()
    {
        try
        {
            connectMe = "server=localhost;database=test;username=root;
            password=admin";
            mySqlConnection = new MySqlConnection(connectMe);
            mySqlConnection.Open();
            Console.WriteLine("Connection to MySQL successful.");
        }
        catch (MySqlException ex)
        {
            Console.WriteLine("Could not connect to the database.Here
            is the problem details.");
            Console.WriteLine(ex.Message);
        }
    }
    private static void CloseDatabaseConnection()
    {
```

```
        try
        {
            mySqlConnection.Close();
        }
        catch (MySqlException ex)
        {
            Console.WriteLine("Could not close the connection.Here is
            the problem details.");
            Console.WriteLine(ex.Message);
        }
    }
  }
}
```

Output

This is the output.

```
***Demonstration-1.Connecting and retrieving details from a MySQL database
table.***
Connection to MySQL successful.
EmployeeId      EmployeeName    Age     Salary
```

EmployeeId	EmployeeName	Age	Salary
1	Amit	25	1200.5
2	Sam	23	1000.25
3	Bob	30	1500

Analysis

At first, the connection is established between the C# application and the MySQL database; and then information from the Employee table could be retrieved. Since it is a connection-oriented architecture, after you fetch records from the database, you cannot close the connection. To test this, let's modify the following block of code and assume that you invoke the CloseDatabaseConnection() method, as follows.

```
while (mySqlDataReader.Read())
{
```

```
Console.WriteLine(mySqlDataReader["EmpId"] + "\t\t" +
mySqlDataReader["Name"] + "\t\t" + mySqlDataReader["Age"] + "\t" +
mySqlDataReader["Salary"]);
// Closing the connection
CloseDatabaseConnection();
}
```

If you execute the program, you get the following output.

```
***Demonstration-1.Connecting and retrieving details from a MySQL database
table.***
Connection to MySQL successful.
EmployeeId      EmployeeName    Age     Salary


1               Amit            25      1200.5
Cannot show the records. Here is the problem details.
Invalid attempt to Read when reader is closed.
```

In demonstration 3, you learn how to continue your work after the connection is closed.

Demonstration 2

Demonstration 1 showed you how to establish a connection, close a connection, and retrieve information from a table in a database. This demonstration introduces three more methods: one to insert a record in the table, one to delete a record from the table, and one to update the table. They are named InsertNewRecordIntoEmployeeTable(), DeleteRecordFromEmployeeTable(), and UpdateExistingRecordIntoEmployeeTable(), respectively.

The program is straightforward, but I want highlight the following points.

- Once the job is done, each method invokes the DisplayRecordsFromEmployeeTable() method to show the current status of the table.

303

- When deleting a record, you saw a way to accept user-provided input from the keyboard. You can refer to the following lines of code in a similar context:

```
mySqlCmd = new MySqlCommand("Delete from employee where
name=@NameToBeDeleted", mySqlConnection);
mySqlCmd.Parameters.AddWithValue("@NameToBeDeleted",
empNameToDelete);
mySqlCmd.Prepare();
mySqlCmd.ExecuteNonQuery();

mySqlCmd is an object of MySqlCmd.
```

- Inside the DeleteRecordFromEmployeeTable() method in the following segment of code, you see a comment prior to the line of code.

```
/* If deletion performs successfully, print this message.*/
Console.WriteLine("One record is deleted from employee table.");
```

- I used this to indicate that I had not validated the user input. For simplicity, I did not include the verification, but you may need to employ similar verification for all the methods. I leave that simple exercise to you. (Still, in demonstration 4, a simple verification is employed after performing a delete operation.)

- In the UpdateExistingRecordIntoEmployeeTable() method, I updated Bob's salary twice. Initially, I changed it to 3000.75, and later I reset it to the old value: 1500.00. I did this to keep the table's original values. In real-world programming, it's better to make a backup of the original table. If needed, you can use the backup table. You can make a backup in various ways. But here we are dealing with a single table called Employee. So, in this case, you can use the following query to create another table (let's say, employee_backup) from an existing employee table and use it as you wish.

```
create table employee_backup as (select * from employee);
```

- It is important to note a situation. The prior command copies the table with data, but it does not copy other database objects, like primary key, foreign key, indexes, and so forth. (If you do not know the keys, please refer to Q&A 7.9). To copy data from an existing table and all the dependent objects, you may use the following two commands (here I assume that you are creating the Employee table by copying employee_backup. I'm also checking whether the table already exists before creating it):

```
create table if not exists employee like employee_backup;
insert employee select * from employee_backup;
```

Now go through the complete demonstration.

```
using System;
using MySql.Data.MySqlClient;

namespace ExercisingSqlCommands
{
    class Program
    {
        static string connectMe = String.Empty;
        static MySqlConnection mySqlConnection = null;
        static MySqlDataReader mySqlDataReader = null;
        static MySqlCommand mySqlCommand = null;
        static void Main(string[] args)
        {
            Console.WriteLine("***Demonstration-2.Connecting and retrieving
            details from a MySQL database table.***");
            try
            {
                /* Open the database connection i.e. connect to a MySQL
                database.*/
                ConnectToMySqlDatabase();
                // Display details of Employee table.
                DisplayRecordsFromEmployeeTable();
```

```csharp
            #region insert and delete a record
            // Insert a new record in Employee table.
            InsertNewRecordIntoEmployeeTable();
            // Delete a record from the Employee table.
            DeleteRecordFromEmployeeTable();
            #endregion

            #region Update and reset a record
            /*
            First updating a record and then resetting the value. So,
            basically there are two updates.
            */
            UpdateExistingRecordIntoEmployeeTable();
            #endregion

            //Close the database connection.
            CloseDatabaseConnection();
        }
        catch (Exception ex)
        {
            Console.WriteLine("Caught exception.Here is the problem
            details.");
            Console.WriteLine(ex.Message);
        }
        Console.ReadKey();
    }

    private static void UpdateExistingRecordIntoEmployeeTable()
    {
        try
        {
            Console.WriteLine("Updating Bob's salary to 3000.75");

            mySqlCommand = new MySqlCommand("update Employee set
            Salary=3000.75 where name='Bob';", mySqlConnection);
            mySqlCommand.ExecuteNonQuery();

            // If update performs successfully , print this message.
```

```
        Console.WriteLine("One record is updated in employee
        table.");
        Console.WriteLine("Here is the current table:");
        DisplayRecordsFromEmployeeTable();

        Console.WriteLine("Now resetting Bob's salary to 1500.00");
        mySqlCommand = new MySqlCommand("update Employee set
        Salary=1500.00 where name='Bob';", mySqlConnection);
        mySqlCommand.ExecuteNonQuery();

        // If update performs successfully , print this  message.
        Console.WriteLine("One record is updated in employee
        table.");
        Console.WriteLine("Here is the current table:");
        DisplayRecordsFromEmployeeTable();

    }
    catch (MySqlException ex)
    {
        Console.WriteLine("Cannot update the record.Here is the
        problem details.");
        Console.WriteLine(ex.Message);

    }
}

private static void DeleteRecordFromEmployeeTable()
{
    try
    {
        Console.WriteLine("Enter the employee name to be deleted
        from Employee table.");
        string empNameToDelete = Console.ReadLine();
        /* Additional validation required to confirm the employee
        name exists in the table.
        Or, whether its a valid entry or not.
        */
```

```
            mySqlCmd = new MySqlCommand("Delete from employee where
            name=@NameToBeDeleted", mySqlConnection);
            mySqlCmd.Parameters.AddWithValue("@NameToBeDeleted",
            empNameToDelete);
            mySqlCmd.Prepare();
            mySqlCmd.ExecuteNonQuery();

            /* If deletion performs successfully , print this message.*/
            Console.WriteLine("One record is deleted from employee
            table.");
            Console.WriteLine("Here is the current table:");
            DisplayRecordsFromEmployeeTable();
        }
        catch (MySqlException ex)
        {
            Console.WriteLine("Cannot delete the record.Here is the
            problem details.");
            Console.WriteLine(ex.Message);
        }
    }

    private static void InsertNewRecordIntoEmployeeTable()
    {
        try
        {
            mySqlCommand = new MySqlCommand("insert into Employee
            values(4,'John',27,975);", mySqlConnection);
            mySqlCommand.ExecuteNonQuery();
            Console.WriteLine("New record insertion successful.");
            Console.WriteLine("Here is the current table:");
            DisplayRecordsFromEmployeeTable();
        }
        catch (MySqlException ex)
```

```
        {
            Console.WriteLine("Cannot insert the new record.Here is the
            problem details.");
            Console.WriteLine(ex.Message);
        }
}

private static void DisplayRecordsFromEmployeeTable()
{
    try
    {
        string sqlQuery = "select * from Employee ;";
        mySqlCommand = new MySqlCommand(sqlQuery, mySqlConnection);
        mySqlDataReader = mySqlCommand.ExecuteReader();
        Console.WriteLine("EmployeeId\t" + "EmployeeName\t" +
        "Age\t" + "Salary");
        Console.WriteLine("_____");
        while (mySqlDataReader.Read())
        {
            Console.WriteLine(mySqlDataReader["EmpId"]
            + "\t\t" + mySqlDataReader["Name"] +
            "\t\t" + mySqlDataReader["Age"] + "\t" +
            mySqlDataReader["Salary"]);
        }
        mySqlDataReader.Close();
    }
    catch (MySqlException ex)
    {
        Console.WriteLine("Cannot show the records.Here is the
        problem details.");
        Console.WriteLine(ex.Message);
    }
}
private static void ConnectToMySqlDatabase()
```

```
        {
            try
            {
                connectMe = "server=localhost;database=test;username=root;
                password=admin";
                mySqlConnection = new MySqlConnection(connectMe);
                mySqlConnection.Open();
                Console.WriteLine("Connection to MySQL successful.");
            }
            catch (MySqlException ex)
            {
                Console.WriteLine("Could not connect to the database.Here
                is the problem details.");
                Console.WriteLine(ex.Message);
            }
        }
        private static void CloseDatabaseConnection()
        {
            try
            {
                mySqlConnection.Close();
            }
            catch (MySqlException ex)
            {
                Console.WriteLine("Could not close the connection.Here is
                the problem details.");
                Console.WriteLine(ex.Message);
            }
        }
    }
}
```

Demonstration-2.Connecting and retrieving details from a MySQL database table.

Connection to MySQL successful.

EmployeeId	EmployeeName	Age	Salary
1	Amit	25	1200.5
2	Sam	23	1000.25
3	Bob	30	1500

New record insertion successful.

Here is the current table:

EmployeeId	EmployeeName	Age	Salary
1	Amit	25	1200.5
2	Sam	23	1000.25
3	Bob	30	1500
4	John	27	975

Enter the employee name to be deleted from Employee table.

John

One record is deleted from employee table.

Here is the current table:

EmployeeId	EmployeeName	Age	Salary
1	Amit	25	1200.5
2	Sam	23	1000.25
3	Bob	30	1500

Updating Bob's salary to 3000.75

One record is updated in employee table.

Here is the current table:

EmployeeId	EmployeeName	Age	Salary
1	Amit	25	1200.5
2	Sam	23	1000.25
3	Bob	30	3000.75

```
Now resetting Bob's salary to 1500.00
One record is updated in employee table.
Here is the current table:
```

EmployeeId	EmployeeName	Age	Salary
1	Amit	25	1200.5
2	Sam	23	1000.25
3	Bob	30	1500

Implementing Disconnected Data Architecture

Now it's time to show you a demo of a disconnected data architecture (also known as a *disconnected layer*). Demonstration 3 is made for this purpose. Here, you see the DataTable, DataRow, and DataSet classes. To get these classes, you need to include the following namespace.

```
using System.Data;
```

System.Data is at the core of the ADO.NET assembly. This namespace contains other important classes, likc DataColumn, DataRelation, and Constraint (it is an abstract class) as well. The following is a brief description of each of them.

- DataSet: It is your local buffer (in-memory cache), which is a collection of tables or record sets.

- DataTable: It contains data in tabular form using rows and columns.

- DataRow: It represents a single row (i.e., record) in a DataTable.

- DataColumn: It represents a column in a DataTable.

- DataRelation: It represents the parent/child relationship between two DataTable objects.

- Constraint: It represents the limitations that are enforced on one or more DataColumn objects.

In this demonstration, you see the following lines of code.

```
static MySqlDataAdapter mySqlDataAdapter = null;
static MySqlCommandBuilder mySqlCommandBuilder = null;
```

So, let's look at them.

MySqlDataAdapter

`MySqlDataAdapter` is a sealed class, so you cannot make another class that inherits from it. The class summary states that it represents a set of data commands and a database connection that you use to fill a dataset and update a MySQL database. Let's see what VS2019 says. Figure 7-14 is a partial screenshot of the `MySqlDataAdapter` class.

```
namespace MySql.Data.MySqlClient
{
    ...public sealed class MySqlDataAdapter : DbDataAdapter, IDbDataAdapter, IDataAdapter
    {
        ...public MySqlDataAdapter();
        ...public MySqlDataAdapter(MySqlCommand selectCommand);
        ...public MySqlDataAdapter(string selectCommandText, MySqlConnection connection);
        ...public MySqlDataAdapter(string selectCommandText, string selectConnString);

        public override int UpdateBatchSize { get; set; }
        ...public MySqlCommand UpdateCommand { get; set; }
        ...public MySqlCommand SelectCommand { get; set; }
        ...public MySqlCommand InsertCommand { get; set; }
        ...public MySqlCommand DeleteCommand { get; set; }
```

Figure 7-14. *Partial screenshot of MySqlDataAdapter class from Visual Studio 2019*

Figure 7-14 tells you that `MySqlDataAdapter` inherits from `DbAdpater`, `IDbDataAdapter`, and `IDataAdapter`. The naming convention indicates that `IDbDataAdapter` and `IDataAdapter` are two interfaces. Let's look at the summaries of these interfaces. Figure 7-15 is a screenshot of `IDbDataAdapter`.

```
namespace System.Data
{
    //
    // Summary:
    //     Represents a set of command-related properties that are used to fill the System.Data.DataSet
    //     and update a data source, and is implemented by .NET Framework data providers
    //     that access relational databases.
    public interface IDbDataAdapter : IDataAdapter
    {
        ...IDbCommand SelectCommand { get; set; }
        ...IDbCommand InsertCommand { get; set; }
        ...IDbCommand UpdateCommand { get; set; }
        ...IDbCommand DeleteCommand { get; set; }
    }
}
```

Figure 7-15. *Partial screenshot of IDbDataAdapter interface from Visual Studio 2019*

You can see that `IDbDataAdapter` has four properties, which are used to select, insert, update, or delete records from a database. Figure 7-15 shows that `IDataAdapter` is the parent of `IDbDataAdapter`.

Figure 7-16 is a screenshot from VS2019; it shows a summary of `IDataAdapter`.

```
namespace System.Data
{
    //
    // Summary:
    //     Allows an object to implement a DataAdapter, and represents a set of methods
    //     and mapping action-related properties that are used to fill and update a System.Data.DataSet
    //     and update a data source. System.Data.IDbDataAdapter instances are for data sources
    //     that are (or resemble) relational databases with textual commands (like Transact-SQL),
    //     while System.Data.IDataAdapter instances could can use any type of data source.
    public interface IDataAdapter
    {
        MissingMappingAction MissingMappingAction { get; set; }
        MissingSchemaAction MissingSchemaAction { get; set; }
        ITableMappingCollection TableMappings { get; }

        int Fill(DataSet dataSet);
        DataTable[] FillSchema(DataSet dataSet, SchemaType schemaType);
        IDataParameter[] GetFillParameters();
        int Update(DataSet dataSet);
    }
}
```

Figure 7-16. *Partial screenshot of IDataAdapter interface from Visual Studio 2019*

In this interface, you can see properties as well as methods. The `Fill`, `FillSchema`, and `Update` methods are very common when you implement a disconnected data architecture. In demonstration 3, you see these methods. The following segment of code from demonstration 3 shows the `Fill` and `FillSchema` methods.

```
// Retrieve details from 'Employee' table
mySqlDataAdapter.FillSchema(localDataSet, SchemaType.Source, "Employee");
mySqlDataAdapter.Fill(localDataSet, "Employee");
```

Prior to using the `Fill()` method, you may need to call `FillSchema()`, which allows you to match the schema of the source table. It is important when you insert a new record offline in your `DataTable`.

In many applications, you may only see the `Fill()` method. In those applications, the `Fill()` method is the most important method because it is the step where the `DataAdapter` object connects to a physical database and fetches the query result (in this example, we called `FillSchema()` prior to `Fill()`).

In this interface, you can see the `TableMappings` property, which maps database column names (from a source table) to more user-friendly display names (to a dataset table).

Lastly, `DbDataAdapter` is an abstract class that inherits from the previous two interfaces. The Method summary states that this class aids the implementation of the `IDbDataAdapter` interface. Figure 7-17 is a partial screenshot from Visual Studio IDE for the `DbDataAdapter` class.

```
namespace System.Data.Common
{
    //
    // Summary:
    //     Aids implementation of the System.Data.IDbDataAdapter interface. Inheritors of
    //     System.Data.Common.DbDataAdapter implement a set of functions to provide strong
    //     typing, but inherit most of the functionality needed to fully implement a DataAdapter.
    public abstract class DbDataAdapter : DataAdapter, IDbDataAdapter, IDataAdapter, ICloneable
    {
        ...public const string DefaultSourceTableName = "Table";

        ...protected DbDataAdapter();
        ...protected DbDataAdapter(DbDataAdapter adapter);

        ...public DbCommand SelectCommand { get; set; }
        ...public DbCommand InsertCommand { get; set; }
        ...public DbCommand DeleteCommand { get; set; }
```

Figure 7-17. *Partial screenshot of DbDataAdapter class from Visual Studio 2019*

MySqlCommandBuilder

`MySqlCommandBuilder` is a sealed class that inherits from `DbCommandBuilder`. The class summary states that it automatically generates single-table commands to reconcile changes made to a `DataSet` with the associated MySQL database.

Figure 7-18 is a partial screenshot of `MySqlCommandBuilder` from Visual Studio IDE.

```
using System.ComponentModel;
using System.Data;
using System.Data.Common;

namespace MySql.Data.MySqlClient
{
    ...public sealed class MySqlCommandBuilder : DbCommandBuilder
    {
        ...public MySqlCommandBuilder();
        ...public MySqlCommandBuilder(MySqlDataAdapter adapter);

        ...public MySqlDataAdapter DataAdapter { get; set; }

        ...public static void DeriveParameters(MySqlCommand command);
        ...public MySqlCommand GetDeleteCommand();
        ...public MySqlCommand GetInsertCommand();
        ...public MySqlCommand GetUpdateCommand();
```

Figure 7-18. *Partial screenshot of MySqlCommandBuilder class from Visual Studio 2019*

In demonstration 3, you see the following lines when you want to reflect your local changes to the actual database.

```
mySqlCommandBuilder = new MySqlCommandBuilder(mySqlDataAdapter);
Console.WriteLine("Syncing with remote database table");
mySqlDataAdapter.Update(localDataSet, "Employee");
```

Here, mySqlDataAdapter is an object of MySqlDataAdapter.

Demonstration 3

This demonstration displays the records from the Employee table, inserts a new record, and then deletes a record. To easily understand the operations, the methods are named DisplayRecordsFromEmployeeTable, InsertRecordIntoEmployeeTable, and DeleteRecordIntoEmployeeTable, respectively. If you go through the class descriptions and the discussions prior to this demonstration, you should have no trouble understanding the code—apart from the following segment of code.

```
// Creates a new record with the same schema as the table
DataRow currentRow = localDataTable.NewRow();
currentRow["EmpId"] = 4;
currentRow["Name"] = "Jack";
currentRow["Age"] = 40;
currentRow["Salary"] = 2500.75;
// Add this record to local table
localDataTable.Rows.Add(currentRow);
```

Yes, you guessed it! The supportive comments tell you that this is a way to add a record to a table. There is an alternative approach that can do the same, however. For example, the following code segment also works in this context.

```
// Also works
currentRow[0] = 4;
currentRow[1] = "Jack";
currentRow[2] = 40;
currentRow[3] = 2500.75;
```

You can choose your preferred approach. If you want to do less typing, choose the second approach. If you want better readability, choose the first one.

Now go through the complete demonstration and the corresponding output.

```
using System;
using System.Data;
using MySql.Data.MySqlClient;

namespace ConnectingDatabase
{
    class Program
    {
        static string connectMe = String.Empty;
        static string sqlCommand = String.Empty;
        static MySqlDataAdapter mySqlDataAdapter = null;
        static MySqlCommandBuilder mySqlCommandBuilder = null;
        static DataSet localDataSet = null;
```

```csharp
static void Main(string[] args)
{
    Console.WriteLine("***Connecting and retrieving details from a
    MySQL database table.***");
    Console.WriteLine("***Testing the disconnected architecture
    now.***");

    try
    {
        // Get a local copy of Employee table
        DataTable localDataTable = CreateLocalTable();
        //Display from the client-side(local)table.
        DisplayRecordsFromEmployeeTable(localDataTable);
        /* Insert a new record into local table and sync it with
        the database*/
        InsertRecordIntoEmployeeTable(localDataTable);
        Console.WriteLine("**After Inserting a record into the
        Employee table...**");
        DisplayRecordsFromEmployeeTable(localDataTable);
        /* Delete an existing record from local table and sync it
        with the database. */
        DeleteRecordIntoEmployeeTable(localDataTable);
        Console.WriteLine("**After deleting a record into the
        Employee table...**");
        DisplayRecordsFromEmployeeTable(localDataTable);
    }
    catch (Exception ex)
    {
        Console.WriteLine("Caught exception.Here is the problem
        details.");
        Console.WriteLine(ex.Message);
    }
    Console.ReadKey();
}
```

```csharp
private static void DeleteRecordIntoEmployeeTable(DataTable
localDataTable)
{
    try
    {
        Console.WriteLine("Now deleting the record for EmpId4.");
        DataTable dataTable = localDataSet.Tables["Employee"];
        // Deleting a record
        DataRow deleteRow = dataTable.Rows.Find(4);
        deleteRow.Delete();

        //If deletion performs successfully, print this message.

        Console.WriteLine("Successfully deleted the record from
        local buffer where EmpId was 4.");
        // Apply the change to MySQL
        mySqlCommandBuilder = new MySqlCommandBuilder(mySqlData
        Adapter);
        Console.WriteLine("Syncing with remote database table");
        mySqlDataAdapter.Update(localDataSet, "Employee");
        Console.WriteLine("Successfullly updated the remote
        table.\n");
    }
    catch (MySqlException ex)
    {
        Console.WriteLine("Could not delete the record.Here is the
        problem details.");
        Console.WriteLine(ex.Message);
    }
}
```

```
private static void InsertRecordIntoEmployeeTable(DataTable
localDataTable)
{
    try
    {
        /* Creates a new record with the same schema as the
        table.*/
        DataRow currentRow = localDataTable.NewRow();
        currentRow["EmpId"] = 4;
        currentRow["Name"] = "Jack";
        currentRow["Age"] = 40;
        currentRow["Salary"] = 2500.75;
        // Add this record to local table
        localDataTable.Rows.Add(currentRow);
        Console.WriteLine("Successfully added a record into local
        buffer.");
        int noOfRecords = localDataTable.Rows.Count;
        Console.WriteLine("Local table currently has {0} number of
        records.", noOfRecords);
        // Apply the change to MySQL
        mySqlCommandBuilder = new MySqlCommandBuilder(mySqlData
        Adapter);
        Console.WriteLine("Syncing with remote database table");
        mySqlDataAdapter.Update(localDataSet, "Employee");
        Console.WriteLine("Successfullly updated the remote
        table");
    }
    catch (MySqlException ex)
    {
        Console.WriteLine("Could not insert the record.Here is the
        problem details.");
        Console.WriteLine(ex.Message);
    }

}
```

```
private static void DisplayRecordsFromEmployeeTable(DataTable
localDataTable)
{
    try
    {
        int noOfRecords = localDataTable.Rows.Count;
        Console.WriteLine("Here is the table for you:");
        Console.WriteLine("EmployeeId\t" + "EmployeeName\t" +
        "Age\t" + "Salary");
        Console.WriteLine("_____");
        for (int currentRow = 0; currentRow < noOfRecords;
        currentRow++)
        {
            Console.WriteLine(
                localDataTable.Rows[currentRow]["EmpId"] + "\t\t" +
                localDataTable.Rows[currentRow]["Name"] + "\t\t" +
                localDataTable.Rows[currentRow]["Age"] + "\t" +
                localDataTable.Rows[currentRow]["Salary"]
                );
        }
    }
    catch (MySqlException ex)
    {
        Console.WriteLine("Cannot show the records.Here is the
        problem details.");
        Console.WriteLine(ex.Message);
    }
}

private static DataTable CreateLocalTable()
{
    connectMe = "datasource=localhost;port=3306;database=test;
    username=root;password=admin";
    sqlCommand = "select * from Employee";
    mySqlDataAdapter = new MySqlDataAdapter(sqlCommand, connectMe);
    // Also works
```

```
            //mySqlConnection = new MySqlConnection(connectMe);
            //mySqlDataAdapter = new MySqlDataAdapter(sqlCommand,
            mySqlConnection);

            // Create a DataSet instance
            /* I recommend you to use the following overloaded constructor
            of DataSet to use.*/
            localDataSet = new DataSet("LocalDataSet");
            // Retrieve details from 'Employee' table
            mySqlDataAdapter.FillSchema(localDataSet, SchemaType.Source,
            "Employee");
            mySqlDataAdapter.Fill(localDataSet, "Employee");
            // Create new instance of DataTable
            DataTable dataTable = localDataSet.Tables["Employee"];
            int noOfRecords = dataTable.Rows.Count;
            Console.WriteLine("Created a local DataTable.Total number of
            records in this table is:{0}", noOfRecords);
            return dataTable;
        }
    }
}
```

Output

This is the output.

```
***Connecting and retrieving details from a MySQL database table.***
***Testing the disconnected architecture now.***
Created a local DataTable.Total number of records in this table is:3
Here is the table for you:
EmployeeId      EmployeeName     Age      Salary

_____

1               Amit             25       1200.5
2               Sam              23       1000.25
3               Bob              30       1500
Successfully added a record into local buffer.
Local table currently has 4 number of records.
```

Syncing with remote database table
Successfullly updated the remote table
After Inserting a record into the Employee table...
Here is the table for you:

EmployeeId	EmployeeName	Age	Salary
1	Amit	25	1200.5
2	Sam	23	1000.25
3	Bob	30	1500
4	Jack	40	2500.75

Now deleting the record for EmpId4.
Successfully deleted the record from local buffer where EmpId was 4.
Syncing with remote database table
Successfullly updated the remote table.

After deleting a record into the Employee table...
Here is the table for you:

EmployeeId	EmployeeName	Age	Salary
1	Amit	25	1200.5
2	Sam	23	1000.25
3	Bob	30	1500

Programming with Stored Procedures

You have seen the use of SQL statements inside all the previous programs. This is fine when you start learning database programming. But this approach has a potential drawback. Using these plain SQL statements, you are exposing the database schema (design) inside the code, which can be changed. This is why in real-world applications, you normally see the use of stored procedures rather than plain SQL statements.

Stored procedures have the following characteristics.

- They are precompiled executable objects.

- You can use one or multiple SQL statements inside a stored procedure.

- Any complex SQL statements can be replaced with a stored procedure.

- They can accept input and return output.

It is already said that I'm using simple SQL statements to demonstrate the idea of database programming in this chapter and if you are new to SQL, I recommended you doing exercises with SQL statements in your preferred database to be familiar with SQL statements. I suggest the same with stored procedures.

Now I'll show you how to replace SQL statements with simple stored procedures.

For demonstration purposes, let's go back to demonstration 1 or demonstration 2. There you saw the use of select, insert, update, and delete SQL statements. In the next demonstration, I replace the select, insert, and delete statements with stored procedures. The remaining case, update, is very easy. I leave that exercise to you.

Now, let's start.

Note   Appendix A includes the complete commands needed to create these stored procedures in the MySQL database. If needed, you can refer to them.

Stored Procedure to Select Records

In my database, I created the following stored procedure, called GetAllEmployees, to replace the select query in demonstration 1 or demonstration 2.

```
DELIMITER $
CREATE PROCEDURE GetAllEmployees()
    BEGIN
        SELECT * FROM EMPLOYEE;
    END $
DELIMITER ;
```

Stored Procedure to Insert One Record

In my database, I created the following stored procedure, called InsertOneNewRecord, to replace the insert query in demonstration 2. This stored procedure inserts a record with predefined values.

```
DELIMITER $
CREATE PROCEDURE InsertOneNewRecord()
    BEGIN
        insert into Employee values(4,'John',27,975);
    END $
DELIMITER ;
```

Stored Procedure to Delete One Record

In my database, I created the following stored procedure, called DeleteOneRecord, to replace the delete query in demonstration 2. This stored procedure deletes a record based on the user's input.

```
DELIMITER //
CREATE PROCEDURE DeleteOneRecord(
  IN NameToBeDeleted varchar(10)
)
BEGIN
  Delete from employee where Name=NameToBeDeleted;
END //
DELIMITER;
```

Note   You can choose the delimiter. Note that in the first two stored procedures, I used $ as a delimiter, but in the last one, I used //.

One Simple Verification

For simplicity and to reduce the code size, I told you to implement your own verification method after different operations. In this demonstration, I show you a simple verification technique using the following code segment (inside the DeleteRecordFromEmployeeTable() method).

```
if (mySqlCommand.ExecuteNonQuery() == 1)
{
        // If deletion performs successfully , print this message.
        Console.WriteLine("One record is deleted from employee table.");
}
else
{
        Console.WriteLine("Couldn't delete the record from employee table.");
}
```

If you see ExecuteNonQuery() method description in Visual Studio IDE, you get the following information.

```
//
// Summary:
//      Executes a SQL statement against the connection and returns the
//      number of rows affected.
//
// Returns:
//      Number of rows affected
//
// Remarks:
//      You can use ExecuteNonQuery to perform any type of database
//      operation, however any resultsets returned will not be available.
//      Any output parameters used in calling a stored procedure will be
//      populated with data and can be retrieved after execution is
//      complete. For UPDATE, INSERT, and DELETE statements, the return
//      value is the number of rows affected by the command. For all other
//      types of statements,the return value is -1.
public override int ExecuteNonQuery();
```

This description is self-explanatory. You can easily use this method for your own verification purposes.

Demonstration 4

Here is the complete demonstration. The method names and operations are similar to demonstration 2, but this time, simple stored procedures are used. I suggest that you refer to the associated comments to get a better understanding.

```
using System;
using System.Data;
using MySql.Data.MySqlClient;

namespace UsingStoredProcedures
{
    class Program
    {
        static string connectMe = String.Empty;
        static MySqlConnection mySqlConnection = null;
        static MySqlCommand mySqlCommand = null;
        static MySqlDataReader mySqlDataReader = null;
        static void Main(string[] args)
        {
            Console.WriteLine("***Demonstration-4.Using stored procedure
            now.***");
            try
            {
                /* Open the database connection i.e. connect to a  MySQL
                database*/
                ConnectToMySqlDatabase();
                // Display details of Employee table.
                DisplayRecordsFromEmployeeTable();
                // Insert a new record in Employee table.
                InsertNewRecordIntoEmployeeTable();
                // Delete a record from the Employee table.
                DeleteRecordFromEmployeeTable();
                // Close the database connection.
                CloseDatabaseConnection();
            }
```

```csharp
        catch (Exception ex)
        {
            Console.WriteLine("Caught exception.Here is the problem
            details.");
            Console.WriteLine(ex.Message);
        }
        Console.ReadKey();
    }

    private static void DisplayRecordsFromEmployeeTable()
    {
        try
        {
            #region old code( which you saw in previous demonstrations)
            //string sqlQuery = "select * from Employee ;";
            //mySqlCommand = new MySqlCommand(sqlQuery,
            mySqlConnection);
            #endregion
            #region new code
            //The following lines are moved to a common place
            //mySqlCommand = new MySqlCommand();
            //mySqlCommand.Connection = mySqlConnection;
            mySqlCommand.CommandText = "SelectAllEmployees";//Using
            Stored Procedure
            mySqlCommand.CommandType = CommandType.StoredProcedure;
            #endregion
            mySqlDataReader = mySqlCommand.ExecuteReader();
            Console.WriteLine("EmployeeId\t" + "EmployeeName\t" +
            "Age\t" + "Salary");
            Console.WriteLine("_____");
            while (mySqlDataReader.Read())
            {
                Console.WriteLine(mySqlDataReader["EmpId"] +
                "\t\t" + mySqlDataReader["Name"] +
                "\t\t" + mySqlDataReader["Age"] + "\t" +
                mySqlDataReader["Salary"]);
```

```
        }
        mySqlDataReader.Close();
    }
    catch (MySqlException ex)
    {
        Console.WriteLine("Cannot show the records.Here is the
        problem details.");
        Console.WriteLine(ex.Message);
    }
}
private static void InsertNewRecordIntoEmployeeTable()
{
    try
    {
        // Old code (you saw in demonstration 2)
        //mySqlCommand = new MySqlCommand("insert into Employee
        values(4,'John',27,975);", mySqlConnection);

        #region new code
        //The following lines are moved to a common place

        //mySqlCommand = new MySqlCommand();
        //mySqlCommand.Connection = mySqlConnection;
        mySqlCommand.CommandText = "InsertOneNewrecord";
        // Using Stored Procedure
        mySqlCommand.CommandType = CommandType.StoredProcedure;
        #endregion

        mySqlCommand.ExecuteNonQuery();
        Console.WriteLine("New record insertion successful.");
        Console.WriteLine("Here is the current table:");
        DisplayRecordsFromEmployeeTable();
    }
    catch (MySqlException ex)
    {
        Console.WriteLine("Cannot insert the new record.Here is the
        problem details.");
```

```
            Console.WriteLine(ex.Message);
        }
    }
    private static void DeleteRecordFromEmployeeTable()
    {
        try
        {
            Console.WriteLine("Enter the employee name to be deleted
            from Employee table.");
            string empNameToDelete = Console.ReadLine();

            #region new code
            MySqlParameter deleteParameter = new MySqlParameter("NameTo
            BeDeleted", MySqlDbType.VarChar);
            mySqlCommand.CommandType = CommandType.StoredProcedure;
            mySqlCommand.CommandText = "DeleteOneRecord";
            // Using Stored Procedure
            /* The following code segment will also work but  in that
            case ,you have to add the value to the parameter  first.*/
            //deleteParameter.Value = empNameToDelete;
            //mySqlCommand.Parameters.Add(deleteParameter);
            mySqlCommand.Parameters.AddWithValue("NameToBeDeleted",
            empNameToDelete);

            #endregion
            if (mySqlCommand.ExecuteNonQuery()==1)
            {
            // If deletion performs successfully , print this message.
                Console.WriteLine("One record is deleted from employee
                table.");
            }
            else
            {
                Console.WriteLine("Couldn't delete the record from
                employee table.");
            }
```

```csharp
        Console.WriteLine("Here is the current table:");
        DisplayRecordsFromEmployeeTable();

    }
    catch (MySqlException ex)
    {
        Console.WriteLine("Cannot delete the record.Here is the
        problem details.");
        Console.WriteLine(ex.Message);
    }
}

private static void ConnectToMySqlDatabase()
{
    try
    {
        // The following will also work
        //connectMe = "datasource=localhost;port=3306;database=test;
        username=root;password=admin";
        connectMe = "server=localhost;database=test;username=root;
        password=admin";
        mySqlConnection = new MySqlConnection(connectMe);
        mySqlConnection.Open();
        Console.WriteLine("Connection to MySQL successful.");
        // Initializing Command here to remove duplicate codes.
        mySqlCommand = new MySqlCommand();
        mySqlCommand.Connection = mySqlConnection;
    }
    catch (MySqlException ex)
    {
        Console.WriteLine("Could not connect to the database.Here
        is the problem details.");
        Console.WriteLine(ex.Message);
    }
}
```

```
        private static void CloseDatabaseConnection()
        {
            try
            {
                mySqlConnection.Close();
            }
            catch (MySqlException ex)
            {
                Console.WriteLine("Could not close the connection.Here is
                the problem details.");
                Console.WriteLine(ex.Message);
            }
        }
    }
}
```

Output

This is the output.

```
***Demonstration-4.Using stored procedure now.***
Connection to MySQL successful.
EmployeeId      EmployeeName    Age     Salary


1               Amit            25      1200.5
2               Sam             23      1000.25
3               Bob             30      1500
New record insertion successful.
Here is the current table:
EmployeeId      EmployeeName    Age     Salary


1               Amit            25      1200.5
2               Sam             23      1000.25
3               Bob             30      1500
4               John            27      975
Enter the employee name to be deleted from Employee table.
```

```
John
One record is deleted from employee table.
Here is the current table:
EmployeeId      EmployeeName    Age     Salary

1               Amit            25      1200.5
2               Sam             23      1000.25
3               Bob             30      1500
```

Q&A Session

7.1 Instead of giving a single set of objects to communicate with various databases, why does ADO.NET support different providers to connect to different databases?

Here are some important benefits that you can get by using this approach.

- A specific provider can help you directly connect to a specific database. As a result, you do not need to support any intermediate layers between the caller and the data store.

- A provider has special and unique features for a specific database. You get the benefit of this specialized support.

7.2 What is the benefit of using a disconnected data architecture in ADO.NET?

In most real-world applications, the required data stays at a remote computer, and you connect to that computer through a network. In disconnected data architecture, once you get the DataSet object, the required data stays in your local machine, so you can access the data quickly. At the same time, since you do not need the Internet connection to access the local data, you can reduce network traffic. As a result, the overall performance of your application is enhanced.

Lastly, you can make any change to the local data and do your own experiments. It is up to you whether you want to reflect those changes in the actual database or not (by calling the Update() method of the adapter). Doing an experiment on an actual database is obviously not a good idea.

7.3 In demonstration 3, you called `FillSchema()` **prior to the** `Fill()` **method in the following code segment. Was this necessary?**

```
// Retrieve details from 'Employee' table
mySqlDataAdapter.FillSchema(localDataSet, SchemaType.Source, "Employee");
mySqlDataAdapter.Fill(localDataSet, "Employee");
```

It's a better practice. To include the constraints from an existing table, I included this line of code. In a case like this, you have two options: use the `FillSchema` method of the `DataAdapter`, or set the `MissingSchemaAction` property of the `DataAdapter` to `AddWithKey` before calling the `Fill` method. In our example, if `FillSchema()` is not used, the line should be commented as follows.

```
//mySqlDataAdapter.FillSchema(localDataSet, SchemaType.Source, "Employee");
```

If you run the application again, you get an exception prior to the delete operation that says *that the t*able doesn't have a primary key.

If you are interested in learning more about these methods, visit `https://docs.microsoft.com/en-us/dotnet/framework/data/adonet/adding-existing-constraints-to-a-dataset`.

7.4 What is a stored procedure?

If you want to repeat a sequence of tasks, create a stored procedure. It's a subroutine (or a subprogram) stored in a database. In our examples, a stored procedure can have a name, parameters, and SQL statements; it is very similar to a method in C#. The steps to create a stored procedure can vary across databases. In this chapter, you were shown three stored procedures in demonstration 4 to serve our needs.

7.5 A stored procedure is similar to a function. Is this correct?

There are some significant differences in stored procedures and functions. For example, in MySQL, a stored procedure can return one or multiple values, or no values at all; whereas a function always returns a single value.

7.6 How can I create a function? A simple demo can help me.

This is a SQL query to create a function called **AddNumbers**:

```
mysql> create function AddNumbers(firstNumber double,secondNumber double) returns double deterministic return firstNumber+secondNumber;
```

Query OK, 0 rows affected (0.45 sec)

The following query confirms the details of the function:

```
mysql> Select Routine_name as "Function Name", routine_Definition as
"Definition", Routine_Schema "Schema", Data_Type as "Types", Created
From  Information_Schema.Routines Where Routine_Name='AddNumbers' and
Routine_Type= 'FUNCTION';
Here is an output:
+---------------+------------------------+--------+--------+-------------------+
| Function Name | Definition             | Schema | Types  | CREATED           |
+---------------+------------------------+--------+--------+-------------------+
| AddNumbers    | return firstNumber+
                  secondNumber           | test   | double | 2020-03-17 10:13:20 |
+---------------+------------------------+--------+--------+-------------------+
1 row in set (0.00 sec)
```

Figure 7-19 is a compact view.

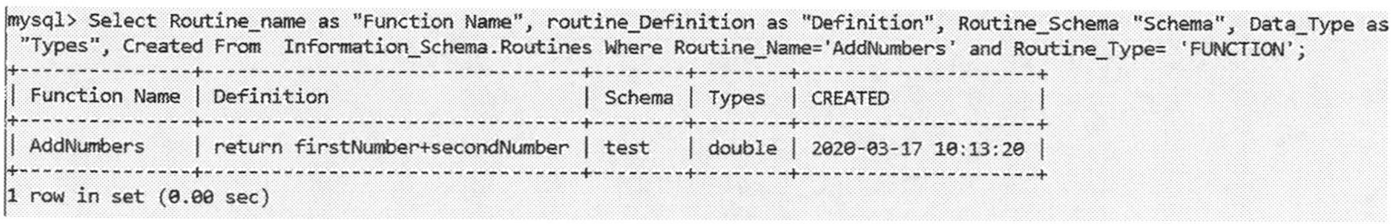

```
mysql> Select Routine_name as "Function Name", routine_Definition as "Definition", Routine_Schema "Schema", Data_Type as
 "Types", Created From  Information_Schema.Routines Where Routine_Name='AddNumbers' and Routine_Type= 'FUNCTION';
+---------------+----------------------------------+--------+--------+---------------------+
| Function Name | Definition                       | Schema | Types  | CREATED             |
+---------------+----------------------------------+--------+--------+---------------------+
| AddNumbers    | return firstNumber+secondNumber  | test   | double | 2020-03-17 10:13:20 |
+---------------+----------------------------------+--------+--------+---------------------+
1 row in set (0.00 sec)
```

***Figure 7-19.** Once the Function called AddNumbers is created in MySQL, the screenshot is taken from the MySQL command prompt.*

Or, you can see all the functions in your current database by using the following query.

```
mysql> show function status where db='test';
```

Now let's execute the function. A function can be invoked in various ways. Here is a sample query with output.

```
mysql> select AddNumbers(25,45) as "Total";
```

```
+-------+
| Total |
+-------+
|    70 |
+-------+
1 row in set (0.00 sec)
```

7.7 I saw the term DDL in the context of SQL in some places. What does it mean?

SQL commands are commonly classified among the following.

- DDL (data definition language) statements create or modify a database object's structure. You use create, alter, drop, and truncate statements in this context.

- DML (data manipulation language) statements retrieve, insert, update, or delete records in a database. For example, you use insert, update, delete, and select statements in this context. Some engineers prefer to put select statements in a separate category called DQL (data query Language).

- DCL (data control language) statements create various roles and permissions to control access to a database. For example, you may use grant and revoke statements in this context.

- TCL (transaction control language) statements manage different transactions that occur in a database. For example, you may use commit and rollback statements in this context.

7.8 How does ADO.NET differ from ADO?

Please refer to the notes in the "A Brief Talk About ADO.NET" section.

7.8 What is a delimiter? Why is it used?

You need to use a delimiter in MySQL to treat a set of statements (functions, stored procedures, etc.) as an entire statement. By default, you use the ; delimiter to separate two statements. But when you need to deal with multiple statements as a whole, you set your own delimiter temporarily and then reset it to the default ;. You can choose different delimiters—like // or $ —when you create your own stored procedures.

7.9 You used the terms *primary keys* and *foreign keys*. What do you mean?

A *primary key* (more correctly, a candidate key) is a single field or a combination of fields used to identify a record correctly. For example, in an organization, two employees can have same name, but their employee IDs are different. So, instead of choosing names, you should choose IDs as primary keys. It is important to note that a primary key not only defines uniqueness, but it also cannot be null. For example, an employee must have an identification number (ID).

Theoretically, in a table you can have several keys that uniquely identify a record. These are called *candidate keys*. Among these candidate keys, you choose only one as the primary key, and the remaining keys are called *alternate keys*. For example, assume that you have a table called `StudentTable` to maintain different student records. And in this table, let's assume that there are columns like `StudentName, StudentAddress, Department`, and so forth. Now you may find that both `RollNumber` and the combination of `StudentName, StudentAddress` can uniquely identify a record. So, if you choose `RollNumber` as the primary key, the other one (`StudentName, StudentAddress`), is an alternate key. When you have multiple columns as a key, those keys are also known as *composite keys*. For example, (StudentName, StudentAddress) is an example of a composite key.

Foreign keys are used to define the relationship between two tables. A foreign key is a column that is primary key of another table. The table containing the foreign key is often called as a *child table*, and the table containing the candidate key is often called the referenced or *parent table*. In this context, the MySQL community says: "A foreign key relationship involves a parent table that holds the initial column values, and a child table with column values that reference the parent column values. A foreign key constraint is defined on the child table." (See `https://dev.mysql.com/doc/refman/5.6/en/create-table-foreign-keys.html`).

Connection Pooling

Let's finish the chapter with a brief discussion about connection pooling. In this chapter, the database is stored locally. You may not see the impact of elapsed time to connect the database, but many real-world applications take a significant amount of time to connect a database (no matter whether using .NET, Java, etc.).

If there are many connections happening rapidly (for example, a web application), initializing (or opening) the connections and then closing the connections can slow down the performance of the application. To overcome this problem, you can use *connection pooling*. Connection pools are specific to a given connection. To enable them, in many applications, you see the presence of "Pooling=true" in the connection string. (For MySqlConnection, pooling is enabled by default).

When connection pooling is enabled, the provider offers a pool of "connected and open" connections, which are immediately given to whoever requests a connection. In this case, the connections seem to be open after invoking the Close() method, which is an expected behavior. The MySQL community says the following at https://dev.mysql.com/doc/connector-net/en/connector-net-connections-pooling.html.

> *The MySQL Connector/NET supports connection pooling for better performance and scalability with database-intensive applications. This is enabled by default. You can turn it off or adjust its performance characteristics using the connection string options Pooling, Connection Reset, Connection Lifetime, Cache Server Properties, Max Pool Size and Min Pool Size.*
>
> *Connection pooling works by keeping the native connection to the server live when the client disposes of a MySqlConnection. Subsequently, if a new MySqlConnection object is opened, it is created from the connection pool, rather than creating a new native connection. This improves performance.*

Lastly, the presence of Max Pool Size and Min Pool Size gives hints that the pool size (of connections) can vary by application.

Final Words

Those are the fundamentals of database programming.

This is not only the end of the chapter, it is also the end of this book. Congratulations, you have finished the book! I believe that you'll find this book useful in the future. Now, you are ready for advanced programming in C#, and hopefully, you can go further with upcoming and new concepts in C#.

Until we meet again, enjoy and happy coding! I wish you all the best.

Summary

This chapter addressed the following key questions.

- What is a database?

- What is a DBMS? What are different types of DBMS?

- What are some common terms used in RDBMS?

- What is SQL?

- What is ADO.NET? How does it differ from classical ADO?

- How do you connect to MySQL?

- How does a C# application talk to a database?

- How do you implement a connected layer using a C# application?

- How do you implement a disconnected layer using a C# application?

- How do you use `MySqlConnection`, `MySqlCommand`, `MySqlDataReader`, `MySqlDataAdapter`, and `MySqlCommandBuilder` in a program?

- What is a stored procedure? How is it different from a stored function?

- How do you use stored procedures in your program?

APPENDIX A

Installing MySQL and Testing SQL Commands

Here I present step-by-step instructions on how to install MySQL on a Windows 10 Home operating system (which I use on my laptop). The instructions were initially written for MySQL community server 8.0.16, but later I upgraded to version 8.0.17. At the time of writing, the most recent version is 8.0.19. Ideally, these steps should not vary much in upcoming versions, but there is no guarantee. I recommend that you visit the official MySQL website at `https://dev.mysql.com/downloads/mysql/` prior to your installation. On this page, you can also get the installer for other operating systems (for example, Debian Linux, Ubuntu Linux, Fedora, macOS, Oracle Solaris, etc.).

I request you to note another minor point. All the MySQL installation steps (and SQL commands execution steps) are clearly described using Figures A-1 to A-42. Except Figure A-20, I didn't extend these figure captions like: *Figure A-1. Downloading MySQL Community Server* etc. For brevity, I kept only simple names like Figure A-1, Figure A-2 and so forth. These are easy to understand and proceed.

Note The installation steps for different operating systems are also available at `https://dev.mysql.com/doc/refman/8.0/en/installing.html`.

---

1. Download the latest MySQL Community server from the official site at `https://dev.mysql.com/downloads/mysql/`. (In my case, initially, it was 8.0.16, but later updated to 8.0.17.) You see a dialog box similar to what's shown in Figure A-1 .

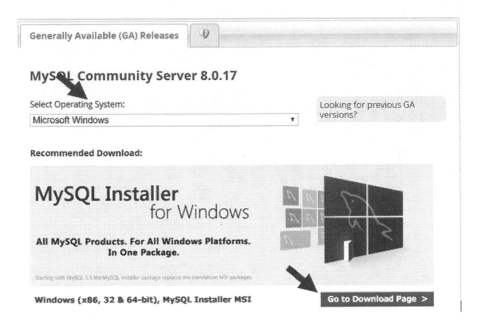

Figure A-1.

2. Select your operating system (Microsoft Windows), and then click **Go to Download Page**. You are redirected to the actual download page for Windows MySQL Server.

3. You see two different installers. Choose the installer with the larger size (i.e., mysql-installer-community-[latest version].msi), as shown in Figure A-2.

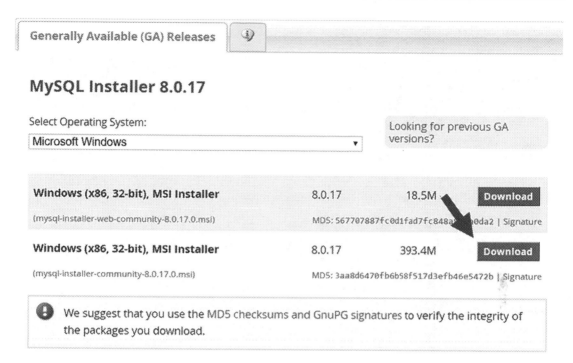

Figure A-2.

4. You are asked for the credentials. You can log in, sign up, or chose the **No thanks, just start my download** option (as I did), as shown in Figure A-3. The installer downloads the selected MySQL on the local machine.

⊕ MySQL Community Downloads

Login Now or Sign Up for a free account.

An Oracle Web Account provides you with the following advantages:

* Fast access to MySQL software downloads
* Download technical White Papers and Presentations
* Post messages in the MySQL Discussion Forums
* Report and track bugs in the MySQL bug system

MySQL.com is using Oracle SSO for authentication. If you already have an Oracle Web account, click the Login link. Otherwise, you can signup for a free account by clicking the Sign Up link and following the instructions.

No thanks, just start my download.

Figure A-3.

5.   Go to your downloads folder and locate the mysql-installer-community file. Double-click the installer, as shown in Figure A-4. (Or, you can right-click on that file and choose the ***Install*** option.)

mysql-connector-java-8.0.16	06-08-2019 09:36	File folder	
mysql-connector-java-8.0.16	19-05-2019 10:40	WinZip File	4,395 KB
mysql-installer-community-8.0.16.0	19-05-2019 09:34	Windows Installer Pa...	3,82,340 KB
mysql-installer-community-8.0.16.0	19-05-2019 09:34	Windows Installer Pa...	3,82,340 KB

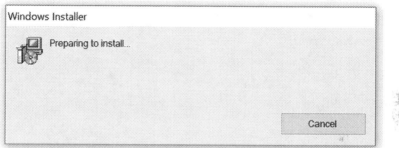

Figure A-4.

During the installation process, you may be asked for permission to change your computer settings or firewall confirmation. Once you accept, the installation proceeds. It may take time to configure the installer (see Figure A-5).

Figure A-5.

6.   Read the license agreement. To proceed further, you need to accept the license terms. Then click **Next**, as shown in Figure A-6.

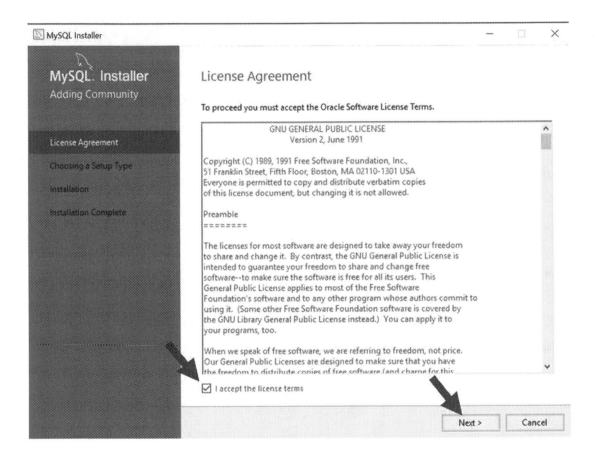

Figure A-6.

7. From a list of various options, I chose Developer Default to serve
    my needs, as shown in Figure A-7. Click **Next**.

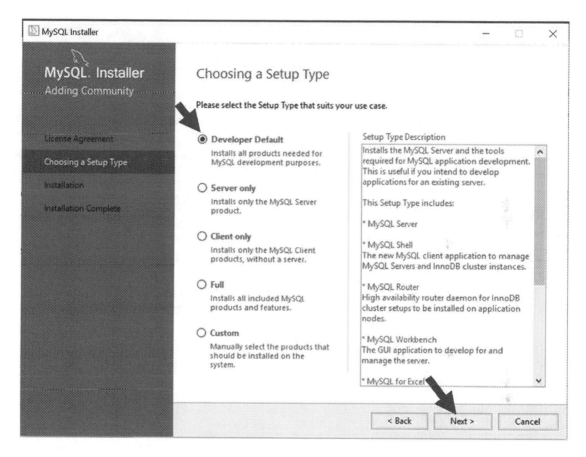

Figure A-7.

8. Note the Check Requirements dialog box. This depends on
    the current configuration of your system. Click **Next**. (Before I
    installed Visual Studio 2019 on my system, I saw what's shown in
    Figure A-8.)

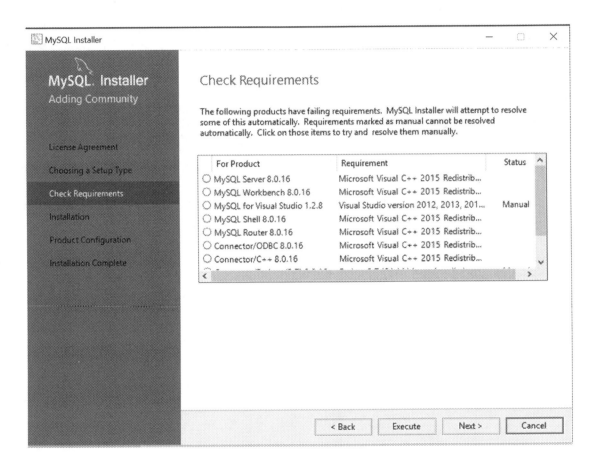

Figure A-8.

(Once I installed Visual Studio Community 2019 on my system, I saw what is shown in Figure A-9.)

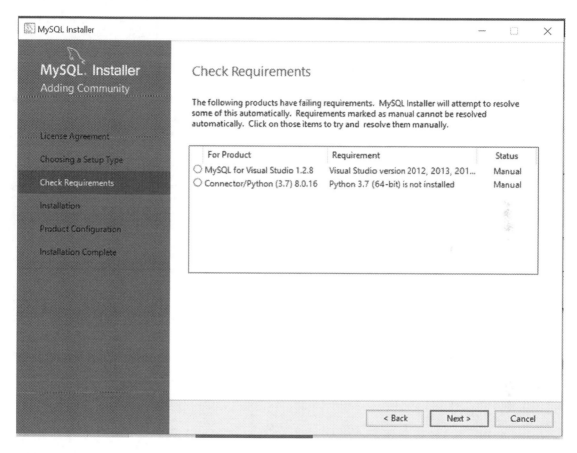

Figure A-9.

9. Based on your current Windows configuration, you may be
    prompted, "One or more product requirements have not been
    satisfied," as shown in Figure A-10. Click **Yes** and then **Next**.

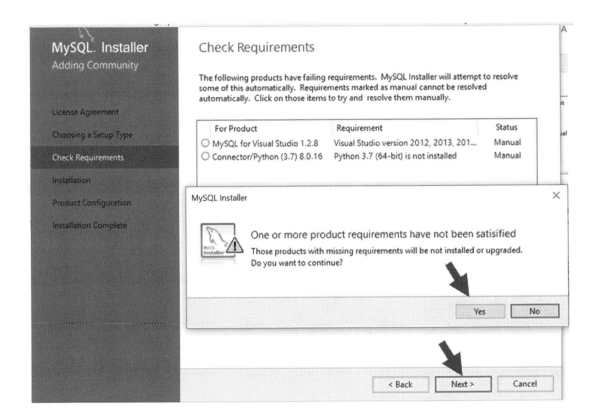

Figure A-10.

10.   You see a screen similar to Figure A-11. (It depends on your current configuration.) Click *Execute*.

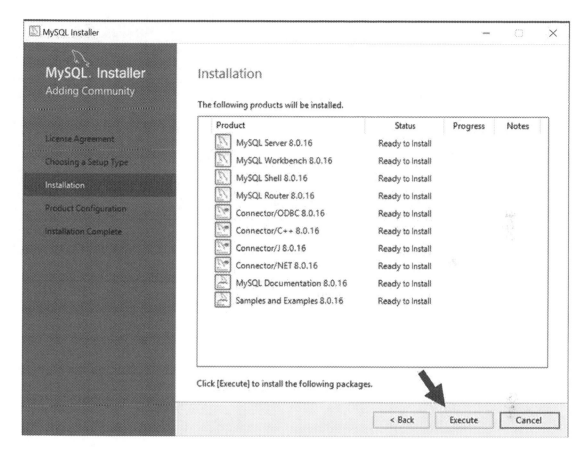

Figure A-11.

Now you see a dialog box similar to what's shown in Figure A-12.

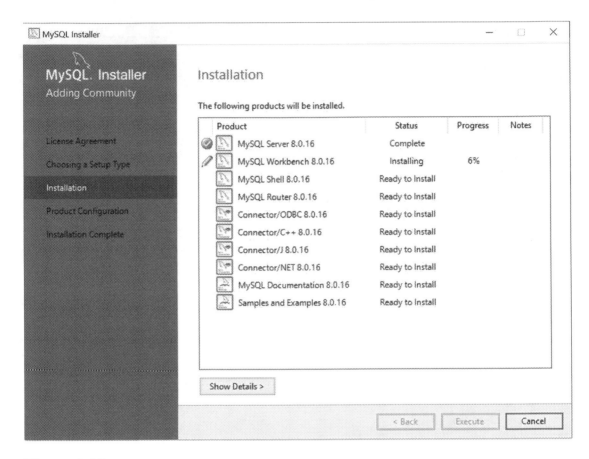

Figure A-12.

11. Once everything is installed, you see the dialog box shown in
Figure A-13. Click **Next**.

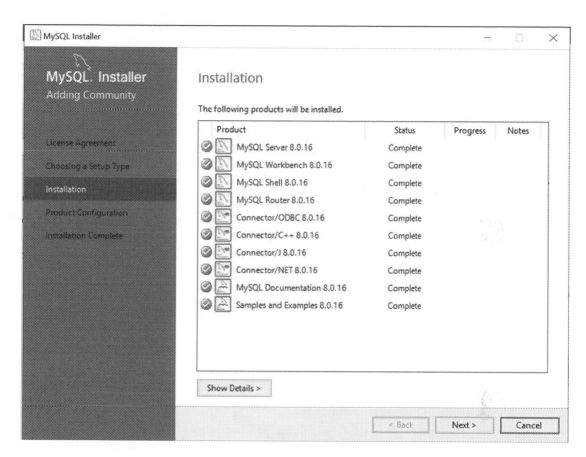

Figure A-13.

12. MySQL suggests configuration of the server settings, as shown in Figure A-14. Click **Next**.

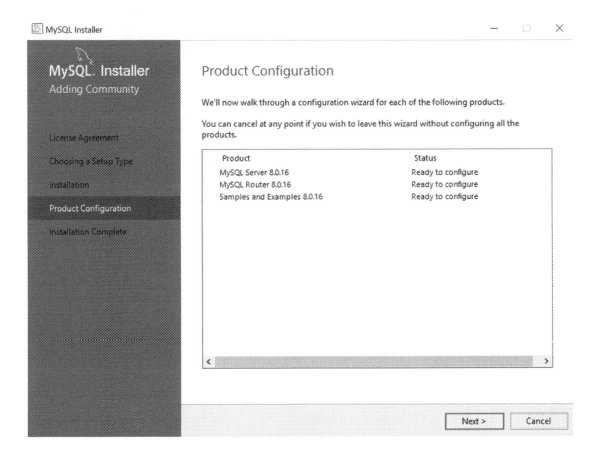

Figure A-14.

13. In Figure A-15, I opted for the default settings (**Standalone MySQL server/Classic MySQL replication**) because I'll use it only for my development, and I do not need a cluster. Click **Next**.

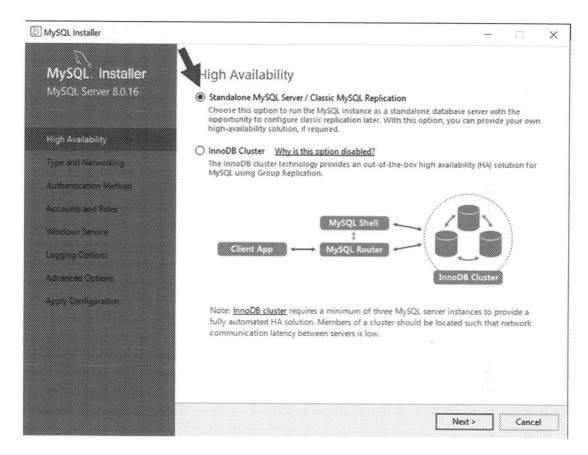

Figure A-15.

14. Keep everything as the default (i.e., I chose *Development Computer*.) Although you can choose other options, per your needs (see Figure A-16). Click **Next**.

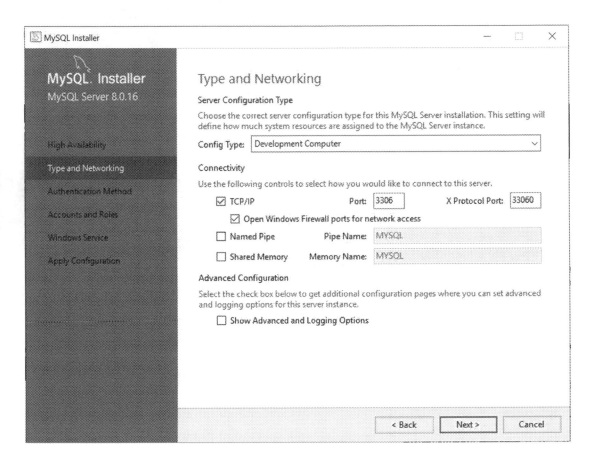

Figure A-16.

15. Choose the default recommended method, and then click **Next**, as shown in Figure A-17.

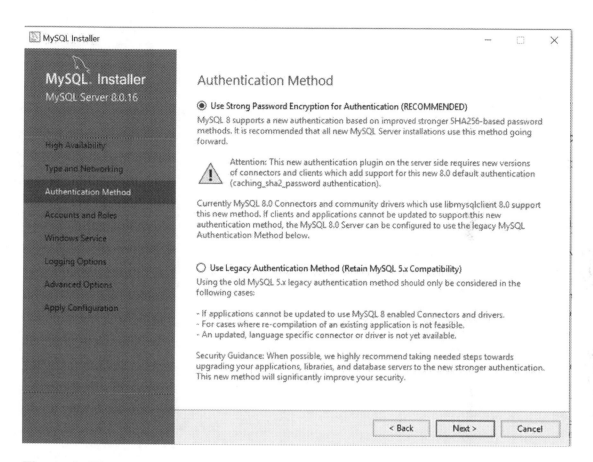

Figure A-17.

16.   Set the MySQL root user password, and then click **Next**, as shown in Figure A-18.

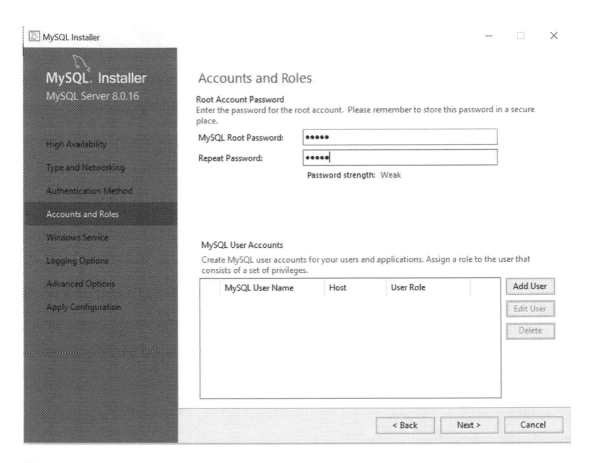

Figure A-18.

17. For now, I am not creating any new user, but you can always create a new user and set the role. In that case, you need to click the **Add User** button to get a dialog box like the one shown in Figure A-19. Provide the required information.

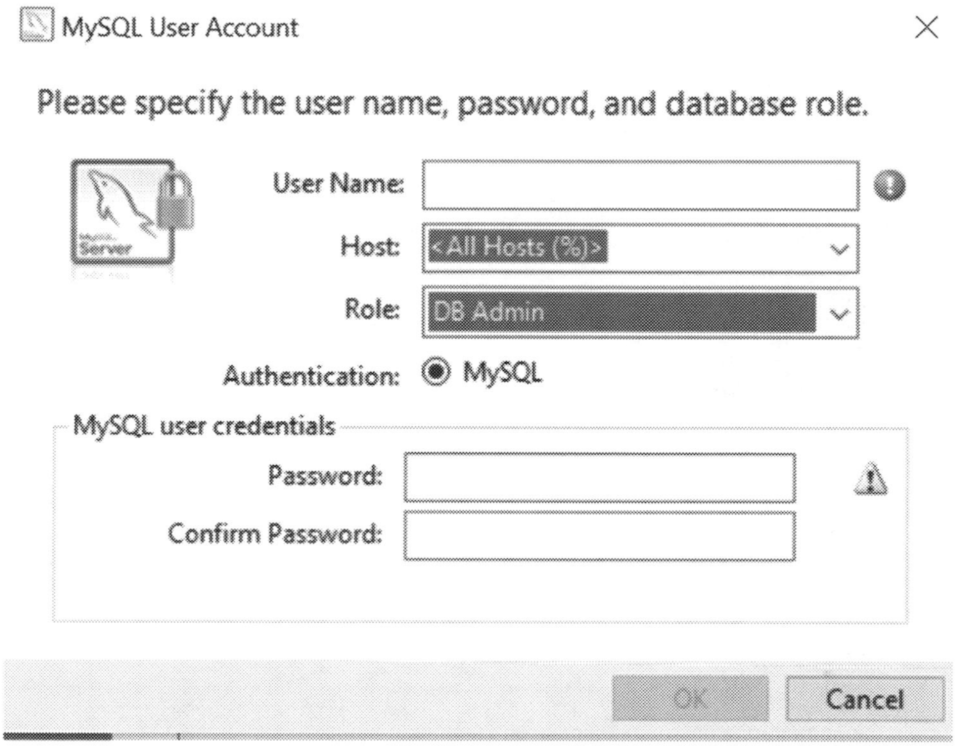

Figure A-19.

18. Keep all the default settings, and click **Next**, as shown in Figure A-20.

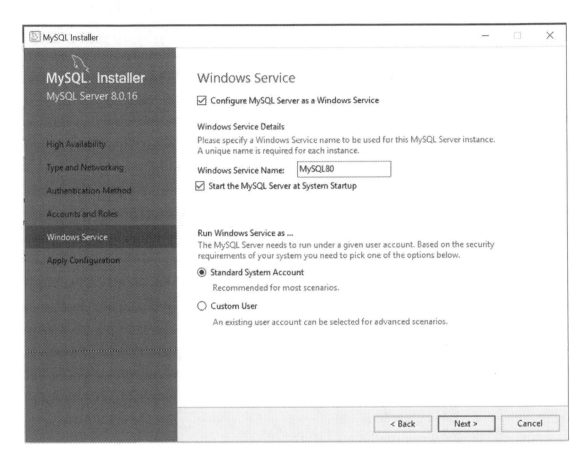

Figure A-20. *Note the MySQL80 service name. Recall that I used version 8.0.16*

19. Click *Execute* to apply the configurations from the previous step, as shown in Figure A-21.

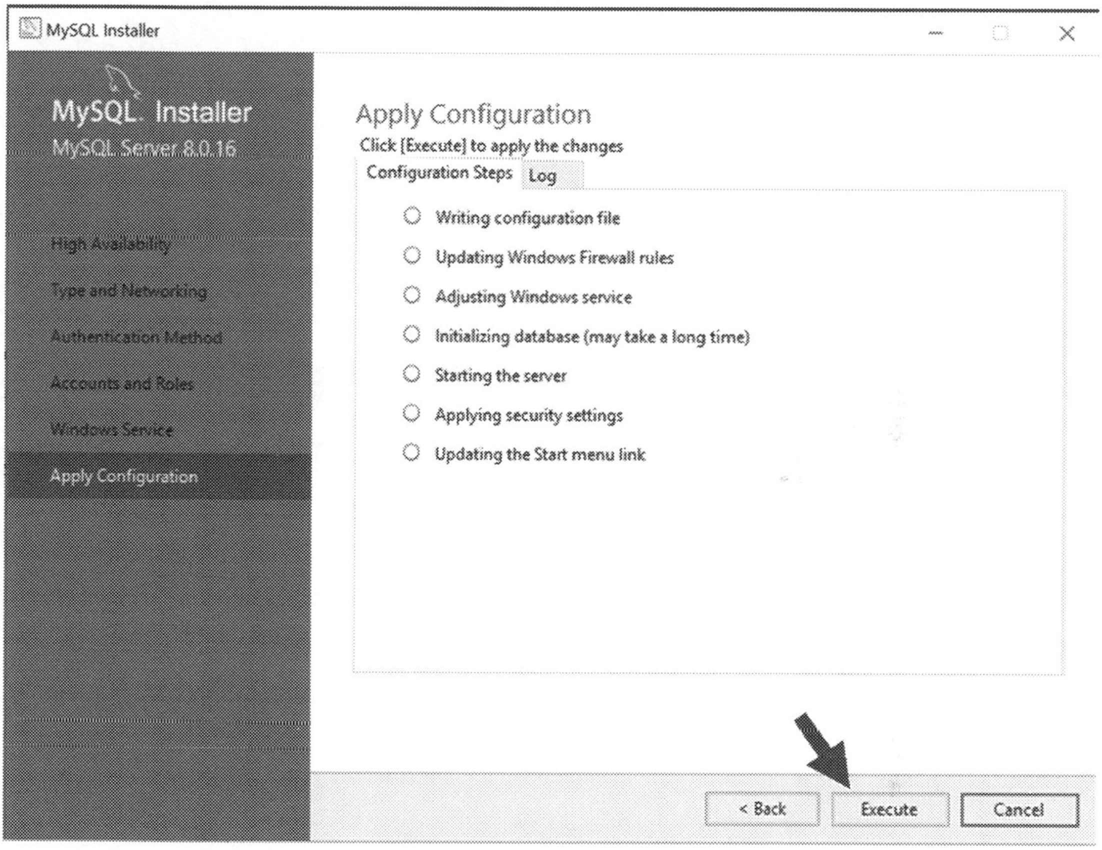

Figure A-21.

Upon execution, you see a dialog box similar to the one shown in Figure A-22.

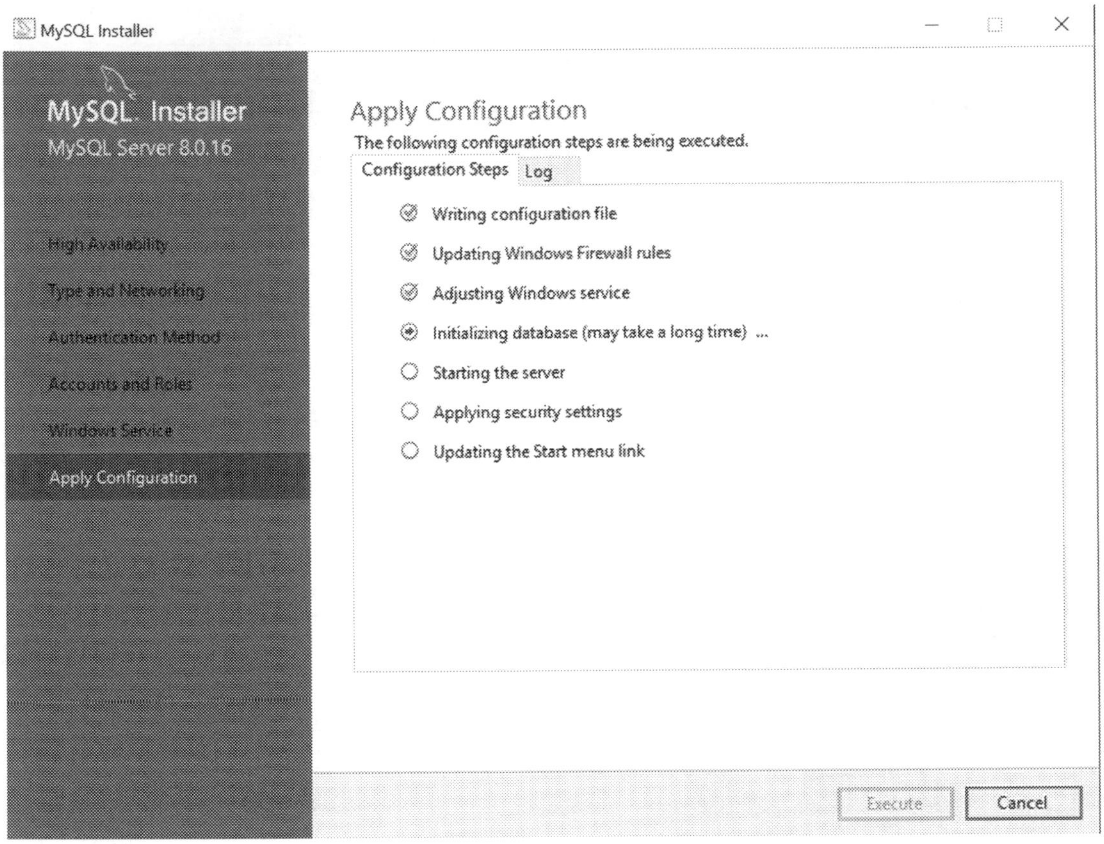

Figure A-22.

20. Once everything is installed, you see the dialog box shown in
    Figure A-23. Click **Finish**.

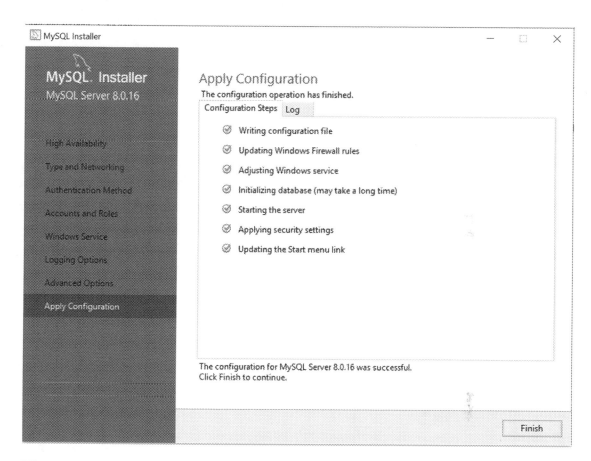

Figure A-23.

21. You see the dialog box shown in Figure A-24. Click **Next**.

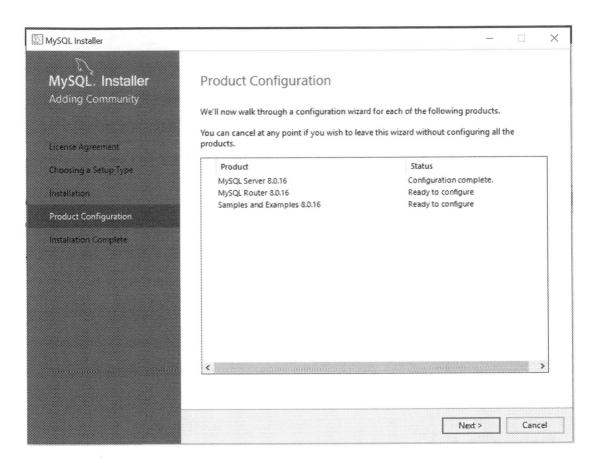

Figure A-24.

22. You do not need to set up the router information for now. Click
    Finish, as shown in Figure A-25.

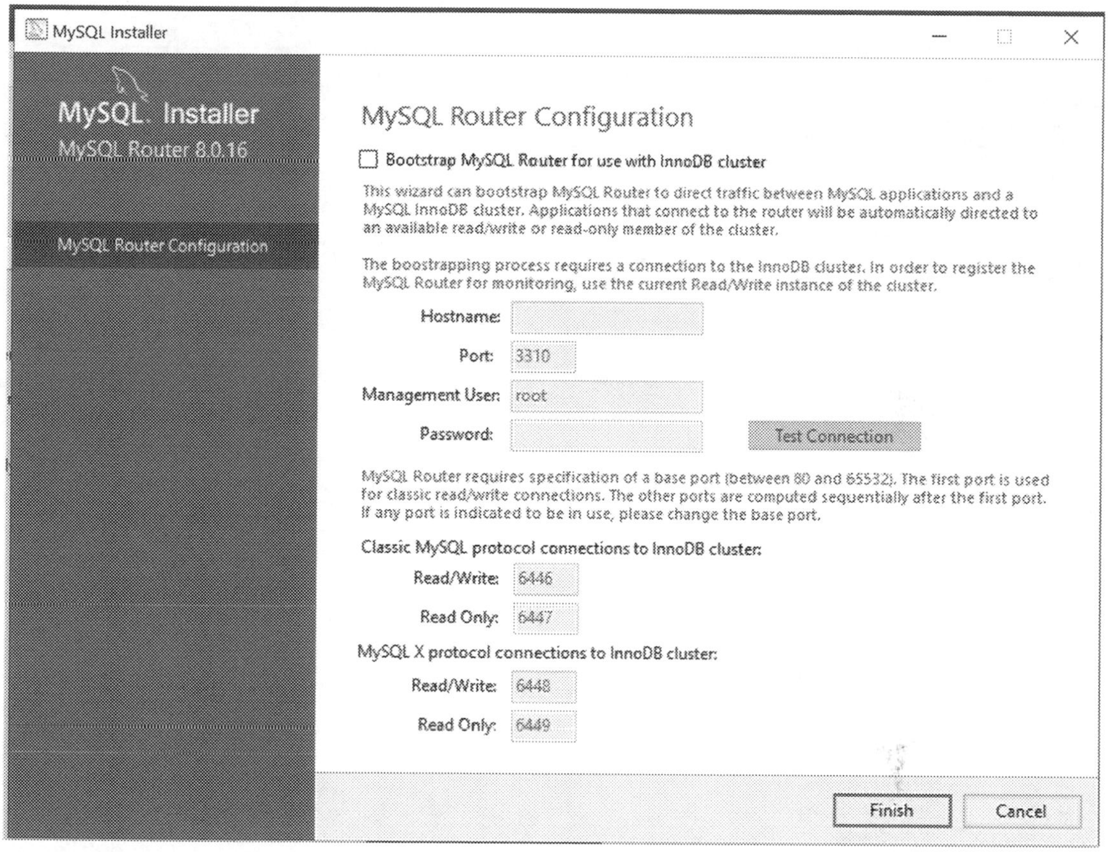

Figure A-25.

23. Note that since you did not provide any settings, "Configuration
     not needed" appears for MySQL Router 8.0.16, as shown in
     Figure A-26. Click **Next**.

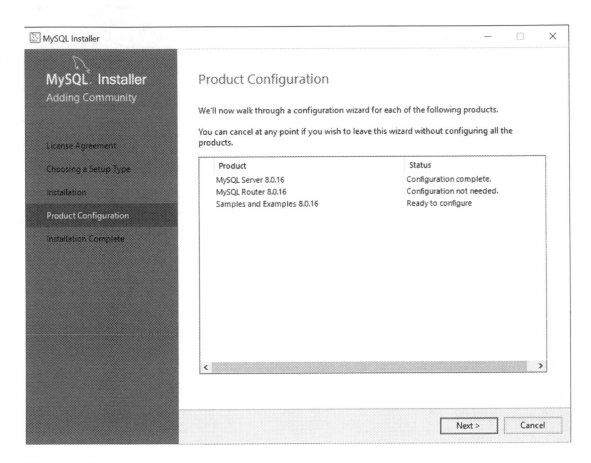

Figure A-26.

24.   Supply a password for the root user, as shown in Figure A-27.

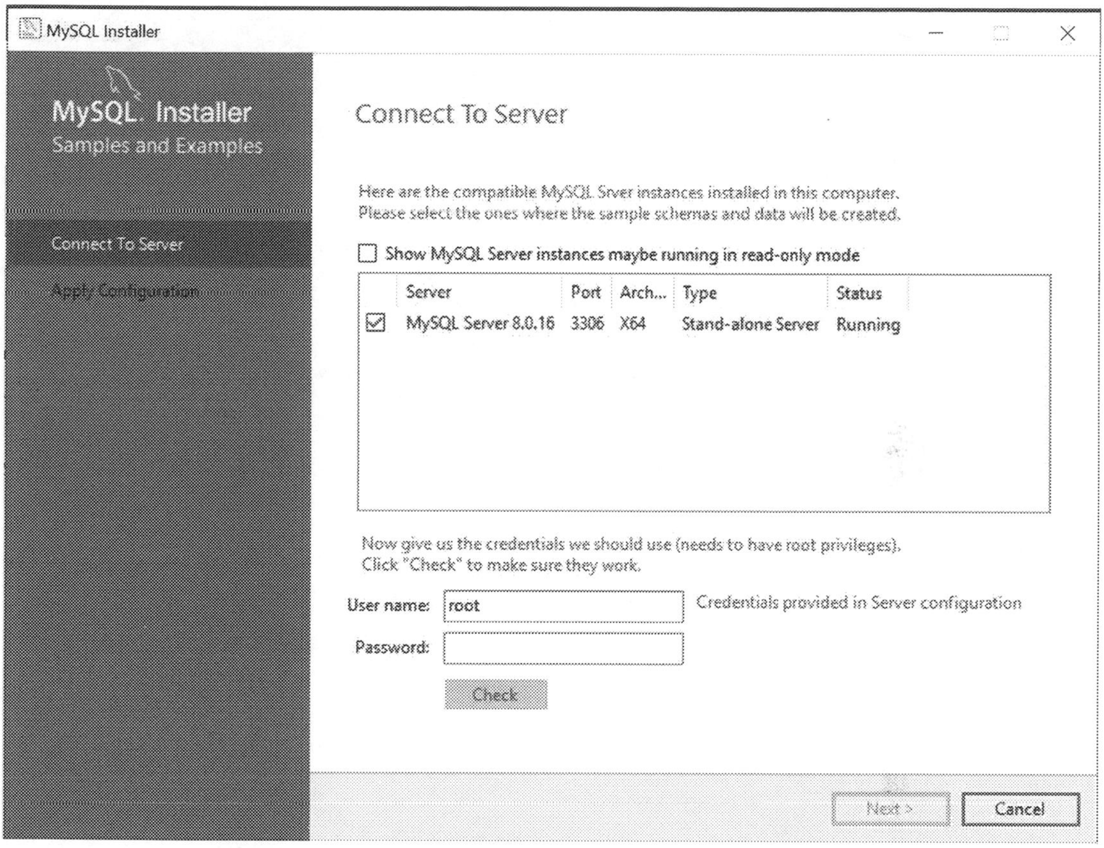

Figure A-27.

25. Click the **Check** button, and then click **Next**, as shown in Figure A-28.

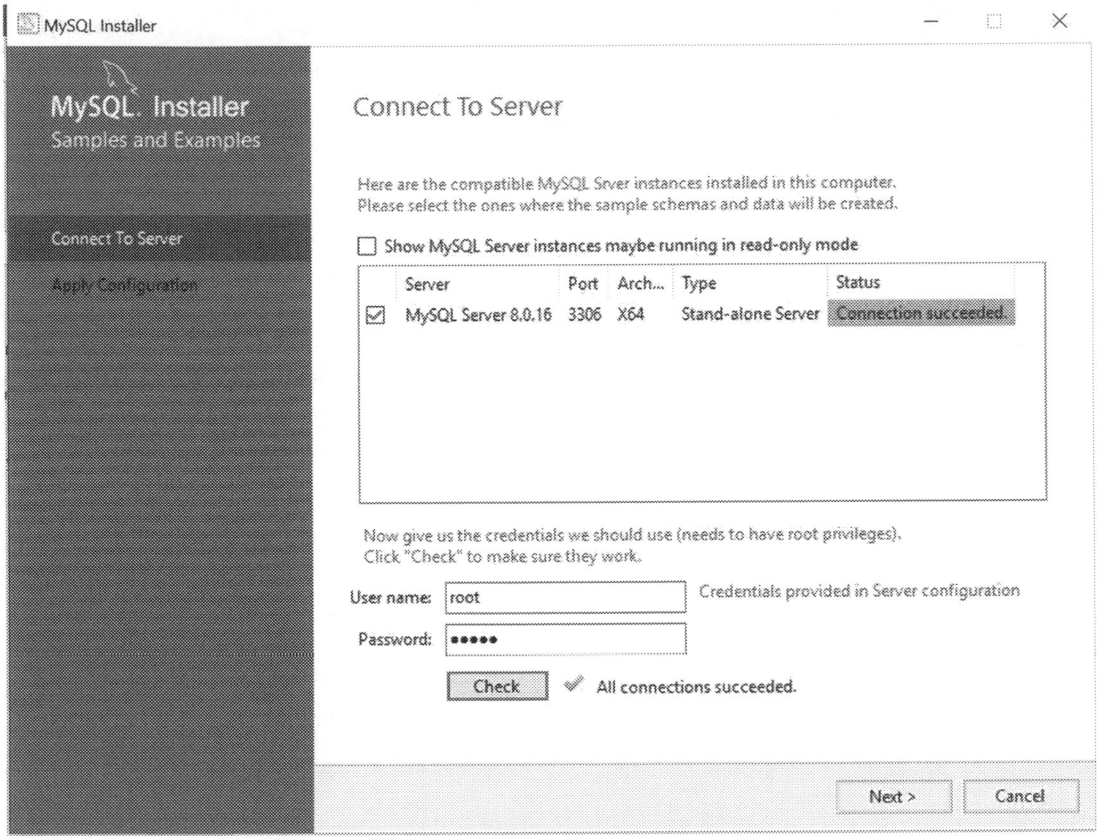

Figure A-28.

26.   The dialog box shown in Figure A-29 appears. Click **Execute**.

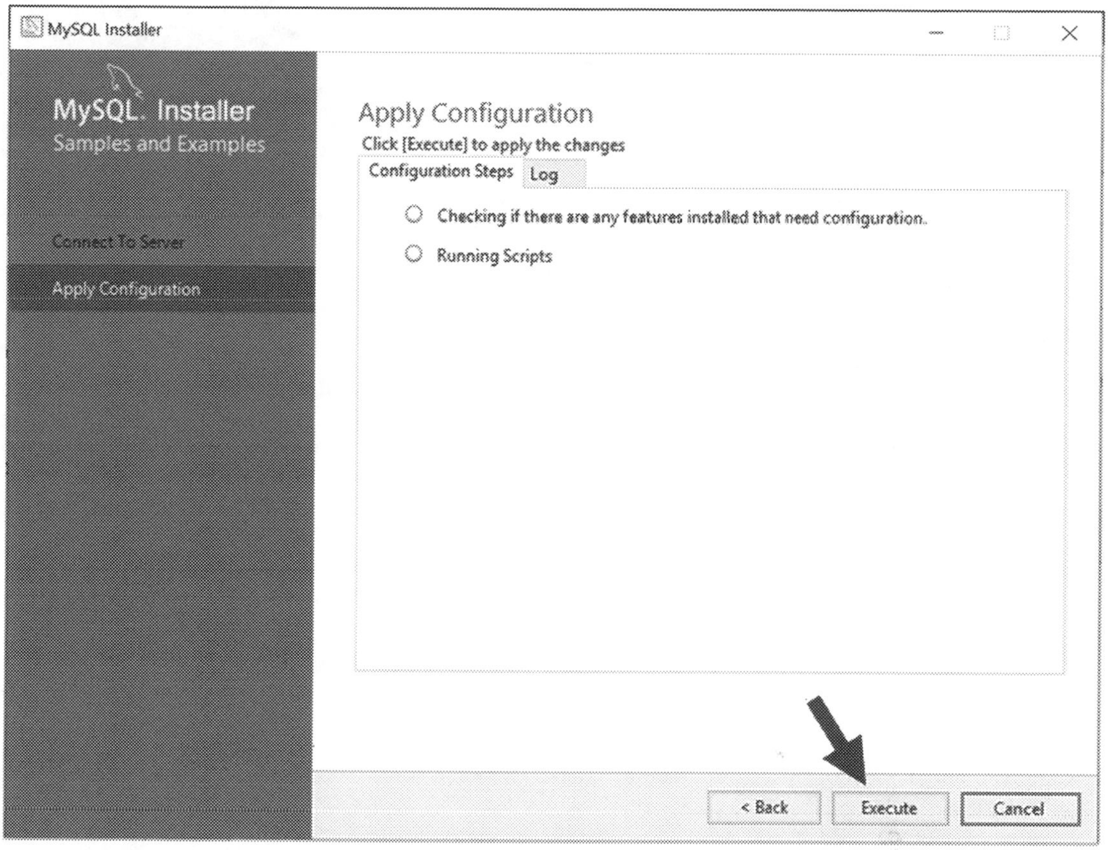

Figure A-29.

27.   Once everything is applied, you see the dialog box shown in
       Figure A-30. Click **Finish**.

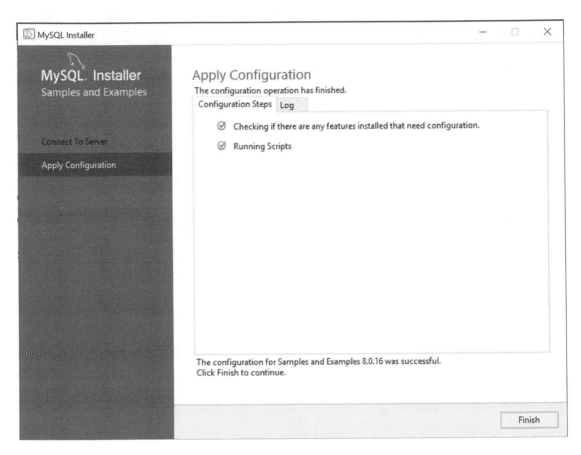

Figure A-30.

28. The dialog box shown in Figure A-31 appears. Click **Next**.

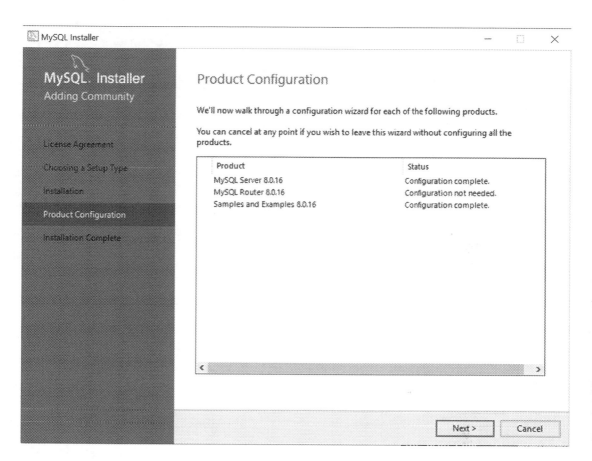

Figure A-31.

29. You see an Installation Complete message, as shown in Figure A-32.
     Click *Finish*.

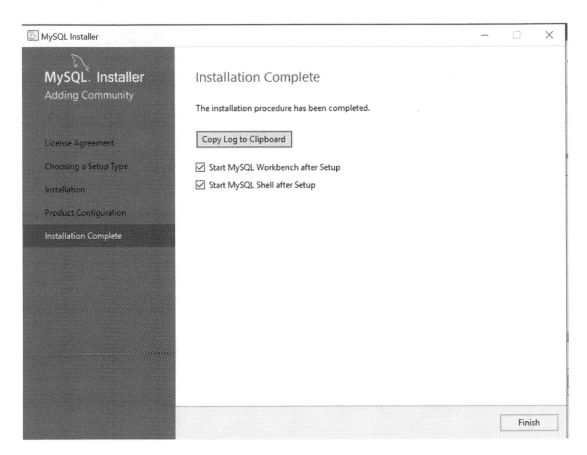

Figure A-32.

Both the MySQL Workbench and MySQL Shell prompts open because they were
selected in the previous step (see Figures A-33 and A-34).

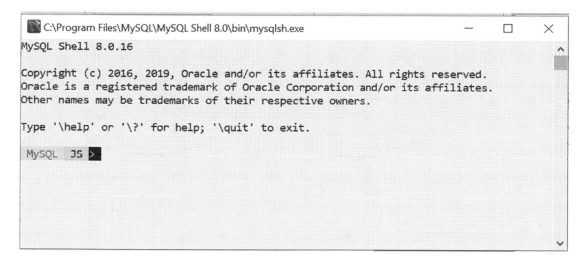

Figure A-33.

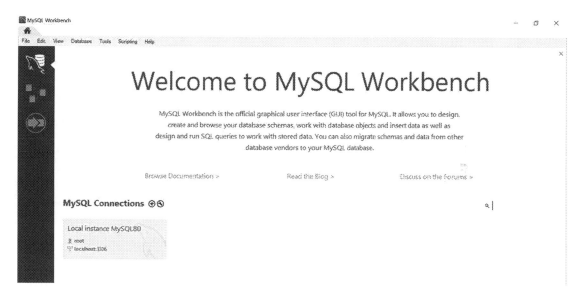

Figure A-34.

Upgrade Scenario

Prior to writing the Chapter 7, I upgraded the software to 8.0.18. This section features some important screenshots to help you understand an upgrade scenario.

When I upgraded to 8.0.18, I saw an increased file size (compare it with Figure A-2), as shown in Figure A-35.

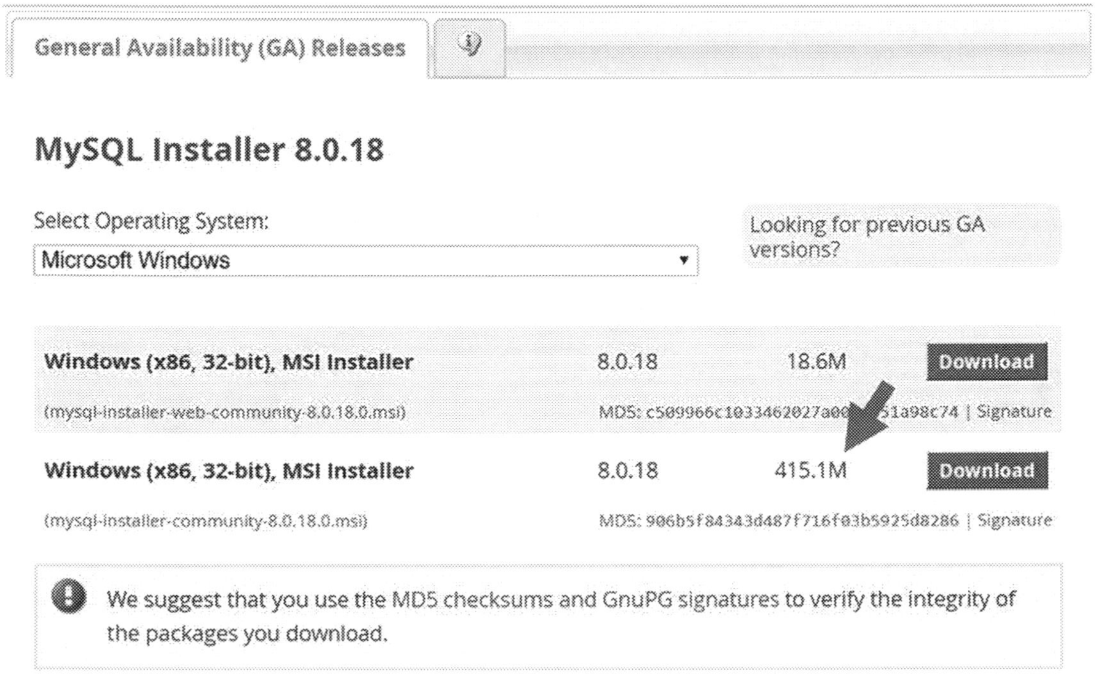

Figure A-35.

In an upgrade scenario, you may see the dialog box shown in Figure A-36 (compare with Figure A-13).

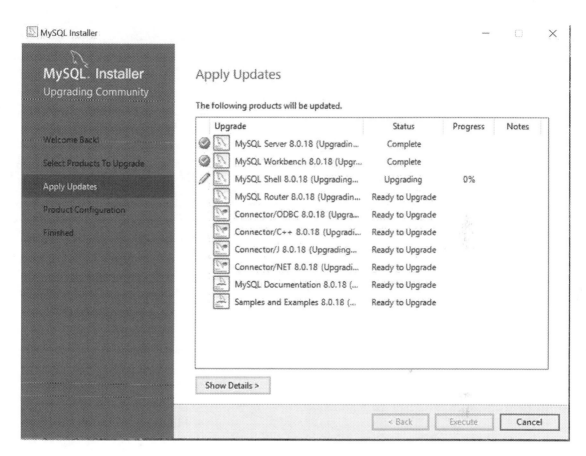

Figure A-36.

Once everything is set up, you may see the dialog box shown in Figure A-37.

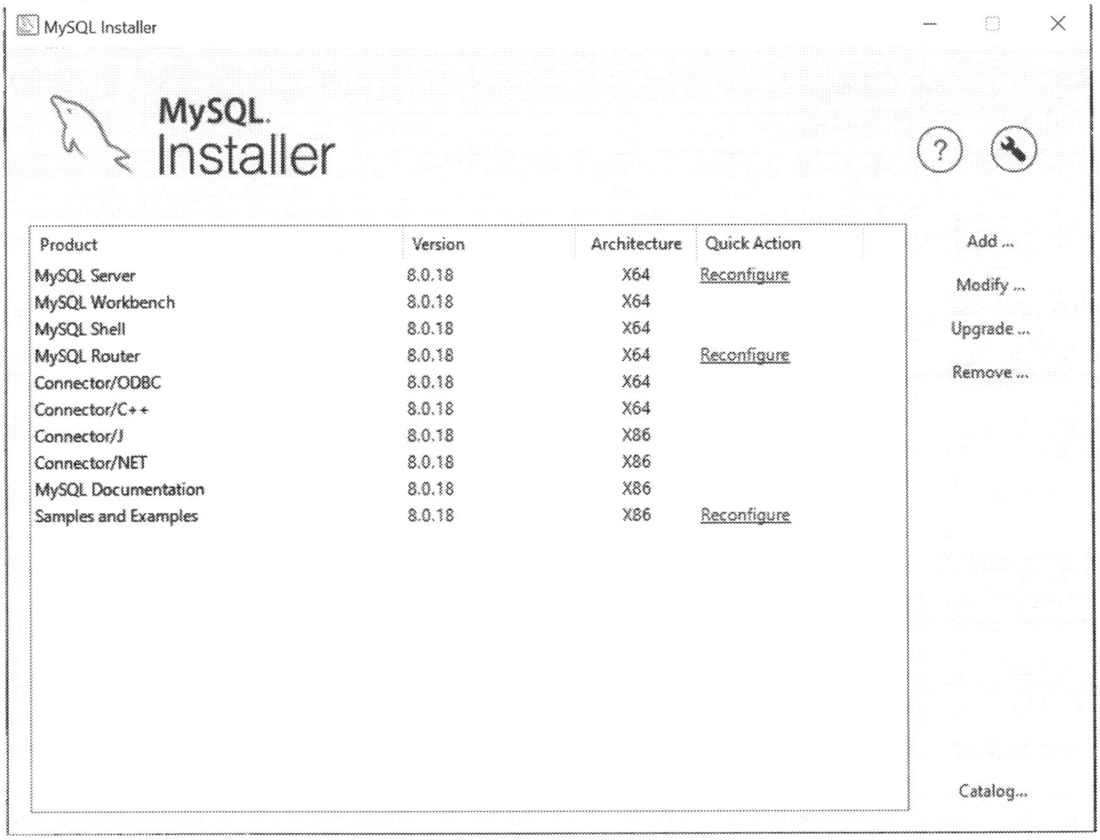

Figure A-37.

Testing the Installation and Executing Simple SQL Statements

Here are some sample SQL queries/statements for your reference. These statements were exercised with a MySQL database using the Command prompt.

Enter password: ✱✱✱✱✱

Welcome to the MySQL monitor. Commands end with ; or \g.

Your MySQL connection id is 8

Server version: 8.0.16 MySQL Community Server - GPL

Copyright (c) 2000, 2019, Oracle and/or its affiliates. All rights reserved.

Oracle is a registered trademark of Oracle Corporation and/or its affiliates. Other names may be trademarks of their respective owners.

Type 'help;' or '\h' for help. Type '\c' to clear the current input statement.

```
mysql> show databases;
+--------------------+
| Database           |
+--------------------+
| information_schema |
| mysql              |
| performance_schema |
| sakila             |
| sys                |
| world              |
+--------------------+
6 rows in set (0.30 sec)
```

[Creating a custom database called test]

```
mysql> create database test;
Query OK, 1 row affected (0.23 sec)
```

[Showing all the currently available database(s)]

```
mysql> show databases;
+--------------------+
| Database           |
+--------------------+
| information_schema |
| mysql              |
| performance_schema |
| sakila             |
| sys                |
| test               |
| world              |
+--------------------+
7 rows in set (0.00 sec)
```

[We'll do all our experiment in test database. So, I'm moving into it.]

```
mysql> use test;
Database changed
```

[Creating a table called employee **in the database. This table is used in the examples of chapter7]**

```
mysql> create table employee(EmpId Integer primary key,Name Varchar(10),Age
Integer not null,Salary Double);
Query OK, 0 rows affected (1.06 sec)
```

[Inserting the records into the employee **table in test database.]**

```
mysql> insert into employee values(1,'Amit',25,1200.5);
Query OK, 1 row affected (0.31 sec)
mysql> insert into employee values(2,'Sam',23,1000.25);
Query OK, 1 row affected (0.22 sec)
mysql> insert into employee values(3,'Bob',30,1500);
Query OK, 1 row affected (0.14 sec)
```

[Fetching all records from employee **table in the database]**

```
mysql> select * from employee;
+-------+------+-----+---------+
| EmpId | Name | Age | Salary  |
+-------+------+-----+---------+
|     1 | Amit |  25 |  1200.5 |
|     2 | Sam  |  23 | 1000.25 |
|     3 | Bob  |  30 |    1500 |
+-------+------+-----+---------+
3 rows in set (0.00 sec)
```

Figure A-38 is a screenshot in a compact view.

```
mysql> select * from employee;
+--------+-------+------+---------+
| EmpId  | Name  | Age  | Salary  |
+--------+-------+------+---------+
|      1 | Amit  |   25 |  1200.5 |
|      2 | Sam   |   23 | 1000.25 |
|      3 | Bob   |   30 |    1500 |
+--------+-------+------+---------+
3 rows in set (0.00 sec)
```

Figure A-38.

[Checking the structure of employee **table in the database]**
mysql> **desc employee;**

```
+--------+-------------+------+-----+---------+-------+
| Field  | Type        | Null | Key | Default | Extra |
+--------+-------------+------+-----+---------+-------+
| EmpId  | int(11)     | NO   | PRI | NULL    |       |
| Name   | varchar(10) | YES  |     | NULL    |       |
| Age    | int(11)     | NO   |     | NULL    |       |
| Salary | double      | YES  |     | NULL    |       |
+--------+-------------+------+-----+---------+-------+
4 rows in set (0.17 sec)
```

Figure A-39 is a screenshot in a compact view.

```
mysql> desc employee;
+--------+-------------+------+-----+---------+-------+
| Field  | Type        | Null | Key | Default | Extra |
+--------+-------------+------+-----+---------+-------+
| EmpId  | int(11)     | NO   | PRI | NULL    |       |
| Name   | varchar(10) | YES  |     | NULL    |       |
| Age    | int(11)     | NO   |     | NULL    |       |
| Salary | double      | YES  |     | NULL    |       |
+--------+-------------+------+-----+---------+-------+
4 rows in set (0.17 sec)
```

Figure A-39.

[Creating another table called NumberTable **in the database. Note that this table is not used in the examples of chapter7]**

mysql> **create table NumberTable(FirstNo Double, SecondNo Double);**
Query OK, 0 rows affected (2.77 sec)

mysql> **show tables;**
```
+----------------+
| Tables_in_test |
+----------------+
| employee       |
| numbertable    |
+----------------+
```
2 rows in set (0.08 sec)

[Inserting the records into the table called numbertable **in test database.]**

mysql> **insert into numbertable values(12.3,15.7);**
Query OK, 1 row affected (2.12 sec)

mysql> **insert into numbertable values(32.3,25.3);**
Query OK, 1 row affected (0.13 sec)

mysql> **insert into numbertable values(25,75);**
Query OK, 1 row affected (0.08 sec)

[Fetching all records from numbertable **table in test database]**
mysql> **select** ∗ **from numbertable;**
```
+---------+----------+
| FirstNo | SecondNo |
+---------+----------+
|    12.3 |     15.7 |
|    32.3 |     25.3 |
|      25 |       75 |
+---------+----------+
```
3 rows in set (0.08 sec)

[Creating a function called AddNumbers **in the current database]**

```
mysql> create function AddNumbers(firstNumber double,secondNumber double)
returns double deterministic return firstNumber+secondNumber;
Query OK, O rows affected (0.45 sec)
```

[Checking the status of the function AddNumbers **in the current database]**

```
mysql> show function status where db='test';
+------+------------+----------+---------------+--------------------+---
----------------+---------------+---------+--------------------+-----
----------------+-------------------+
| Db   | Name       | Type     | Definer       | Modified           |
Created                | Security_type | Comment | character_set_client |
collation_connection | Database Collation |
+------+------------+----------+---------------+--------------------+--
----------------+---------------+---------+--------------------+-----
----------------+-------------------+
| test | AddNumbers | FUNCTION | root@localhost | 2020-03-17 10:13:20 |
2020-03-17 10:13:20 | DEFINER       |         | cp850                |
cp850_general_ci     | utf8mb4_0900_ai_ci |
| test | total      | FUNCTION | root@localhost | 2019-09-02 19:41:28 |
2019-09-02 19:41:28 | DEFINER       |         | cp850                |
cp850_general_ci     | utf8mb4_0900_ai_ci |
+------+------------+----------+---------------+--------------------+---
----------------+---------------+---------+--------------------+-----
----------------+-------------------+
2 rows in set (0.11 sec)
```

```
mysql> Select Routine_name as "Function Name", routine_Definition as
"Definition", Routine_Schema "Schema", Data_Type as "Types", Created
From  Information_Schema.Routines Where Routine_Name='AddNumbers' and
Routine_Type= 'FUNCTION';
```

```
+---------------+-------------------------------+--------+--------+------
---------------+
| Function Name | Definition                    | Schema | Types  |
CREATED         |
+---------------+-------------------------------+--------+--------+------
---------------+
| AddNumbers    | return firstNumber+secondNumber | test   | double | 2020-
03-17 10:13:20 |
+---------------+-------------------------------+--------+--------+------
---------------+
1 row in set (0.00 sec)
```

Figure A-40 offers a compact view.

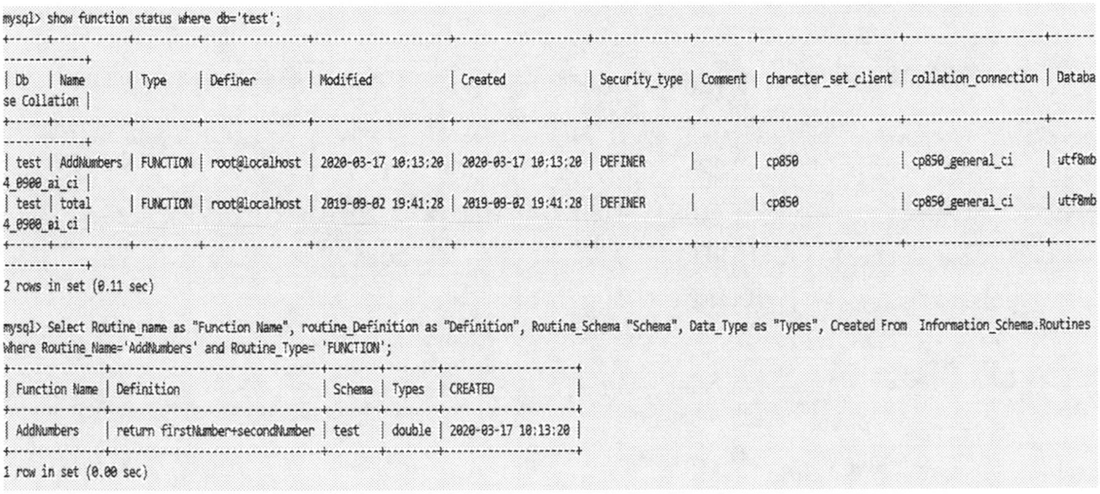

Figure A-40.

[Invoking the AddNumbers **function with two arguments (25 and 45) in the current database]**

```
mysql> select AddNumbers (25,45);
+-------------------+
| AddNumbers(25,45) |
+-------------------+
|                70 |
+-------------------+
```

1 row in set (0.21 sec)

[Invoking the AddNumbers **function with two arguments (25 and 45) in the current database and setting the column name(which is holding the result of the function) as "Total"]**

mysql> **select AddNumbers(25,45) as "Total";**

```
+-------+
| Total |
+-------+
|    70 |
+-------+
```

1 row in set (0.00 sec)

[Creating another table called employee_backup **from exiting table** employee**]**

mysql> **create table employee_backup**
    -> as (select * from employee);
Query OK, 3 rows affected (1.99 sec)
Records: 3 Duplicates: 0 Warnings: 0
Note.

The prior command copies the table with data, but it does not copy other database objects, such as primary keys, foreign keys, indexes, and so forth. To copy data and all the dependent objects from an existing table, you can use the following two commands. (I assume that you are creating an employee table by copying employee_backup. I also check whether a table already exists before creating it.)

---

create table if not exists employee like employee_backup;
insert employee select * from employee_backup;

[Fetching all records from employee_backup **table in test database]**

```
mysql> select * from employee_backup;
+-------+------+-----+---------+
| EmpId | Name | Age | Salary  |
+-------+------+-----+---------+
|     1 | Amit |  25 |  1200.5 |
|     2 | Sam  |  23 | 1000.25 |
|     3 | Bob  |  30 |    1500 |
+-------+------+-----+---------+
3 rows in set (0.00 sec)
```

[Checking the structure of employee_backup **table in the database]**

```
mysql> desc employee_backup;
+--------+-------------+------+-----+---------+-------+
| Field  | Type        | Null | Key | Default | Extra |
+--------+-------------+------+-----+---------+-------+
| EmpId  | int(11)     | NO   |     | NULL    |       |
| Name   | varchar(10) | YES  |     | NULL    |       |
| Age    | int(11)     | NO   |     | NULL    |       |
| Salary | double      | YES  |     | NULL    |       |
+--------+-------------+------+-----+---------+-------+
4 rows in set (0.01 sec)
```

[Creating the procedure 'GetAllEmployees' **in the current database]**

```
mysql> DELIMITER $
mysql> CREATE PROCEDURE GetAllEmployees()
    -> BEGIN
    -> SELECT * FROM EMPLOYEE;
    -> END $
Query OK, 0 rows affected (0.30 sec)

mysql>
mysql> DELIMITER ;
```

[Creating the procedure 'InsertOneNewRecord' **in the current database]**

```
mysql> DELIMITER $
mysql> CREATE PROCEDURE InsertOneNewRecord()
    -> BEGIN
    -> insert into Employee values(4,'John',27,975);
    -> END $
Query OK, 0 rows affected (0.47 sec)
```

[Creating the procedure 'DeleteOneRecord' in the current database]

```
mysql> DELIMITER //
mysql> CREATE PROCEDURE DeleteOneRecord(
    -> IN NameToBeDeleted varchar(10)
    -> )
    -> BEGIN
    -> Delete from employee where Name=NameToBeDeleted;
    -> END //
Query OK, 0 rows affected (0.23 sec)

mysql> DELIMITER ;
```

[To display all procedures in current database]

mysql> **show procedure status where db='test';**

Figure A-41 is a partial screenshot in a compact view.

```
mysql> show procedure status where db='test';
+------+-------------------+-----------+--------------+---------------------+---------------------+---------------+---
------+-------------------+----------------------+-------------------+
| Db   | Name              | Type      | Definer      | Modified            | Created             | Security_type | C
omment | character_set_client | collation_connection | Database Collation |
+------+-------------------+-----------+--------------+---------------------+---------------------+---------------+---
------+-------------------+----------------------+-------------------+
| test | DeleteOneRecord   | PROCEDURE | root@localhost | 2020-03-16 09:36:26 | 2020-03-16 09:36:26 | DEFINER       |
       | cp850             | cp850_general_ci     | utf8mb4_0900_ai_ci |
| test | InsertOneNewRecord | PROCEDURE | root@localhost | 2020-03-15 09:44:26 | 2020-03-15 09:44:26 | DEFINER      |
       | cp850             | cp850_general_ci     | utf8mb4_0900_ai_ci |
| test | SelectAllEmployees | PROCEDURE | root@localhost | 2020-03-14 18:04:15 | 2020-03-14 18:04:15 | DEFINER      |
       | cp850             | cp850_general_ci     | utf8mb4_0900_ai_ci |
+------+-------------------+-----------+--------------+---------------------+---------------------+---------------+---
------+-------------------+----------------------+-------------------+
3 rows in set (0.00 sec)
```

Figure A-41.

[Dropping a procedure from database 'test']

mysql> **drop procedure if exists DeleteOneRecord;**

After dropping the procedure, Figure A-42 shows a partial screenshot in a compact view.

```
mysql> drop procedure if exists DeleteOneRecord;
Query OK, 0 rows affected (2.14 sec)

mysql> show procedure status where db='test';
+------+--------------------+-----------+---------------+--------------------+--------------------+-----
------+--------------------+--------------------+
| Db   | Name               | Type      | Definer       | Modified           | Created            | Sec
lient | collation_connection | Database Collation |
+------+--------------------+-----------+---------------+--------------------+--------------------+-----
------+--------------------+--------------------+
| test | InsertOneNewRecord | PROCEDURE | root@localhost | 2020-03-15 09:44:26 | 2020-03-15 09:44:26 | DEF
      | cp850_general_ci    | utf8mb4_0900_ai_ci |
| test | SelectAllEmployees | PROCEDURE | root@localhost | 2020-03-14 18:04:15 | 2020-03-14 18:04:15 | DEF
      | cp850_general_ci    | utf8mb4_0900_ai_ci |
+------+--------------------+-----------+---------------+--------------------+--------------------+-----
------+--------------------+--------------------+
2 rows in set (0.07 sec)
```

Figure A-42.

APPENDIX B

Recommended Reading

I recommend that you read the following books(or, the updated editions).

- *C# 7.0 in a Nutshell* by Joseph Albahari and Ben Albahari(O'Reilly, 2018).

- *Professional C# 4.0 and .NET 4* by Christian Nagel, Bill Evjen, Jay Glynn, Karli Watson, and Morgan Skinner (Wrox, 2010).

- *Design Patterns in C#* by Vaskaran Sarcar (Apress, 2018).

- *The C# Player's Guide* by R. B. Whitaker (Starbound Software, 2015).

- *C#4.0 : The Complete Reference* by Herbert Schildt (McGraw-Hill Education, 2010).

You can also visit the following online resources/websites to get useful information on C#.

- https://docs.microsoft.com/en-us/dotnet/csharp/

- https://devblogs.microsoft.com/csharpfaq/

- www.c-sharpcorner.com

- www.codeproject.com

- www.artima.com/intv/generics.html

- https://docs.microsoft.com/en-us/dotnet/standard/asynchronous-programming-patterns/

- www.c-sharpcorner.com

- www.csharp-station.com

- https://csharp.2000things.com

- www.tutorialsteacher.com/csharp/csharp-tutorials

- https://en.wikipedia.org/wiki/C_Sharp_(programming_language)

© Vaskaran Sarcar 2020
V. Sarcar, *Getting Started with Advanced C#*, https://doi.org/10.1007/978-1-4842-5934-4

Index

© Vaskaran Sarcar 2020
V. Sarcar, *Getting Started with Advanced C#*, https://doi.org/10.1007/978-1-4842-5934-4

Printed in the United States
By Bookmasters